World Youth Day

From Catholicism to Counterchurch

Cornelia R. Ferreira
John Vennari

Canisius Books
Toronto

Library and Archives Canada Cataloguing in Publication

Ferreira, Cornelia R.
    World Youth Day: from Catholicism to counterchurch /
Cornelia Ferreira, John Vennari.

Includes bibliographical references.
ISBN 0-9697103-8-0

    1. World Youth Day. 2. Catholic youth--Religious life.
I. Vennari, John II. Title.

BX2347.8.Y7F47 2005   282'.0835   C2003-903941-2

COVER: Photo taken by John Vennari at the World Youth Day sleepover at
         12:45 a.m., Sunday, July 28, 2002. (See Chapters 12-14.)

I saw in vision ... [a] black, filthy, four-cornered, false church.... This church is full of impurity, vanity, sottishness and darkness, but scarcely one of those men knew in what obscurity he labored. It is all proud presumption.... a stool is the altar, and on the table is a death's head veiled, a light on either side. In their worship they use naked swords, and at certain parts of the ceremonies the death's head is unveiled. It is all bad, thoroughly bad, the communion of the unholy. I cannot say how abominable, how pernicious and empty are their ceremonies. Many of the members know it not themselves. They wish to be one single body in some other than the Lord....

When science separated from Faith, this church was born without a Saviour, good works without faith, the communion of the unbelieving with the appearance but not the reality of virtue; in a word, the anti-Church whose centre is malice, error, falsehood, hypocrisy, tepidity, and the cunning of all the demons of the period. It forms a body, a community outside the Body of Jesus, the Church. It is a false church without a Redeemer. Its mysteries are to have no mysteries and, consequently, its action is temporal, finite, full of pride and presumption, a teacher of evil clothed in specious raiment.

Its danger lies in its apparent innocence. It wills differently, acts differently everywhere. In many places its action is harmless, in others it aims at corrupting a few of the learned. But all tends to one end, to something bad in its origin, an action outside Jesus Christ, through whom alone every life is sanctified, and outside of whom every action, every work remains in death and in the demon.

Blessed Anne Catherine Emmerich

Foreword

In July 2002, Mr. John Vennari came to Toronto to cover World Youth Day for his newspaper, *Catholic Family News*. Like the youthful pilgrims, he rode the subway to the main venues and participated in the major events of that week. He also filmed many happenings that were not seen in official television coverage.

In Toronto, he enjoyed the hospitality of the home of Mrs. Cornelia Ferreira and her family. Mrs. Ferreira had already been speaking and writing on World Youth Day and its connection to the post-conciliar agenda for a "new" humanist Catholicism that could be merged with the one-world religion. A plan was soon born for a book combining Mrs. Ferreira's trenchant Catholicism-to-Counterchurch research with Mr. Vennari's vivid World Youth Day reports.

This book, therefore, is not just about World Youth Day, but about how World Youth Day fits into the larger agenda of erecting a modernist Counterchurch, operating within the structure of the Roman Catholic Church. Construction of this Counterchurch has been going on since Vatican II. It has produced a community-oriented democratic church devoted to social justice, interfaith unity, and the establishment of the Masonic universal brotherhood.

This book explains the terminology, ideologies and methodologies used in crafting this new religion, also known as Adult Church. World Youth Day has showcased its progression over the last twenty years. The youth on display at WYD in Toronto represented the first through-and-through Counterchurch generation, born and raised in Adult Faith.

If this mass "pilgrimage" of Catholics to the new church is not halted by God Himself, all our churches and cathedrals will shortly resound with the riotous worship of Antichrist — whilst the remnant One, Holy, Catholic and Apostolic Church will find herself once more a Church of the catacombs.

Feast of St. Peter Canisius · April 27, 2005

Contents

Part I
World Youth Day: Change Agent for the Counterchurch

Part II
World Youth Day:
An Eyewitness Account

Part I

World Youth Day: Change Agent for the Counterchurch

By Cornelia R. Ferreira

Chapter 1
Journeying Out of the Church

Two words heard commonly in the Catholic Church today are *community* and *pilgrimage*. One may think these are just trendy terms, but they are the keys to a subversive agenda, delineated in the literature of the community *movement*. Upon these words *community* and *pilgrimage* rests a revolutionary blueprint for inserting the Church into the occult Masonic one-world religion,[1] whilst enabling it still to *look* Catholic, thus ensnaring the grassroots.

This masquerade tricks Catholics into accepting a new and "better" Catholicism, one devoted to social improvement rather than saving souls. Forty years of progressively abandoning her divine mandate to teach, govern and sanctify has led to the Church's resembling more and more what Archbishop Fulton Sheen predicted in 1948 — a Counterchurch of the Antichrist. The Counterchurch, he said, will "in all *externals* resemble the mystical body of Christ," but will be "emptied of its divine content."[2]

This anti-Church was also foretold by Blessed Anne Catherine Emmerich in 1819:

> ... this church was born without a Saviour, good works without faith, the communion of the unbelieving with the appearance but not the reality of virtue; in a word, the anti-Church whose centre is malice, error, falsehood, hypocrisy,

---

[1]For an explanation of the Masonic plan for a one-world government and religion, see Cornelia R. Ferreira, *The New Age Movement: The Kingdom of Satan on Earth* (Scarborough, ON: Canisius Books, 1991). The one-world community, to be run by the Antichrist, is being prepared by the New Age/New World Order Movement. This is an occult, socio-political movement that is the umbrella for all heretical and seditious movements. Its aim is a complete cultural transformation in which occultism will replace Christianity, and totalitarian socialism will replace all other forms of government.

[2]Archbishop Fulton J. Sheen, *Communism and the Conscience of the West* (n.p.: [The Bobbs-Merrill Co.], 1948; reprint ed., Garden City, NY: Garden City Books, 1951), pp. 22-24. (Emphasis added.)

tepidity, and the cunning of all the demons of the period. It forms a body, a community outside the Body of Jesus, the Church. It is a false church without a Redeemer. Its mysteries are to have no mysteries and, consequently, its action is temporal, finite, full of pride and presumption, a teacher of evil clothed in specious raiment.[3]

Archbishop Sheen described the Antichrist as one who will *pose* as the "Great Humanitarian" who will "talk peace, prosperity and plenty." He will "spread the lie that men will never be better until they make society better." That profile exactly fits Maitreya or "The Christ," the world leader New Agers expect to appear any day. The Counterchurch, *operating within the structure of the true Church* like cockle amidst the wheat, smoothly melds unsuspecting Catholics with the Masonic New Age/New World Order movement. One way it does this is through the promotion of humanitarianism or *service*.

Archbishop Sheen predicted a conflict between "the God Who became man, and the man who makes himself God." The Antichrist, disguised as the Great Humanitarian, will tempt Christians with the same temptations with which he tempted Jesus:

> The temptation to turn stones into bread as an earthly Messias will become the temptation to sell freedom for security, making bread [i.e., all earthly goods] a political weapon which only those who think his way may eat. The temptation to work a miracle by recklessly throwing himself from a steeple will become a plea to desert the lofty pinnacles of truth ... for those lower depths where the masses live on slogans and propaganda. He wants no proclamation of immutable principles from the lofty heights of a steeple, but mass organization through propaganda.... Opinions not truths, ... nature not grace — to these golden calves will men toss themselves from their Christ.

---

[3]Father Carl E. Schmöger, CSSR, *The Life of Anne Catherine Emmerich*, 2 vols. (n.p., English ed., 1885; reprint ed., Rockford, IL: Tan Books and Publishers, 1976), 1:475.

We recognize in the first temptation the social justice and human rights movements, in the second, the principles of *pilgrimage* and *community*. As we shall see, these principles epitomize the flight today from the pinnacles of truth to the abyss in which propaganda and pious-sounding slogans lure Catholics into the collectivist universal brotherhood.

The third temptation is the crucial one. Satan asked Jesus to worship him, promising in exchange all the kingdoms of the world. This is the temptation to have

> a new religion without a Cross, a liturgy without a world to come, a religion to destroy a religion, or a politics which is a religion — one that renders unto Caesar even the things that are God's.

The atheistic Great Humanitarian, said Archbishop Sheen, will "identify tolerance with indifference to right and wrong, truth and error." He "will set up a counterchurch,"

> which will be the ape of the Church, because he, the Devil, is the ape of God. It will have all the notes and characteristics of the Church, but in reverse and emptied of its divine content. It will be a mystical body of the Antichrist that will in all *externals* resemble the mystical body of Christ.

In other words, the Counterchurch will be a gnostic, Arian church. It will resemble the Catholic Church, having Her structure and what *looks* like the usual religious practices; but the meaning of everything will be perverted so that Catholics will unknowingly (in most cases) be following Antichrist. *The* Antichrist prophesied by Scripture for the last days may not be here yet, but his occult anti-Church and kingdom are being prepared by his forerunners within the Church today.

This Counterchurch is *exactly the one designed by the Masonic architects of Satan's new world order*. Their plan was promulgated by New Age leader Alice Bailey,[4] and it is being

---

[4]Alice A. Bailey, *The Externalisation of the Hierarchy* (New York: Lucis Pub-

meticulously followed. The "Guides of our evolution," wrote Bailey, recognize that for "the general public ... [i]t is the *form* which matters to them the most, for they are conservative and cling to the familiar. The church is intended to serve the masses and is not intended to be of use (except as a field of service) to the esotericists" because they are more interested in inner spirituality, not external structures.

How is the Church to serve Masonic occultists?

> The Christian church in its many branches can serve as a St. John the Baptist [i.e., as a precursor for *Antichrist*!] ... and as a nucleus through which world illumination may be accomplished.... Its work is intended to be the holding of a broad platform. The church must show a wide tolerance and teach no revolutionary doctrines or cling to any reactionary ideas [i.e., Tradition].... *The prime work of the church is ... preserving the outer appearance in order to reach the many who are accustomed to church usages.*

In this illuminized or occultized Counterchurch, "the sacraments must be mystically interpreted," i.e., given a new meaning suited to the religion of Antichrist. We shall see later on that, indeed, all our sacraments today have new meanings. The Church, Masonry and education are the "three main channels through which the preparation for the new age is going on," said Bailey.

The only way the Catholic Church could help usher in the new world order is for its members to be thoroughly re-educated to accept the restructuring of their religion. This is being done both by illuminizing their minds through destroying traditional Catholicism,[5] and by immersing them in collective humanitarianism. They will practise the "religion [of] brotherhood without the fatherhood of God," explained

---

lishing Co., 1957), pp. 510-11. (Emphases added.)

[5]Illuminism requires the destruction of "all old-established systems and religions." From the ashes arises the "new kingdom of Lucifer — the Great Perversion." This technique is termed "destruction and reconstruction." See Inquire Within [pseudonym of a former Rosicrucian chief], *Light-bearers of Darkness* (London: Boswell Printing & Publishing Co., 1930), pp. 5, 64, 42, 81, 122.

Archbishop Sheen.

> In desperate need for God, whom he nevertheless refuses to adore, modern man in his loneliness and frustration will hunger more and more for membership in a *community* that will give him enlargement of purpose, but at the cost of losing himself in some vague collectivity.[6]

We're there now! Under the heading, "Made to be Together," a Toronto parish bulletin recently stated,

> We were created for community.[7] There is a built-in need in us for other people.... We belong to a local community and to a worldwide community.... When I admit that I belong to a worldwide community there are many consequences that follow.... Hunger in the world becomes my issue. Land mines, deforestation, injustice of any kind. We begin to see that we are all tied together [New Agers call this *interdependence*], and so must all work together to solve common problems.

This is the "enlargement of purpose" Archbishop Sheen said would be furnished by community membership. It fuels the social justice movement. So let us see how the concepts of *community* and *pilgrimage* are producing the gnostic, Arian Counterchurch of the Antichrist, the one called for by the Illuminati planners of the New World Order.

Dewey Restructures the Church

Let us start with *pilgrimage*. The youth descending on

---

[6]Archbishop Sheen, p. 24. (Emphasis added.) In the 1970s and '80s, there were studies and conferences by the Canadian and American bishops, as well as Belgian Catholics, on "hunger for community": "Faith Community as Educator," *Adult Faith, Adult Church* (Ottawa: Canadian Conference of Catholic Bishops, 1986), p. 23 (see p. 24.)

[7]Contrast this with what the Church teaches through the *Baltimore Catechism*: God made us to know, love and serve Him in this world, and to be happy with Him for ever in the next.

Toronto for World Youth Day in 2002 were said to be on "pilgrimage." Now, a pilgrimage is a journey to a *sacred* place for a pious reason. "Pilgrimage" also refers to our mortal life, which is a journey through this world to our *most* sacred goal: Heaven. Since Toronto is hardly a sacred place, obviously *pilgrimage* is one of the innumerable Catholic terms that have been redefined.[8]

The modernist meaning of *pilgrimage* is derived from humanists, especially John Dewey (1859-1952), the father of modern education. In 1989, an article explaining the humanistic meaning of pilgrimage appeared in *Religious Education*, the journal of the interreligious Religious Education Association.[9] Reading it, one realizes that Dewey's ideas have not only destroyed Catholicism in Catholic schools, as is widely recognized today, but they've also played a major role in restructuring the Church itself, building the Counterchurch through the concepts of *pilgrimage* and *community*. Dewey, a drafter of the first *Humanist Manifesto* (1933), was a product of Hegelian and Illuminati training, which also produced Communism. Indeed, humanists and Karl Marx himself equate naturalistic humanism with Communism.[10] In other words, as recognized by Archbishop Sheen, the ideology of the Counterchurch is rooted in Communism[11] — and illuminized Masonry.

There are four key concepts involved in the humanistic restructuring of the Church: spirituality, pilgrimage, community and lived experience. In order to understand how the humanist idea of pilgrimage got entrenched in the

---

[8]This is the typical modernist technique of destroying doctrine indirectly by using Catholic words with altered meanings.

[9]Iris M. Yob, "The Pragmatist and Pilgrimage: Revitalizing an Old Metaphor for Religious Education," *Religious Education*, Fall 1989, p. 521.

[10]Paul Kurtz, ed., *Humanist Manifestos I and II* (Buffalo: Prometheus Books, 1973, pp. 11, 15; Antony C. Sutton, *America's Secret Establishment* (Billings, MT: Liberty House Press, 1986), pp. 79, 84, 86, 91; *The Encyclopedia of Education* (n.p.: The Macmillan Company & The Free Press,1971), s.v. "Dewey, John," by Jonas F. Soltis. Marx acknowledged, "Communism, as fully developed naturalism, equals humanism": cited in D. L. Cuddy, "The Deceptive New Age 'Service' and 'Light,'" *The Christian News*, April 30, 1990, p. 22.

[11]Cf. Archbishop Sheen, pp. 25-26.

Church, we need first to consider the role of "spirituality."

For humanists, religion is different from a religious *attitude* — or *spirituality*, as it's known today. Religion, complained Dewey, "provides a set of ready-made beliefs and practices based on the idea of the supernatural." Further, it entails obedience, "takes away responsibility from the believer," and so it diminishes the dignity of man. A religious *attitude*, or spirituality, on the other hand, is naturalistic and communistic. Involving imagination and feeling, it "helps one to adjust to the world and bring about changes ... to meet collective ... demands." It is thus "meaningful" and upholds human dignity, and so is preferable to religion.[12] "Spirituality" is a *change agent* that is experiential and "dynamic," i.e., evolutionary.[13] It reflects two planks of Freemasonry: *Liberty* (freedom from dogma) and *Equality* (freedom from authority, the basis of the democratic Church).

A typical comment of young Catholics attending World Youth Day in Toronto was that they were searching for a spirituality "that feels right." They wanted to find this spirituality independently of the Church.[14] Youth were officially denominated "the light of the world" at World Youth Day 2002 — because they "shine as advocates for change." They are allegedly "leading efforts to create a just world." As one Canadian student boldly told a high school assembly,

> Each of us can be a spark to fuel the fires of change. We will be the ones living with the consequences of other people's decisions unless we take action and let our wills be known. Starting right now, you have a chance to improve

---

[12]Michael Kesterton, in "The Rise of the Nones," *The Globe and Mail* (Toronto), October 19, 2004, p. A24, quotes Douglas Todd of Religion News Service as saying, "The fastest-growing 'religious' group on the North American continent is the spiritual-but-not-religious." Called "nones" because they do not identify with any religion, they "have more than doubled their numbers in the past 10 years. There are an estimated 30 million in the United States." According to the 2001 Canadian census, there are nearly 4.8 million "nones" in Canada. Three quarters of them are under the age of 45. See "Seekers and Nones: Canada's Spiritual Portrait," listenuptv.com/programs/030605seek.htm, June 5, 2003.

[13]Yob, pp. 523, 525, 531, 535-36.

[14]Michael Valpy, "So Far, Volunteers Outnumber Local Registrants," *Globe and Mail*, July 22, 2002, p. A4.

our world.[15]

Improving the world is the rationale for *pilgrimage*, the second concept for restructuring Catholicism. The humanist definition of pilgrimage is "a journey away from a less desirable state of affairs" to something better. The starting point of pilgrimage is said to be *chaos*, a state of "social oppression and injustice." It is a life-long evolutionary journey of constant change as each step forward "brings new problems that require readjustment." The endpoint of pilgrimage is the "sacred objective" of social well-being, the ideal society.[16] Clearly, the humanistic pilgrimage reflects the Masonic slogan, "Out of chaos, order." *Pilgrimage* thus underpins the social justice and volunteer/service movements, as well as liberation theology,[17] and the concept has been implemented through humanistic religious education:

> [W]hen religious education is conceived in terms of pilgrimage, it leads students to identify and be concerned about the social, moral, and personal problems that afflict modern society. Dewey ... was inclined to reduce religion to morality and see modern problems in terms of social concerns.... pragmatists remind us, religion seeks to redress injustice....[18]

That is, humanistic "morality" is divorced from God's law, sin and virtue; it is merely a concern for social problems.[19] It involves a set of changing values for making life comfortable, whilst posing as altruism:

---

[15]"Young People Acting for Justice," *Development and Peace* (Toronto), Lent 2002, p. 4.

[16]Yob, pp. 521, 528, 532-34. Some pragmatists see the endpoint as perfection or godhood (p. 532).

[17]Ibid., pp. 535, 522-23; cf. William Adamson, "Nurturing and Empowering Adults in the Church," *Insight, Number 2* (Ottawa: Canadian Conference of Catholic Bishops, 1988), p. 40 (see p. 41); "Faith Community as Educator," p. 27.

[18]Yob, pp. 534-35.

[19]Thus Pope John Paul II could call for the United Nations "to rise ... above the cold status of an administrative institution and to become a moral centre": World Day of Peace message, January 1, 2004, initiative no. 7.

> ... religious impulses are ... effective forces for change.... they substitute and empower a better way of living for a less desirable way.... Treated as positive responses rather than as rules that bind behavior, religious meanings will not ... inhibit creative action but appeal to and enliven youthful commitments.[20]

When man is God, his "religious impulses" are rationalistic and naturalistic:

> In Dewey's mind, all finally turns on humankind. Human beings have a heritage of values ... in embryonic form, which can take on more effective ... roles through intervention and direction. Human aspirations are religious impulses; and when these are freed from theological dogma, the practices and inhibitions of institutionalized religion, and particularly the belief that humanity is dependent on a Supreme Being, they will produce an effective "social intelligence" to dispose of social evils and direct social change.[21]

Since the pilgrimage involves continuous reorganization to deal with new problems, the focus is on the *process* rather than on the product.[22] The pilgrimage process brings about equity as participants "slip out of their social constraints and enter 'a state of unmediated egalitarian association' with other pilgrims."[23] The "pilgrimage mentality" is that everyone is a "co-learner" and "companion on the journey of discipleship."[24]

The third humanistic concept used in restructuring proposes that pilgrimage be done in *community*. Dewey con-

---

[20]Yob, p. 535.

[21]Ibid., p. 531. Pope Pius IX condemned naturalism and rationalism in his *Syllabus of Modern Errors*, December 8, 1864: Henry Denzinger, *The Sources of Catholic Dogma*, 30th ed., trans. Roy J. Deferrari (St. Louis, MO: B. Herder Book Co., 1957; reprint ed., Powers Lake, ND: Marian House, n.d.), nos. 1702-9.

[22]Yob, p. 533.

[23]John Allemang, "To Boldly Go Where No Brain Has Gone Before," *Globe and Mail*, May 28, 1996, p. A8.

[24]The National Advisory Committee on Adult Religious Education, Canadian Conference of Catholic Bishops, "Christian Orientation in Adult Education: A Synthesis of Our Vision," *Insight 2*, p. 8 (see p. 13).

sidered the human being only in a social context. The "less-desirable state of affairs" from which one journeys is the "problem-afflicted society," such as one's family, nation, the Church, or even the international community. Human *progress*, *growth* or *development* (synonyms for *pilgrimage*) is seen as taking place *only* by "individuals united by a common [experiential] knowledge and shared purposes," i.e., individuals working together. This is because collaboration (the process) *builds community*, brotherhood[25] or solidarity, which are all synonyms for *Fraternity*, the third plank of Masonry.

Chiara Lubich, the founder and head of the syncretic world brotherhood organization Focolare, recently "pointed out that of the three ideas of the great political project of the modern world, expressed through the French Revolution, one was still just getting on its feet. Liberty and equality have been more or less pursued, but brotherhood has been all but ignored." The French Revolution was the first great attack by Freemasonry upon the Catholic Church in an ongoing war which aims to make the Church an illuminized member of the Masonic world community. Grand Orient Freemasonry defines Masonry as "a society of *Universal Brotherhood.*" Yet, bringing about universal brotherhood is the constantly-stated goal of Focolare.[26]

Aloysius Cardinal Ambrozic of Toronto, host of World Youth Day 2002, described it in terms that clearly show *World Youth Day is a program to build world brotherhood*:

> The World Youth Day is a *pilgrimage....* It is a journey *creating a community of its own*, motivated by the goal it sets for itself. This goal consists in meeting other young people, strengthening and being strengthened by the faith they share....[27]

[25]Yob, pp. 523, 529-30, 532, 535.

[26]Antonio M. Baggio, "Chiara Lubich Meets Interested Politicians," *Living City* (New York), March 2001, p. 8 (*Living City* is Focolare's magazine); *Light-bearers*, pp. 14, 17. Focolare's own gathering during World Youth Day in Toronto was entitled "Interfaith Dialogue to Build the Universal Family," i.e., the global community.

[27]Aloysius Cardinal Ambrozic, Pastoral Letter *The People who sat in Darkness*

Pope John Paul II was even clearer. He exhorted attendees:

> In the quest for justice, in the promotion of peace, in your commitment to brotherhood and solidarity, let no one surpass you![28]

> The world you are inheriting ... desperately needs a new sense of brotherhood and human solidarity.[29]

Dewey encouraged every individual to make a contribution to his community, as that links him to the "universe and infinity," i.e., to the one-world community and its pantheistic divinity. "Only a society that recognizes the needs and contributions" of each member "can move forward" to this divine global community. The "ideal world" is a "genuine community created by thinkers and doers,"[30] thinking and acting, of course, along world brotherhood lines.[31]

Obviously, the Catholic Church can *not* join the one-world community unless she dismantles her hierarchical authority, treats all her members as equals, and focuses on man's temporal rather than supernatural needs. This new orientation of the Church began at Vatican II and is now being rapidly implemented, making the Counterchurch more visible.

From Parish to Community

Today we are bombarded with talk of "building community" and "service" (to the community). This is where the "new evangelization" fits in. Every Catholic is expected to evangelize, and in practice this has become the blind leading

---

have seen a great Light, November 2001. (Emphases added.)

[28]"Build a Civilization of Love," statement at Papal Vigil, *The Catholic Register* (Toronto), August 11-18, 2002, p. 17.

[29]"You are Called to be Transformed," homily at closing Mass, ibid., p. 22.

[30]Yob, p. 531.

[31]Illuminism's stated goal is: "creating single-eyed fanatics, false idealists, soft peacemongers," willing to destroy "national, tribal and family unity ... [so that] Universal Brotherhood can become a fact": See Inquire Within, *The Trail of the Serpent* (London: Boswell Publishing Co., 1936), p. 221.

the blind. For example, student retreats are given by students; the European bishops "are committed to allowing themselves" to be evangelized by youth; and Ralph Martin's charismatic Renewal Ministries uses *unbaptized* "Christians" to evangelize in the former Soviet Union.[32] As missionary magazines make clear, conversions are not the goal of today's evangelization — building community is, which happens when people dialogue and work together.

Today the word "parish" is being replaced by "community." The name change is very significant. A parish, you see, is not necessarily a community. A parish consists of people who attend a local church merely to worship God and receive the sacraments and graces necessary to save their souls. They attend church as individuals, not "linked" to anyone else in the parish "by effective latitudinal bonds." "Different social and ethnic classes can remain apart," and the pastor is an "authoritarian" who does not encourage lay "co-responsibility."[33] Today, the parish is despised as the selfish, pre-Vatican II or "Old Age" — i.e., traditional — model of Church.

Consciousness-raising about individualistic parishioners is seen in this instruction given to ushers a quarter century ago:

> In many city parishes those who gather for Sunday worship may well be strangers to one another.... [Some] may labor under the misapprehension that the Eucharist is an opportunity to be alone with God, coming with neither the desire nor a felt need for fellowship.... On Sunday it is *people* who are important. *The gathering itself is the most sig-*

---

[32]"How Adults Learn," *Adult Faith*, p. 49 (see p. 50); Paula Antonello, "Youth Retreats Are an Experience That Can be Fruitful," *Catholic Register*, March 1, 1999, p. 13; Lisa Becker, "NET Ministries Spread the Word to Youth," ibid., April 23, 2001, p. 7; "European Bishops Decide on 'Quality Leap' in Youth Pastoral Care," Zenit.org, April 30, 2002; Ralph Martin, *Renewal Ministries*, November 1999, p. 1.

[33]Cf. "Faith Community as Educator," pp. 23, 28, 30; "Structures Which Support Adult Religious Education," *Adult Faith*, p. 59 (see p. 65). For how to *convert* a parish to a community, see Father Philip J. Lewis, "Learning Through Stewardship: A Parish Experience," *Insight* (Ottawa: Canadian Conference of Catholic Bishops, 1987), p. 70.

nificant element of the worship environment….   The ushers' role is decisive in creating an atmosphere of hospitality and friendliness….   It is crucial in helping people to shed the inhibitions and rigidity too long associated with "going to church."[34]

At their recent conference, the Consolata Missionaries heaped contempt on the traditional parishes and parishioners their missionary "animators" encounter:

Since the parish has failed to become a communion of communities as the Vatican Council projected and instead it continues to be a mass of Christians that individually practice the sacraments in hope of eternal salvation, it is increasingly becoming irrelevant to the society and to the individual who sees no connection between faith and everyday life. It goes without saying that *such lifeless and socially irrelevant faith* is not worth passing on to others.[35]

So the new compassionate Counterchurch has to be *built* by moving away from this undesirable state of affairs. This is where the pilgrimage starts.   The collaboration involved in the pilgrimage is called *community building*. It is a *process* in which people are led from where they are to where they are wanted by clever facilitators versed in humanistic psychology and sociology.[36] They fool the community into believing its goals and plans of action are its own original ideas to solve perceived problems. As John Dewey said,

through education [i.e., indoctrination] society can formulate its own purposes, can organize its own means and resources, and thus shape itself … in the direction in which it wishes to move….[37]

---

[34]Father Gregory F. Smith, OC, *The Ministry of Ushers* (Collegeville, MN: Order of St. Benedict, 1980), pp. 10-11, 15. (Emphases added.)

[35]Father George Amaro, IMC, "A Vocation for All," *Consolata Missionaries* (Toronto), April-June 2004, p. 10. (Emphasis added.)

[36]"Christian Orientation," p. 13; Marge Denis and Caryl Green, "What is This Thing Called Process?", *Insight 2*, p. 45 (see p. 46).

[37]*Encyclopedia of Education*, ibid.

And so consciousness-raising programs form communities, independent of the Church, that journey on to create a better temporal world. Once you are used to being part
of a local community, it's a small step to join the global community of the new world order. In the early '80s most parishes were not communities. They were seen as *supporters* of
community, as "the organizational umbrella under which
many communal groups [could] be formed" and encouraged
to interact with each other.[38] This networking spread the
subversion, so that today most parishes *are* communities.

The Counterchurch will be "authentically" Catholic.
As Hans Küng, the dissident theologian who was banned
from teaching as a Catholic theologian by Pope John Paul II,
has said, we need a Vatican III "which will lead this church
from Roman Catholicism to an authentic Catholicity" if the
Church "is to have a future as an institution in the 21st Century."[39] Note the pilgrimage idea: lead the whole Church
from the old to the new model.

What will be the chief characteristics of this new
church? It will be non-structured, anti-authoritarian, led by
lay men and women who are equals; it will be experiential,
tolerant of heresy, indifferentist, inculturated and syncretic.
Inculturation will make the Church "truly universal" instead
of "essentially Western" in her theology, liturgy and philosophical systems, according to Karl Rahner, the modernist Jesuit who highly influenced Vatican II and whose heresies run
rampant in the Church today. In 1978, the Asian Colloquium
in Ministries, sponsored by the Federation of Asian Bishops'
Conferences, observed we were entering "a new era that will
make the Catholic Church for the first time really 'catholic' by
introducing into its life the riches of all nations...." They
urged we collect the "seminal reasons," i.e., core meanings, in
"man's old and new religions and integrate them into a *new
synthesis of the Gospel* as it is experienced by today's man."

---

[38]"Faith Community as Educator," pp. 28-29.
[39]Michael McAteer, "Praying for a Pope John XXIV," *The Toronto Star*, May 26,
2001, p. M14.

The meaning of "Gospel," therefore, is also changed.   It now means a synthesis of teachings from different religions, including the religion of humanism.   So the role of adult religious educators is "to help believers accept the value of pluralism in religious expression," and "to move beyond their own relatively narrow paths of belief and practice.   This means that ecumenical, interfaith [i.e., syncretic] and multicultural experiences will need to be a more integral part of what they do."[40]

Since pilgrimage is an evolutionary process in which the "Church is becoming church" and Catholics are becoming catholic, it involves constant change.[41]   Vatican II started the Church on pilgrimage, as the community movement's literature continually points out.   In 1983, *Time* magazine published this interesting observation on the Council by English Benedictine abbot Dom Christopher Butler:

> Before, the church looked like an immense and immovable colossus, the city set on a hill, the stable bulwark against the *revolutionary* change.   Now it has become a people on the march — or at least a people which is packing its bags for a *pilgrimage*. [42]

Marxist Pilgrimages for Every Taste

Now, a community is a group of people sharing the

---

[40]Neil Parent, "Adult Religious Education: Challenges for the Future," *Insight*, p. 13 (see pp. 13-16), emphasis added; Hayden Roberts, "The Church: Its Gift to Alternative Adult Education," ibid., p. 8 (see pp.10-12); "How Adults Learn," p. 55; "Structures Which Support," pp. 63-65; "Maturing Adult Believers," *Adult Faith*, p. 33 (see p. 45).   Non-inculturated Catholicism allegedly "disturbs" Africans and Asians because it is "European": Father John Duggan, SJ, "The Multicultural Parish: Building Community," *Insight 2*, p. 58 (see p. 62).   As we shall see later, the small-c "catholic" denotes a universalist "Catholicism" which preaches that everyone is saved.

[41]Denis and Green, p. 47; Yob, pp. 532-34, 536.   "The heart" of the RCIA program (the Rite of Christian Initiation of Adults) is "the church becoming church": Sister Nancy Burkin, SSJ, "The Parish Community and the RCIA," *Insight 2*, p. 80 (see p. 85); cf. "How Adults Learn," p. 55.

[42]"Vatican II: Turning the Church Toward the World," October 5, 1983, p. 84. (Emphases added.)

same beliefs, problems, goals or activities. It can range from two people to the world community of all nations. *Faith community* just means a community of a particular religion — Catholic, Buddhist, Lutheran, etc.[43] A parish can be a single faith community, or it can contain several smaller communities. *For the Counterchurch, the title "community" is applied to a group that is leading its members on pilgrimage away from Roman Catholicism.* Amongst the groups cited as communities or as "building" community or church are new ecclesial movements (Focolare, The Neocatechumenal Way, etc.); prayer/discussion/Bible study/social-justice groups; RENEW, Marriage Encounter, RCIA, *World Youth Day*, Cursillo, Charismatic Renewal and 12-Step Programs (like Alcoholics Anonymous). There are even communities within religious orders.[44]

Overlapping these groups are the basic Christian communities or small faith communities, which "serve as important balances to ... highly traditional parish structures." Popes Paul VI and John Paul II saw these base communities as "a force for evangelization," Pope John Paul also calling them "a solid starting point for a new society based on a civilization of love."[45] His speeches at World Youth Day in Denver, Rome and Toronto indicate that he also saw the youth faith community being generated by World Youth Days as necessary for constructing the civilization of love.[46]

Inspired by the Marxist liberation theology of base

---

[43]Kenneth Stokes, Executive Director of Adult Faith Resources (Minneapolis, MN), explained in a letter dated October 18, 1991: "'Faith Community' is a generic term used increasingly in interfaith discussions to refer to *all kinds of local religious settings*: Jewish synagogues, Catholic parishes, Protestant congregations, Unitarian fellowships, etc."

[44]"Faith Community as Educator," pp. 23, 27; "How Adults Learn," p. 50; "Structures Which Support," pp. 59, 61, 63; Father John English, SJ, cited in a pamphlet advertising a Toronto conference on "The Spirituality of Community" in January 2000; "World Youth Day," *Development and Peace*, p. 4; Cardinal Ambrozic, ibid.

[45]Reynolds R. Ekstrom, *The New Concise Catholic Dictionary*, rev. ed. (Mystic, CT: Twenty-Third Publications, 1995), s.v. "Community" and "Small Faith Communities."

[46]"Pope Denounces 'Culture of Death,'" *Toronto Star*, August 16, 1993, p. A3; Domenico Bettinelli, Jr., "An Unprecedented Gathering," us.catholic.net/rcc/Periodicals/lgpress/2000-10/Vatican.html; "Called to be Transformed."

communities, all faith communities teach and practise auton-omy in religion.   Following humanist and pantheist John Dewey, they make their members feel they are special and *not anonymous sheep* in the flock; *everybody's a leader* who deserves a *visible* "role" in the Church and his "talents recognized." Unless you have a visible role or "ministry" and receive offi-cial recognition, you are not a valued member of the Church. World Youth Day is *dedicated* to making young Catholics feel valued; like the feminists, youth now expect to be treated as special.

Two 20-year-old Knights of Columbus considered John Paul II "a good guy for the Catholic faith" because he "lets us know we're *important* and we're *needed*, ... part of the Church right now."[47] Father Thomas Rosica, CSB, national director and chief executive officer of World Youth Day 2002, and himself a Knight, stated that "hundreds of thousands" of youth "are waiting to be welcomed into the life of the Church, and to be given credible and visible roles. We must ... go out to meet them and welcome them into our midst."[48] Not surprisingly, then, youth believe "the church would benefit from new ideas," such as "the possible ordination of women." And to keep the Mass from being "boring," asserts a callow 14-year-old, "They need to involve us young people more.... They need to put it into terms that teenagers can understand."[49]

Increasingly today, faith communities are being merged around "shared concerns" like debt relief or peace, or activities like the Jubilee 2000 celebrations, thus moving the "evolution" of the world forward to a pantheistic godhood. This brings us to the fourth concept for restructuring the Church: the pilgrimage must involve what's called *lived experience* (as a community) — activities that unite participants,

---

[47]Mike Latona, "Lighting the Way," *Columbia* (New Haven, CT), May 2002, p. 16 (emphases added). *Columbia* is the Knights of Columbus magazine.

[48]"Toronto Still Abuzz in the Wake of World Youth Day," Zenit.org, August 22, 2002.

[49]David Crary, "Pontiff Joins Youth Day Pilgrims in Prayer," HoustonChronicle.com, July 27, 2002.

like World Youth Day or social justice projects. Only learning by doing something together (instead of by being taught) constitutes "true" Christian learning and creates the bond of community. Members of the parish or classroom community must be introduced to a wider community to "experience the ties they have with others." "Authentic adult learning" must "develop social consciousness and moral response," i.e., lead to "problem solving" and "world-making." "From personal engagement in some issue, they will feel the *outrage* ... and apply personal effort to its solution." Adult faith is nothing else, therefore, than a socio-political change agent to make the world a humanist utopia.[50] Its God-talk and religiosity entrap Catholics looking for spirituality.

Dewey believed one could unite nature and grace in lived experience.[51] Following Dewey, pragmatists and religious educators propose that knowledge obtained from *experiencing* the "unity" of evil and good (i.e., by not striving against sin) is the only genuine form of religious knowledge; "theologies and creeds that are divorced from lived experience," are not forms of genuine knowledge. Religion "is not something we inherit but something we appropriate anew ... and shape according to present realities. It becomes ours only as we make it so within our own experience...." It means being open to the changing world and continually modifying beliefs and practices to fit in. If we don't, religion will become anachronistic.[52] In practice, this means, for instance, not making a fuss about the increasing acceptance and legalization of moral depravity. Dewey's proposal recycles man's first temptation: eating (experiencing) the fruit of the Tree of Knowledge of good and evil will lead to godhood. It is also pantheism, the belief that one can unite things displeasing to God with things pleasing to Him.[53]

---

[50]Yob, p. 535 (emphasis added); "Faith Community as Educator," pp. 24-27.

[51]Yob, p. 529. Contrast this with *The Imitation of Christ* (Book 3, Chaps. 54 and 55), which teaches that nature is worldly and corrupt, due to original sin, whereas grace shuns the world, is concerned only with the things of God, is contrary to nature and fights against it.

[52]Yob, pp. 529-30, 536-37.

[53]Pantheism is the heresy underlying ecumenism, syncretism and inculturation.

Perhaps the most malign influence in the Catholic Church in the attempt to unify good and evil has been the gnostic psychologist and occultist Carl Jung (1875-1961). A Masonic Grand Master, Jung has been likened to the Roman emperor Julian the Apostate, because of his serious under-mining of Christianity through his pagan polytheism. One of the "prophets" of the New Age Movement, he himself was a follower of New Age founder Helena Blavatsky's Theoso-phy.[54]   His ideas have become entrenched in the Church through religious feminism, whilst retreat houses and self-help programs are drenched in Jungian psychotherapy.

Jung believed the gnostic concept of creation: "the cosmos arises from a separation of opposites," so that "evil can be no less essential than the good." Good and evil are two sides of the same coin, complementary aspects of the same reality. Hence, "to do good and eschew evil" is an im-possibility, as striving to do so will lead to disequilibrium and breakdown.[55] "Wholeness" is therefore the goal. It can only come about by the union of our good and evil sides. The ho-mosexual who accepts his "darker and opposite-sex side" becomes whole, and cannot be condemned. Now, since Jesus was infinitely good, He lacked "wholeness." He had no evil, dark side; He "receives wholeness in the person of the Anti-christ."[56] This is probably why New Agers, who strive after "wholeness," look forward to the Antichrist, whom they term "The Christ."   This is also probably why the New Agers within the Church are working to establish the Counter-church of the Antichrist, a combination of nature and grace, evil and good — true religion in their eyes.

Jung also believed everyone is on a journey to divin-

---

[54]Richard Noll, *The Aryan Christ: The Secret Life of Carl Jung* (New York: Ran-dom House, 1997), pp. xv-xvi, 15, 126; id., *The Jung Cult* (New York: Free Press Paperbacks, 1997), pp. 68-69; Dusty Sklar, *The Nazis and the Occult* (New York: Dorset Press, 1989), pp. 130-39; Robert Eady, "Carl Jung and the Aryan God Within," *The Orator* (Ottawa, ON), May/June 1995, p. 1.

[55]Wolfgang Smith, *Cosmos and Transcendence* (Peru, IL: Sherwood Sugden & Company, 1984), pp. 122-23.

[56]Pravin Thevathansan, "Carl Gustav Jung: Enemy of the Church," *Christian Order*, December 1998, p. 635; "Introduction," p. 634.

ity. The occult techniques of Jungian psychotherapy that are being used for building community include story-telling, role-playing, drama, dance, music, childish "creative" rituals, mime, etc. The concept of a safe, non-judgemental atmosphere or support group within which to practise these techniques is Jungian. "Spirituality" (Dewey's "religious attitude") is one's personal experience of the divine (obtained through occult means to access the "inner self" or "god within") and the actions it inspires. "Lived experiences" that constitute one's "personal spirituality" can include sins such as abortion or contraception. Hence traditional Catholics and priests endanger the "health" (or "wholeness") of the faith community and are ruthlessly suppressed by Jungians.[57]

For Dewey, the truly religious pilgrimage is a social-justice journey meant to produce peace, harmony and justice, "the kingdom of God on earth now," by means of the knowledge gained on the pilgrimage.[58] Since all religions are seen as building the kingdom of God together, you know it is *not* the kingdom of Christ (the Catholic Church), but a naturalistic kingdom of man-as-god, i.e., the kingdom of Antichrist, the one-world community called for in *The Humanist Manifesto*.[59] In fact, one of the chief voices in the Counterchurch movement, ex-priest Thomas Groome, talks of "leading people *out* toward the Kingdom of God."[60] Out of what? Obvi-

---

[57]Cf. Paul Likoudis, "Jung Replaces Jesus in Catholic Spirituality," and "Jungians Believe Traditional Catholics Impede 'Renewal'," *The Wanderer*, January 5, 1995, pp. 1 and 7, respectively. Jung believed in his own divinity, having merged with his "god within," the Mithraic snake-wrapped lion-god Aion, as well as with "Christ within": Noll, *Jung Cult*, pp. 214-15, 222-23.

[58]Yob, pp. 528-30, 532.

[59]Maria Ferrazzi, "Working for Workers," *Living City*, March 2001, p. 25; cf. Yob, p. 534; Kurtz, p. 23.

[60]"Adult Religious Education," *Adult Faith,* p. 13 (see p. 15; emphasis added). Groome is professor of theology and religious education at the Jesuit Boston College. His "perversion of catechesis" is "normative" in religious education. He is a popular speaker at education conferences. Groome wishes to destroy "the present structures of diocesan priesthood." He considers it "an elitist sect" that is "pedestalized, … accepting that there is a real … difference between the ordained and the baptized." The pro-abortion Groome would open ordination to women, married men and homosexuals. See Eamonn Keane, *A Generation Betrayed: Deconstructing Catholic Education in the English-Speaking World* (Long Island City, NY: W. W. Norton and Co., 2002), pp. xiv-xv, xx-xxi; Fred Mar-

ously the Catholic Church.

The pilgrimage away from the rigid doctrine and tradition that are blamed for causing divisions and wars began at Vatican II, as confirmed by Dom Christopher Butler. That it is an ongoing evolutionary process was indicated by the Papal/Curial Day of Pardon ceremony on March 12, 2000, when Bernard Cardinal Gantin, dean of the College of Cardinals, prayed that the Church "will be committed to the *path* of true conversion," implying a continuous journey from Old Age to New Age Catholicism. The pre-conciliar, i.e., Old Age, Church allegedly damaged human dignity, so the overriding concern today is human rights.[61]

One of the identifying characteristics of the Counterchurch is that it is *futuristic* — constantly striving for a future world that is peaceful (in spite of its being atheistic). This Kingdom of God, where "God" is man, living in a peaceful "civilization of love," was sought by Catholics a century ago. Their quest was condemned by Pope St. Pius X:

> … alarming and saddening … are the audacity and frivolity of men who call themselves Catholics and dream of reshaping society … and of establishing on earth, over and beyond the pale of the Catholic Church, "the reign of love and justice" with workers … of all religions and of no religion….
>
> … the beneficiary of this cosmopolitan social action can only be a Democracy … more universal than the Catholic Church, uniting all men to become brothers … at last in the "Kingdom of God"….[62]

---

tinez, "What is VOTF's Real Agenda?", *The Wanderer*, September 5, 2002, p. 1; Ted Schmidt, "Thomas Groome: the Demise of Clericalism and Breaking Open of Priesthood," *Catholic New Times* (Toronto), November 16, 2003, p. 11.

[61]Cf. Cornelia R. Ferreira, "Red Flag Over the Vatican," *Catholic Family News*, January 2001, p. 13.

[62]Pius X, Encyclical *Our Apostolic Mandate*, August 25, 1910, trans. and commentary by Yves Dupont (Kansas City, MO: Angelus Press, 1998), nos. 38-39.

Chapter 2
Church Becoming Counterchurch

In order to lead the grassroots out of the Church, a whole international industry called *adult religious education* or *adult catechesis* has sprung up, based on the ideas of John Dewey. You might think "adult religious education" refers to teaching the Catholic faith to adults, but the term is concerned neither with true religion nor exclusively with adults. It is a *conditioning* pedagogy, used also in teaching children and at World Youth Day.

The principles of today's religious education or catechetics are derived from the religious education *movement*. This movement began with the formation in 1902 of the *interfaith* Religious Education Association by American biblical scholars and teachers, led by Baptist William Rainey Harper, founder and first president of the University of Chicago. Harper's vision was partly inspired by the 1893 syncretic World Parliament of Religions held in Chicago. The REA intended to promote a religious and moral education "transformed" by psychology and the new educational pedagogy being spread at that time.[63] This psychology and pedagogy had been imported from Germany by Yale's Illuminati-connected Skull and Bones Society. It spread the totalitarianism of Hegel, who stressed community over individualism, with the individual only having value if he served society, i.e., the State; the experimental psychology of Wilhelm Wundt, which helped develop mass conditioning; and the educational theories of Johann Herbart, who was strongly

---

[63]Theodore Brelsford, "Editorial," *Religious Education*, Fall 2003, and Helen Allan Archibald, "Originating Visions and Visionaries of the REA," ibid., p. 414, both posted on religiouseducation.net; Martha Lund Smalley and Joan R. Duffy, *Guide to the Archives of the Religious Education Association (Record Group No. 74)*, Yale University Library, September 1989, webtext.library.yale.edu; Religious Education Association information pamphlet (New Haven, CT). The REA's address is that of the Yale University Library.

connected with the Illuminati. Hegel and Herbart, followers of Freemason Johann Fichte, who devised the dialectical process, influenced Wundt. Wundt then trained the American doctoral students who spread the Masonic "new learning" with the help of Skull and Bones. Dewey studied under these hand-picked academics. His promotion of education as a change agent to prepare students to fit into a totalitarian socialist global community has penetrated not just the Catholic school system, but also the Church itself, through the religious education movement.[64]

Father of Modern Religious Education

Helping to shape the objectives and strategies of the Religious Education Association, Dewey addressed its first convention in Chicago in 1903. He was then director of the University of Chicago's Rockefeller-funded School of Education, one of the main sources of modern education. One conference organizer was a co-founder of the National Herbartian Society. Another organizer and speaker, George Coe, was involved in experimental psychology. He had a great influence on religious education and the REA in the first half of the 20th century. The REA prospered with grants from the Rockefeller and Carnegie Foundations (controlled by Skull and Bones). Its first president was the Dean of Yale Divinity School, another stronghold of Skull and Bones ideology. Catholics have long been associated with the Masonic-influenced REA, even holding executive positions. For instance, along with Dewey, Bishop John Spalding of Peoria, Illinois, was elected to the Council of the REA in 1904 (when ecumenical activity was forbidden), whilst Joanne Chafe, head of the Adult Education Portfolio of the Canadian Bishops' National Office of Religious Education and editor of its adult faith resources cited in this book, has served as presi-

---

[64]Sutton, pp. 31-35, 84, 101-3; Cornelia R. Ferreira, "What is New Age Education?", *Catholic Family News*, September and October 2003.

dent of the Religious Education Association of the United States and Canada.[65]

In his 1903 speech,[66] Dewey set the parameters for religious education that are followed in the Church today. First, religious education must incorporate the psychological principle of *growth*.   Second, applying the Hegelian-Hebartian-Wundtian philosophy that education is not meant to impart knowledge, but to condition students to live as collectivists in a world society,[67] Dewey maintained that *religious* education is also not for imparting knowledge.   Religious knowledge is the sum of one's own *experience* and sense evidence.   It is not taught.   Dewey complained that "too much education ... has been carried on, in spiritual as well as in other matters," utilizing the principle that "the child is to be taught down to, or talked down to, from the standpoint of the adult."

Effectively relegating objective magisterial teaching to the category of mere subjective adult *experience*, Dewey said children must not be "inoculated externally" with the views and emotions *adults* (i.e., the *Church*) "have found serviceable to themselves."   Children must be led to discover and appreciate the "religious aspects" of their "own growing life."   It is wrong to use adult ideas "to supply the standard of the religious nature of the child."   Dewey repudiated "[t]he habit of basing religious instruction upon a formulated statement of the doctrines and beliefs of the church," and upon the belief that "since a catechism represents the wisdom and truth of the adult mind," the child can be given "at once the benefit of adult experience."[68]   Further, since the "consciousness of sin,

---

[65]Archibald, ibid.; Brelsford, ibid.; Smalley and Duffy, ibid.; Sutton, pp. 32, 84, 91, 97, 101; George Vander Zanden, "Committee Chairperson Receives Award," *Caravan* (a publication of the Canadian Bishops' National Office of Religious Education, Ottawa), Spring 1990, p. 5.

[66]John Dewey, "Religious Education as Conditioned by Modern Psychology and Pedagogy," *The Religious Education Association: Proceedings of the First Convention, Chicago 1903* (Chicago: The Religious Education Association, 1903), p. 60, religiouseducation.net.

[67]Ferreira, ibid.; Sutton, pp. 71, 75, 77.

[68]Repudiation of catechism is consistent with Dewey's anti-educational creed, which he expressed as follows: "Genuine ignorance [is] profitable because it is

repentance, redemption, etc.," stem only from the adult's spiritual and emotional experiences, children cannot be expected to have the same consciousness. Clearly, foreseeing that Dewey's monstrous error would infect the Church, Heaven itself took the unprecedented step of refuting it. In 1917, Our Lady of Fatima was sent to show three young children a vision of hell in all its horror. She made clear that God wants children to have the same consciousness of sin, repentance, and redemption as adults. She told the seers: "You have seen hell, where the souls of poor *sinners* go [having not *repented*]. To save them [*redemption*], God wishes to establish in the world devotion to My Immaculate Heart."[69]

Like the other convention speakers, Dewey was influenced by Darwin.[70] So he emphasized that ignoring the "fundamental principle of continuity of development" would cause "maladjustment resulting from the premature fixation of intellectual and emotional habits" in childhood. It could produce "shock and upheaval" and "crises of frightful doubt" when a soul realizes "it has been passively accepting … ideas and feelings which it now recognizes are not a vital part of its own being." Dewey thus planted, a century ago, the seeds of evolutionary *pilgrimage* and *constant change*, as well as personal, experiential spirituality. Those seeds have produced the harvest of adult faith, the Counterchurch.

Now, humanists consider so-called "secular" humanism a religion, which they term *religious humanism*. Hence, they gladly promote religious education if they can control its content, because what they actually teach is *religious humanism*. The deity of this religion is Man. Its goal is a world community of peace and prosperity created by man, without

---

likely to be accompanied by … open-mindedness; whereas ability to repeat catch phrases, cant terms, familiar propositions … coats the mind with varnish waterproof to new ideas" (Ferreira, ibid.). In other words, Dewey recognized that memorization of catechism is a bulwark against heresy and brainwashing; after Vatican II, catechism was thrown out of religion class by his followers.

[69]Sister Lucia's memoirs, *Fatima in Lucia's Own Words*, ed. Father Louis Kondor, SVD, trans. Dominican Nuns of Perpetual Rosary (Fatima: Postulation Centre, 1976), edition without photographs, p. 167.

[70]Archibald, ibid.

any dependence on God.[71]   Remember that according to Dewey, religion harms the dignity of man, so it's a religious *attitude* — spirituality — that must be inculcated. Religious education is thus a *change agent* to help one adjust his thinking to the world, and to change institutions to meet the needs of the world — what Dewey calls "reorganiz[ing] the social consciousness of the race."   And so, religious education is "understood as pilgrimage."[72] It produces an "adult" faith and "adult" church.

Highly promoted and funded by the hierarchy, the adult religious education industry[73] is not here to teach the unchanging truths of the Roman Catholic Faith, but to *destroy* them in whatever pre-Vatican II mindsets still exist. A report by the National Office of Religious Education of the Canadian Conference of Catholic Bishops said that adult religious education is needed "as some people are still bound to pre-Vatican II notions of church" and need "faith updating."[74] The report, titled *Adult Faith, Adult Church,* was approved by then-Bishops Aloysius Ambrozic, Emmett Doyle, Adam Exner and Marcel Gervais. It was edited by Joanne Chafe. Most of the information on adult catechesis cited herein is from this report and the bishops' resource books *Insight* and *Insight, Number 2,* also edited by Chafe.[75]

Journey to Godhood

According to the Canadian bishops' National Advi-

---

[71]Kurtz, pp. 3, 7-10.

[72]Yob, pp. 522-24, 528-29, 534-37.

[73]The reason given for this industry is "Pope John Paul II's Apostolic exhortation on catechesis, *Catechesi tradendae,* [which] affirms article 20 of the *General catechetical directory* [*sic*]" that adult education is "the chief form of catechesis": "Adult Religious Education," p. 15. For an outline of the American bishops' program, see *Our Hearts Were Burning Within Us: A Pastoral Plan for Adult Faith Formation in the United States,* November 17, 1999, nccbuscc.org.

[74]"Adult Religious Education," ibid.

[75]*Insight* was approved by Bishops Ambrozic, Exner, Gervais and Faber MacDonald, whilst *Insight 2* was approved by Bishops Exner, Gervais, MacDonald and Frederick Henry.

sory Committee on Adult Religious Education (chaired by Chafe), "we are all pilgrims and companions on this journey towards adult faith."[76] What does "adult" mean? *An adult is simply a person who has reached godhood.* Christ is the Word, but the National Advisory Committee, attempting like Dewey and Jung to combine nature and grace, exhorted an international conference of religious educators in 1988: "... the adult should be wholistic ..., avoiding all kinds of dualisms and encompassing the human and the divine. Each person is a 'word' to be spoken and to be heard." Adults, therefore, "will not accept unconditionally anything that the authority of the church proposes or suggests, but they will want to ... argue or think it over." In Jungian style, adult religious education is meant "to facilitate inner-direction within the community of faith, and it aims at building small Christian communities." The inner-directed adult is a person who "make[s] judgments and take[s] decisions by being guided from the inside by the indwelling Spirit of Christ,"[77] i.e., not from the outside by God speaking through His Church. Being our own authority (gnosticism) makes us gods, so we need not pray to God, the Blessed Mother and the saints for help.

Belief in "inner guidance" is similar to the pantheistic New Age belief that God, the universe, and we are one unified force,[78] so we can each evolve towards individual godhood by using occult means to access the supposedly divine knowledge of this force hidden *within* us. Adult religious education indeed involves occult techniques to get in touch with one's unconscious.[79] *Adult faith* and *adult church* are,

---

[76]"Christian Orientation," p. 8.

[77]Ibid., pp. 8, 10-11. Skipping the God-talk, humanist Erich Fromm describes the rationale for inner direction: "... only man himself can determine the criterion for virtue and sin and not an authority transcending him." See *The Humanist Postion and Organization*, Pamphlet 601 of the American Humanist Association.

[78]For Dewey, "'God' denoted the force that brings about a union between the actual and the ideal.... His complaint against religion was that this force is shackled by ... beliefs and practices that isolate believers from their natural selves and their environments": Yob, p. 526.

[79]Parent, p. 14; Denis and Green, p. 49; id., "Facilitating Right Brain Learning," *Caravan*, Spring 1988, p. 10. *Caravan* is another adult faith resource of the Ca-

therefore, just terms for the pantheistic, gnostic Counterchurch that will *pose as* Catholicism in the one-world religion.

In practice, adult faith uses the humanistic technique of *faith* values clarification — discovering *your* faith through the process (searching for a spirituality that "feels right"), then *living* according to the faith you devise for yourself. The local church must accept all faith interpretations. Therefore, by logical extension, adult faith must also be indifferentist. In fact, since its beginnings in 1903, the adult faith industry has always been syncretic as diversity helps growth.[80]

Now, it takes pride to believe we have all the answers within our god-selves, so adult religious education has to "foster self-esteem." It builds communities to act as *support groups*, termed "secure learning environments" or "private survival units," where converts to adult faith feel accepted. This is important, because the newly enlightened often find themselves unappreciated by the unconverted grassroots in the parish.[81] *World Youth Day is an adult faith support group* for young Catholics whose values are at odds with their elders.

Another reason for building community is that promoting autonomy is only half the agenda; a person then has to be led towards the *desired outcome*, which is union with the global religion. Individualism is forbidden in the collectivist one-world. As the bishops' literature admits, there is a

---

nadian bishops.

[80]Roberts, p. 11; Yob, pp. 530, 534. Adult faith spokesman Stokes explains its humanistic values-clarification nature: "Our working definition is 'Faith is ... making meaning of life's significant ... issues, adhering to this meaning, and acting it out.' The *adult* factor emphasizes that faith is *not* just something learned in childhood, but rather an *ongoing process* throughout the adult life cycle...." Stokes also explains its syncretic nature: "Perceptions of 'God,' 'Jesus Christ' and other dimensions of faith *are highly personal* ... because of one's family upbringing, religious tradition, life style.... *it is this wide variety of faith interpretations* that makes it so necessary that the local church ... accept all individual persons, regardless of their beliefs.... Adult faith has no denominational limitations." Participants in workshops and conferences come from all religious traditions, including Humanism, he adds, "and we ... grow through the diversity of shared understandings of adult faith." (Emphases in original.)

[81]"Christian Orientation," pp. 8, 12; Denis and Green, "Process," p. 49; "Maturing Adult Believers," p. 43; "Structures Which Support," pp. 60, 64; "Faith Community as Educator," pp. 23, 25.

risk involved in putting much emphasis on the person's growth, autonomy, self-direction and responsibility: it is the risk of promoting an individualistic conception of Christian existence.... the risk is lessened when growth is fostered within a community setting. This is why it is *vital* for adult religious education that small faith communities be brought into existence....[82]

"Marks" of the Counterchurch

Adult catechesis is outcomes-based education. It uses the conditioning techniques of discussion, story-telling, role-playing, situation-ethics games, music, drama, etc., to implant desired values.[83] Since the pilgrimage is a process of learning, adult catechesis must be experiential and personal. We allegedly learn only from ourselves, so we start with our own experiences or "stories." According to an article in one of the Canadian bishops' adult faith books, the justification for experiential religion is none other than Jesus — stripped of His divinity. Since Jesus "increased in wisdom and stature and favour" as a child (Lk. 2:52), then "Jesus, like all of us, learned through his experience and developed because of it."[84] In other words, Christianity is mere religious humanism.

This is the Church shorn of her divinity, the Arian Counterchurch described by Archbishop Sheen. Its members — the community — equate themselves with Christ and proclaim *they* are the body of Christ (not members of His Mystical Body), *they* are the Church. Since they are creating the "authentic" Church, they appropriate to themselves a gnostic divinity, and the community supplants Christ and His Mystical Body.[85]

---

[82]"Christian Orientation," p. 13 (emphasis added). Cf. Parent, p. 15.

[83]Also used in schools, Outcomes-Based Education (OBE) is a manipulative methodology for instilling New World Order values or "outcomes." The same conditioning techniques are utilized in World Youth Day activities, including the catechesis sessions.

[84]Walter Vogels, "Biblical Wisdom: A Trust in Human Experience," *Insight 2*, p. 15 (see p. 23).

[85]Sister Burkin, p. 82; cf. Cornelia R. Ferreira, "Our Blessed Mother and the

The following quotations from *The New Concise Catholic Dictionary*[86] show how the marks of the true Church have been modified to become the humanistic marks of the community, the Counterchurch.

"Church teachers today note that the church community — the body of Christ and the people of God — has four basic Christian marks...." These marks are as follows:

"1) [I]t is one in faith." True: it is founded around a common set of humanistic beliefs, but not the doctrines of the Catholic Church; furthermore, the true Catholic Church is one not *just* in her faith, but also in her hierarchical government, sacraments and liturgy.[87]

"2) [I]t is holy, as Jesus of Nazareth, the founder of the Christian community, was holy." Saying Jesus *was* (past tense) a holy man from Nazareth imputes to Him only a human nature, and denies that as God He is alive and still running His Church. Furthermore, the Catholic Church is holy not just in her Founder, but also in her purpose, which is the glory of God and the sanctification of men; holy in her means to attain her purpose, which are her doctrines, laws, liturgy and religious institutions; and holy in her fruits, which are the countless saints produced.[88]

"3) [I]t is catholic or universal." The universalism denoted by the small-c "catholic" does not refer to the worldwide extent of the Roman Catholic Church, but to what is termed "the universality of God's saving will and action"[89] — everyone is saved. This is opposed to the exclusivity of Catholicism, which teaches salvation only through the Catholic Church.

The religion of Unitarian Universalism, which postulates universal salvation and a world religion, seems to be the

---

Return to Holiness, Part II," *Catholic Family News*, November 2001, p. 1. The Arian church poses a physical danger to traditionalists, as Church history attests.

[86]S.v. "Ecclesiology."

[87]Ludwig Ott, *Fundamentals of Catholic Dogma*, ed. James Canon Bastible, trans. Patrick Lynch (Cork, Ireland: The Mercier Press, 1955; 4th ed., 1960; reprint ed., Rockford, IL: Tan Books and Publishers, 1974), p. 303.

[88]Ibid., p. 305.

[89]Father Duggan, p. 64.

basis of the Counterchurch. It, too, teaches religious humanism, i.e., the purpose of religion is to improve the temporal lot
of man. It is rationalistic, experiential and pantheistic, believing God is the universal *force* of Love. There's no original sin;
and Jesus was just a great teacher whose death was not an
atonement for sin, but a demonstration of God's love for His
children. Because God is a power or force, not a living Person, its adherents praise God not by liturgical worship, but by
service or love.[90] *Universalist* "Catholicism," therefore, encourages Catholics, especially converts, to retain the pagan
beliefs and practices of their nation, i.e., it encourages inculturation. Through inculturation, "our church [is] now becoming a world church," with "a people prepared to be world
church in a global community." That is, inculturation is vital
for turning the Church into the Counterchurch that will be
admitted to the Masonic one-world religion (the calling card
of Masonry being religious indifferentism). Because Catholicism is considered European and Western, Counterchurch
members are genuinely disturbed when they see "traditional
European patterns of religious expression" still holding sway
over people from other cultures.[91]

We will see later that World Youth Day encourages
inculturation and social service, whilst its cross promulgates
the *Unitarian Universalist* notion of Christ's death.

"4) [I]t is apostolic. The church community is thus to
remain a true continuation of the apostolic community and
fundamentally dedicated to the apostles' mission...." However, since this *Catholic Dictionary* also states (falsely) that the
"hierarchy of ordained leaders" only developed centuries after the Church's founding, it implies the "apostolic community" was one of equals.[92] Hence, claiming the church com-

---

[90]*The New Encyclopaedia Britannica*, 15th ed. (1992), s.v. "Unitarians and
Universalists," by John Charles Godbey; *The New Encyclopaedia Britannica
Micropaedia*, 15th ed. (1992), s.v. "Universalism"; K. D. D. Henderson, "Francis
Younghusband and the Mysticism of Shared Endeavour" (London: World Con-
gress of Faiths, 1976), pp. 6-8.

[91]Father Duggan, pp. 61-64. The merger of paganism with Catholicism is pantheism.

[92]A vocations booklet for youth, advertising the various religious orders in

munity is a continuation of the apostolic community equates the community with the hierarchy and gives the community the power to appoint bishops. [93]

Appropriating the Power of Teaching

The adult faith literature makes it clear that the community is replacing the Church by usurping her threefold power to teach, govern and sanctify.

But first, the community replaces God. Faith is said to come through the *community*, not from God.[94] "Faith," you see, is another word whose meaning has been altered. Faith is not belief in the true God and His Revelation. Nor is it an infused gift distributed by God to whomever He wishes. This undemocratic way of behaving is unacceptable to Deweyites. Hence, faith is defined as a *relationship*, "not referring specifically or exclusively to a relationship with God. Faith could be a relationship with people, causes, ideas...."[95] Allegedly, "one of the great hungers of modern men and women is relatedness" (as Archbishop Sheen said, "hunger to belong to a community").[96] Since the community provides relationships, it

---

Canada, and published by vocation *directors*, states that bishops and priests "emerged in response to the needs of the church." See Br. Rodney Warman, OFM Cap., "Responding to the Needs of the People, the 'Church'," *Vocations.ca*, 3d ed. (Toronto: Toronto Area Vocation Directors Association, 2001), p. vii.

[93]The Modernist proposition that the Church hierarchy is the result of a general historical development, rather than divinely instituted by Christ, was condemned by Popes St. Pius X and Pius XII. Moreover, the errors that (a) the power of the Church belongs to the *community*, making the faithful one with Christ as sole priest and victim; and (b) the power of ecclesiastical rule is derived from the community, have also been condemned by the Church. See Ott, pp. 276-77, and Denzinger, nos. 960, 966-67, 1502, 1515.

[94]Sister Elizabeth Bellefontaine, SC, "Living Christian Community: A Biblical Perspective," *Insight 2*, p. 31 (see p. 33). Cf. "Adult Religious Education," p. 14.

[95]Jack D. Spiro, Editorial, *Religious Education*, Fall 1989, p. 482. Naturalistic "faith" can even be a relationship with pagans or atheists (cf. "Faith Community as Educator," p. 23). *Indifferentism is thus an integral part of adult catechesis* and its heretical notion of faith. The RCIA, the catechesis program for converts, also teaches that faith is "relational": it "can come from and lead to communal religious experiences." See "Adult Religious Education," ibid.

[96]Spiro, ibid. Adult faith educators themselves speak of "a hunger for community": see "Faith Community as Educator," pp. 23-24.

provides faith (which adds another dimension to the term "faith community"). It is God.

Now, the first step in the Church's task of saving souls is to *teach* all the truths of God's Revelation. This is Her mandate from Christ. However, adult faith literature reveals the *faith community* is the pre-eminent educator.[97] But since catechesis is not about teaching the Catholic Faith, what the community does is *develop*, i.e., "update" faith,[98] especially of those "still bound to pre-Vatican II notions."

Faith development is today's term for Dewey's evolutionary concept of "continuity of development." Thus, religious educators recognize that faith development is a revolutionary idea that differs from *having* faith, i.e., belief in God and the unchanging truths He teaches through the Catholic Church:

> … the term "faith development" also presents a problem of incongruity for people whose "faith" is essentially belief, doctrine, or dogma…. [U]ntil one understands and accepts the basic concept of faith as <u>dynamic</u>, faith as <u>process</u>, faith as <u>ever becoming</u>, "faith development" is but a juxtaposition of *mutually exclusive* words.

Their basic definitions of faith and faith development are as follows:

Faith: The finding and making meaning of life's significant questions and issues, adhering to this meaning, and acting it out.

Faith development: The dynamics by which a person finds and makes meaning of life's significant questions and is-

---

[97]"Faith Community as Educator," ibid. The community is not only the chief educator, but also the catechesis *text* (i.e., one learns from its members' experiences), says Michael Warren in *Faith, Culture, and the Worshipping Community: Shaping Practice in the Local Church* (New York: Paulist Press, 1989), reviewed by Diane J. Hymans, *Religious Education*, p. 635. Also see "Faith Community as Educator," p. 25.

[98]Adamson, pp. 40-44.

sues, adheres to this meaning, and acts it out....[99]

This is pure humanism: find the values that define your spirituality, then apply them to your life. This is *your* personal
faith. Hence articles on youth constantly refer to *their* faith.
There is a near universal, unthinking acceptance today of heretical *my*-faith, *your*-faith, *their*-faith terminology.

Developmentalist James Fowler has postulated six
stages in "faith development," the "journey in faith," or "life-
long conversion." A person moves beyond a certain stage
when it no longer helps him derive "meaning out of life";
each stage involves "the working out of new values." The
pre-Vatican II Church was at the immature stage three of dependent and conformist believers. This stage is inhabited by
non-rebels, equivalent to children of eleven or twelve, "anxious to respond faithfully to the expectations and judgments
of significant others." Faith after Vatican II has reached the
"more mature" stage five in which believers are questioners,
indifferentist, interdependent and concerned about the global
community. Those involved in social activism are at a
"higher stage" of faith than those concerned merely with religious and moral beliefs.[100]

Journeying to a Democratic Church

The Catholic Church also has the power to *govern*,
through the papacy and episcopacy. However, hierarchy
does not suit the Masonic tenet of equality and democracy.
Therefore, since all are equal in the community, the *community* is appropriating the Church's hierarchical power of governing. As seen earlier, the pilgrimage itself is the equalizer.

A fine example of how pilgrimage acts as an equalizer, following the principles of John Dewey, is seen in Re-

---

[99]Religious Education Association of the United States and Canada, *Faith Development in the Adult Life Cycle*, (1987), Module 1, pp. 3-4. (Underlinings in
original; italicized emphasis added.)
    [100]"Maturing Adult Believers," pp. 37, 40-41.

gina, Saskatchewan. At the invitation of its bishop, the entire archdiocese started on pilgrimage in 2001 to form a diocesan-wide community by turning all parishes into communities having a common direction and goals. Since the new church must reflect the values of the pilgrims, a "new vision" is needed. The visioning *process* is the pilgrimage, and it's called "VisionQuest." Its propaganda pamphlet states:

> Standing at the dawn of a new millennium, this is a time of new beginnings. The paramount question we face is "What is the church of the Archdiocese of Regina going to look like in the coming decade?" It is a question we must ... answer as a *community*. Decisions need to be made based on a *new vision* and comprehensive plan that will give a *common direction* to bring unity and dynamism to meet future challenges.[101]

Note the built-in evolutionary Dewey principle that the pilgrimage never reaches a goal, but is dynamic, i.e., continually moving and modifying beliefs in order to be relevant ("meet future challenges"). So Regina is only planning changes for the first decade and then it will modify its direction as needed. The discerning is being directed by a "process facilitator" who is training parish facilitators. Illustrating that pilgrimage is an outcomes-based educational process, a *standardized* format will be utilized by these facilitators in parish discussion groups.[102]

The equalizing aspect is apparent in the pamphlet's stated aims that "*together* the ordained and the laity" will "craft a vision," "create a strategic plan," and "determine the changes required" to move towards the vision "as a diocesan community." The process seeks to "problem solve" (the Dewey principle of starting from "a less desirable state of affairs"). Yet, in spite of 2,000 years of problem solving, the

---

[101] Archdiocese of Regina, *Visioning for the New Millennium*.   (Emphases added.)
[102] "VISIONQUEST 2001," *The Arch* [archdiocesan paper], September 2001, p. 1; Frank Flegel, "Facilitator Hired for Regina Archdiocese," [*Prairie Messenger*, Muenster, SK, ca. Fall 2001].

hierarchy is no longer able to do this by itself — that's because the hierarchy *is* one of the "problems"! In the new vision, committees, teams and facilitators are the hierarchy. These Counterchurch "bishops" or "approved party leaders," as Archbishop Sheen titled them, "derive their authority fom the apostles Marx and Lenin."[103]

Another "problem" is obviously the Church's exclusivity, because the visioning process is meant to facilitate universalism. The propaganda pamphlet says the process will also consider the input of non-practising Catholics and *other faith communities*, i.e., other religions. The "operating principles" are that everyone must listen respectfully to everyone else and seek "the common good *over* personal preferences *faithful to our Catholic foundations*." In other words, as in the days of the Arian heresy, the only thing suppressed is Tradition, whilst no one — not even a priest — is allowed to correct error as the *foundations* of the Church are destroyed in Regina and the Counterchurch erected on the rubble.

Montreal launched its 5-year plan for equality in October 2003, "aimed at ensuring another generation of Christians in Montreal." "Faith education" has to be "a priority" in all parishes. It will be outcomes-based; *everyone* will have to be "on the same wavelength" by following authorized catechetical programs. Community will be built by the use of volunteer teachers (aided by trained "master catechists"). The goal is "to have Christian communities where the life experienced there is desirable, *different* and exciting. We can't be strictly about rituals." Roman Catholicism is obviously neither exciting nor Christian, because the people are "to be initiated into a different kind of life, a Christian life," i.e., a new church.[104]

Kingston, Ontario, is also implementing a democratizing process.[105] Its "new pastoral vision" "calls for an expanded

---

[103]Archbishop Sheen, p. 26.
[104]Christina Parsons, "Montreal Pastoral Plan Crosses Generations," *Catholic Register*, November 30, 2003, p. 13. (Emphasis added.)
[105]Therese Greenwood, "Kingston Pastoral Vision Calls for Living out of Faith," ibid., January 18, 2004, p. 8.

relationship between clergy and laypeople, noting that 'This conversion should move us from seeing the church as primarily bishops, priests and religious, to seeing it as the Body of Christ, in which each one of us is an important member.'"

Following the 1999 document *Ecclesia in America*, Abp. Anthony Meagher[106] holds the laity "largely responsible for the future [and "renewal"] of the church." In "an ongoing process [of] collaboration between laypeople and priests," the priest is merely a *facilitator*, he says. The priest's role is "not telling people what to do," but "to step back and say, hey, a layperson can have a vision of the Gospel that is as good as mine." The bishop admits this abdication "can be a frightening thing" for a priest to do. His reassuring propaganda for the role reversal is, "But a layperson is going to take that vision into places where a priest doesn't go, such as his ... workplace." Of course, lay people have always done this, without considering themselves equal to priests.

As per the outcomes-based formula, Kingston has hired "a full-time resource person [i.e., facilitator] to assist both priests and parishioners with implementing the vision," i.e., to ensure everyone joins Adult Church. Notice how lay facilitators fit Archbishop Sheen's description of "approved party leaders" or "secret police [who] keep the errant in the party line."[107]

Halifax, Nova Scotia, facing the closing and consolidation of inner-city parishes, a 17.5 per cent Mass attendance rate, and a declining number of priests, has also jumped on the community bandwagon. Archbishop Terrence Prendergast, SJ, wants "fewer, but more vibrant centres." An adult faith process and bureaucracy is being set up, with special emphasis on involving *youth* "in all aspects of parish life."[108]

There is another agenda to forming parish communities. It involves money and jobs. Forty years of subversive Catholic education, accompanied by the revolution in doc-

---

[106]Prior to his Kingston appointment, Archbishop Meagher was an auxiliary bishop of Toronto and chairman of the World Youth Day Committee.

[107]Archbishop Sheen, p. 26.

[108]"Halifax Launches Renewal Plan," *Catholic Register*, February 15, 2004, p. 5.

trine and liturgy, has produced a dearth of vocations and the empty pew. Worldwide, churches are closing, parishes and dioceses are merging, priests' pension funds are drying up, clerical criminality is increasing financial stress, and diocesan personnel and lay leaders face "downsizing." However, in many areas, the Counterchurch is capitalizing on the shrinking clerical base to build community and keep the money flowing in. The strategy is found in the following report that cites a member of Regina's Visioning Steering Committee:

> The bottom line, according to [Fr. John] Weekend, is to try and maintain the parishes as viable Christian communities "even in light of the fact that a lot of them won't have resident priests. I think the philosophy is that we don't want to go around closing parishes, but let the parishes decide whether they are viable," Weekend said. He suggested there may have to be greater sharing of resources and personnel, ordained and non-ordained, among all parishes.[109]

This philosophy is also being put into practice in the United States. Sixteen percent of its parishes — 3,000 churches — are now "priestless parishes." They are "high on community, volunteer participation and competent, professional lay leadership." This is where all those graduates of leadership courses come into their own. People have been "empowered" "to assume responsibility for their own parish family church," says a nun who is a "parish director." Parishioners seemingly "adapt" to lay leaders holding Communion services "in lieu of Mass," so much so *that often community appears to eclipse Eucharist [i.e., Mass] in importance.*" Hence, "most agree that having lay leaders is better than closing parishes."[110] What we see here is the *realization* of lay equality.

---

[109]Flegel, ibid.

[110]"O Father Where Art Thou? How Catholics are Coping Without Resident Priests," *Catholic New Times*, June 6, 2004, p. 13 (emphasis added). Lay presiders also lead priestless parishes on Canada's native reserves: Sister Norma Samar, OLM, "The Sacred Journey," *Catholic Missions in* Canada, Fall 2003, p. 13; Sister Carmen Catellier, SNJM, "Lay Leaders Give Their Love and Service," ibid., p. 30. Some lay leaders are even called lay pastors now.

Viable priestless parishes are the back door to the democratic church. Of course, if traditional orders and priests were not suppressed, as they are in huge numbers today, there would be no priest "shortage" — but then, community would suffer a great setback.

A Counterchurch needs bodies and money to be viable, so building community is critical. Besides the conversion of parishes and dioceses worldwide into local branches of the universal Counterchurch,[111] Catholics are being recruited for this church through programs like World Youth Day, as will be shown later.

God the Community

Now let's look at how the community is trying to usurp the Church's power to *sanctify*, in particular through the sacraments. Christ conferred this power on His *ordained* ministers. But today, the *community* "administers" sacraments, and sometimes considers *itself* the sacrament. Father Ronald Oakham of the North American Forum on the Catechumenate elucidates: "... we often refer to the action of the Church (*especially* the celebration of sacraments) as being done by the parish community and not just by the parish priest."[112] Further, as per New Age leader Alice Bailey's plan, the sacraments are being "mystically" interpreted. As she required, their meanings have been altered so that they are no longer means of passing on true doctrine, whilst their outward appearances are being preserved just enough to fool "the many who are accustomed to church usages."

Baptism incorporates us into the Mystical Body of Christ, infuses supernatural life into the soul through sanctifying grace, and confers the right to eternal life through the forgiveness of original sin. It also infuses the theological virtues of faith, hope and charity. However, the Canadian bish-

---

[111]Ron Stang, "London [ON] Diocese Looks to Embrace a 'Future Full of Hope,'" *Catholic Register*, June 20, 2004, p. 16.
[112]Father Ronald A. Oakham, OC, letter, May 4, 1992. (Emphasis added.)

ops' adult church literature says:

> Faith comes through the *community* and unites one into the community.... From the vine who is Jesus *and* the body [i.e., the community] whose head is Christ, the members receive *life*, the same divine life coursing through the branching vine and the whole body.[113]

In other words, the community considers *itself* the "sacrament" of Baptism, giving faith and a "life" that apes sanctifying grace. That's why we find statements in church bulletins like, "Through this Community we receive eternal life."[114] Writing in Toronto's archdiocesan paper, syndicated columnist Fr. Ron Rolheiser, OMI, former General Councillor for Canada for the Oblates of Mary Immaculate, also implies the community opens heaven to us:

> God is a flow of relationships ... to be experienced in community.... God *is* community, family, parish, friendship, hospitality.... in coming to know God, the dinner table is more important than the theology classroom, the practice of grateful hospitality is more important than the practice of right dogma.... we can't go to hell if we stick close to family, community and parish....[115]

This statement illustrates that pantheism, the belief that God is one with the universe, and hence with the community, undergirds the heresy that salvation is obtained through the community if we "go with the flow" — of relationships. The community is God, a flow of relationships. So faith is a gift of "God the Community."

That is why community is the *focus* of the Rite of Christian Initiation of Adults (RCIA), the catechumenate program to instruct converts — and *re-educate parishioners* — for the Adult Church. The genealogy of the RCIA reveals it was

---

[113]Bellefontaine, ibid. (Emphases added.)

[114]A Regina church bulletin, cited in a personal communication with the author.

[115]"God is to be Experienced Within the Community," *Catholic Register*, June 25, 2001, p. 23. (Emphasis added.)

devised as one of Vatican II's subversive tools. It reintro-
duced a perverted form of the adult catechumenate used by
the early Church. That original catechumenate was a prolonged intellectual and moral preparation to strengthen the
faith of new converts aginst pagan doctrines and persecu-
tion.[116] Today's "catechumenate" does just the opposite.
Adult church and RCIA literature make it plain that its intent
is not to protect the faith of converts, but to train them in
Counterchurch doctrine.

The RCIA: Begotten by Bugnini

The genealogy of the RCIA is as follows. The implementation of Vatican II's liturgical revolution was entrusted
to a group of bishops and *periti* (experts) known as the Consilium.   The Consilium was headed by Freemason Father
(later Archbishop) Annibale Bugnini, architect of the Novus
Ordo Mass. He assigned its work to several committees.
Consilium member and *peritus* Msgr. Balthasar Fischer, who
served on the preparatory commission for Vatican II, was put
in charge of the committee to restore the catechumenate. Ecu-
menist Fischer was a "pioneer and giant of the liturgical reform." He co-founded the Liturgical Institute at Trier, Germany, in 1947, and trained thirty-five disciples from different
countries who then spread his revolution worldwide.[117]
One of his graduates, Boston's Msgr. Frederick
McManus, was a founder of the language-wrecking International Committee on English in the Liturgy (ICEL) and long-
time member of its Advisory Board. Monsignor McManus

---

[116]*The Catholic Encyclopedia* (NY: The Encyclopedia Press, 1913), s.v.
"Catechumen" and "Doctrine, Christian," both by T. B. Scannell.

[117]Father John K. McKenna, CM, "In Memoriam: Balthasar Fischer," naal-
liturgy.org/memoriam; Father Paul Turner, "Balthasar Fischer, 1912-2001," paul-
turner.org/fischer; "Requiescat in Pace: Msgr. Balthasar Fischer," U.S. Bishops
Committee on the Liturgy newsletter, nccbuscc.org, February 2002.   In the
1970s, Monsignor Fischer observed, "We priests, theologians, and especially we
liturgists are going to have a lot to answer to God for, because we deprived the
people of the whole devotional life":   Oswald Sobrino, "A Ray of Light in the
Smoke," catholicanalysis.blogspot.com, October 13, 2003.

worked on Fischer's committee to develop the RCIA, which was approved by Paul VI in 1972.[118]

The RCIA is considered "the showpiece document of the Post Vatican II Church. It is the document which most clearly articulates the vision of the Council."   It "sets a course" for a new ecclesiology, a new idea of the Church. That idea or vision is to have communities of equals, co-responsible for "ministries and mission." The RCIA is "prophecy of the highest order" in parishes, where "prophecy" is a euphemism for *change agent*. It is "such a radical shift" in "vision and practice" that the RENEW program was introduced to help pre-condition Catholics for the change, and so create a "welcoming environment" for RCIA in the parish. Both programs are "essential" tools in adult faith formation.[119]

In line with the lay-empowering goal of Vatican II, the RCIA switched responsibility for baptismal preparation from the parish priest to the parish. Catechumenate leaders boast it is "helping us redefine leadership in our Church," bringing about "a change in the leadership models the Church has formerly embraced." Monsignor Fischer's slogan was, "Not the shepherds make sheep. Sheep make sheep." Hence, the catechumenate was promoted "as a means for entire parishes to celebrate, catechize, *form community* and serve."[120]

The "Adults" in the RCIA name refers not just to converts, but also to everyone in the parish. This is because the RCIA "is much more than a recipe book for making new Catholics"; it is "the church becoming church," "the community of faith ... express[ing] themselves as a church giving birth to new members," "giving and nourishing new life"[121] — like the Sacrament of Baptism. The goal is achieved by in-

---

[118]Susan Benofy, "What Have we Done to Our Children?", Part I, *Adoremus Bulletin*, adoremus.org, November 2003; Father Turner, ibid.

[119]Father Thomas J. Caroluzza, *RENEW and the RCIA* (Kearny, NJ: National Office of RENEW, [1984]), pp. 1-3, 5-7, 9, 16, 27, 29.

[120]Thea Jarvis, "Forum on the Catechumenate Comes to Emory," *Bulletin* (Atlanta's archdiocesan newspaper, online ed.), georgiabulletin.org, May 2, 1985; Father Turner, ibid. (emphasis added).

[121]Sister Burkin, pp. 84-85.

volving the whole parish in the *process* of initiation, in order to *turn* it into a community. Father Oakham says, "[W]e use the term ... 'initiating community' to refer to the *parishioners* in *their* duty to initiate new members into the Church."[122]

The emphasis is not on regeneration from original sin and the salvation of souls, but on increasing membership in the Counterchurch[123] through the "conversion" of both parishioners and catechumens to community ideology. New converts are incorporated into the Counterchurch, not the Catholic Church. This makes a mockery of the very reason for the drawn-out catechumenal program of the early centuries. To guard against pagan philosophy infiltrating the Church and the danger of apostasy, a stringent intellectual and moral preparation was needed.[124] Today's catechumenate is, however, a primer in error. The RCIA is able to "reconvert" or "reform" the Church "precisely because of its openness to new members with new ideas and insights," i.e., because it welcomes heresy. "A catechumenal model of Church is a Church that is open, pilgrim," and "fit[s] the postmodern world." The RCIA is a process and journey that builds community.[125]

Thus, RCIA belief is that Baptism does not make one a member of the *Catholic* Church, but of the local community. Writing in the Canadian bishops' adult faith resource book, *Insight, Number 2*, liturgist Sr. Nancy Burkin, SSJ, says:

> Entrance into the church means entrance into a people, becoming one in faith and life with the people of God *particularized* in this *local* community.[126]

Note that the terms "church," "people of God" and "commu-

---

[122]Father Oakham, ibid. (Emphasis added.)

[123]In his book, *Christ Denied* (Rockford, IL: TAN Books and Publishers, 1982), Fr. Paul A. Wickens says (p. 13) that, in talking about Baptism and the Eucharist, modernists "concentrate their catechesis on the *secondary* effects of these sacraments, thereby implicitly *denying the primary* (and *de fide*) effects. Baptism becomes 'Initiation' rather than 'Regeneration from Original Sin'...."

[124]*Catholic Encyclopedia*, ibid.

[125]Jarvis, ibid.

[126]Sister Burkin, p. 81. (Emphases added.)

nity" are used interchangeably. They do not refer to the Catholic Church.

Sister Burkin explains several articles of the Rite of Christian Initiation to show its purpose is to produce a community of equals through which salvation is obtained[127]:

> Article 9: "… the people of God, as represented by the local church, should understand … that the initiation of adults is the responsibility of all the baptized…. Hence the entire community must help…."

This shows, says Sister Burkin, that "active participation belongs not only to those few who take on the ministerial roles, for example, sponsors or catechists, but also to the entire congregation itself." Note that priests are missing from the list, as the true ministerial role has been hijacked.

> It is the church who "admits those who intend to become members" (Article 41); the church who makes "the choice and admission of the catechumens" (Article 106); … it is the church, "the community and the neophytes who move forward together" (Article 234).

Article 234 means that the RCIA facilitates the "conversion" of the entire parish into becoming what's labelled an "RCIA Community."[128]

"The RCIA *begins*, then, with the parish community and *not* with potential candidates for membership," comments Sister Burkin. The community is "essential to the process." The process involves core teams and facilitators whose "focus is always on the parish community" to make sure it stays on its faith journey of "continual conversion" to the new church (the "secret police" making sure everyone toes the party line). So important is this pilgrimage that even if there are *no* Baptismal candidates, a "way [must be] devised to help the parish continue its process of conversion." According to

---

[127]Ibid., pp. 80-81.
[128]Ibid., photograph, p. 81.

Sister Burkin, belief in the continual need for "conversion" (journeying away from Catholicism) reflects Teilhard de Chardin's evolutionary theory of human development as "movement to the Omega point." She adds, "The RCIA is built upon this foundation" of continual conversion.[129]

In other words, the *primary* goal and true purpose of the RCIA is to facilitate the entry of whole parishes into the Counterchurch. The RCIA's touted role in the preparation of converts to Catholicism is only the *cover* for its revolutionary agenda. Indeed, according to the Canadian bishops' adult faith literature, the RCIA is an important tool in "the process of building Church" (the Counterchurch): "People are having an experience of being co-creators of a spirit of Church: *the Rite of Christian initiation of adults* [*sic*] supports this process." The RCIA is "process learning" because it is experiential and communal: "it calls for the total engagement of the learners, facilitator and community."[130] This is a highly significant disclosure of the RCIA's revolutionary nature because process learning borrows from Dewey, Jung and the occult.

Adult faith and process learning facilitators Marge Denis and Caryl Green tell us in the Canadian bishops' *Insight, Number 2* manual that process is a journey, an exodus, "to an unknown promised land." In line with the humanist teaching on pilgrimage, "[g]ood process does not favour the strong; it *equalizes*. There is no room for ... dominant power...." Process leads to "empowerment of the *group*" and, by implication, to revolution and the destruction of hierarchy and authority. Process learning is also "spiritual," as it "connects with both our unconscious and our conscious selves." Denis and Green explain that "to be in touch with the unconscious is to be in touch with the shadow."[131] Jung popularized the occult concept of "shadow," one's dark or evil side, with which one must come to terms by lowering one's Christian standards. According to a study of Jung's psychology,

---

[129]Ibid., pp. 80-82, 84. (Emphases added.)
[130]"How Adults Learn," p. 50; Denis and Green, pp. 47-48.
[131]Denis and Green, pp. 48-49. (Emphases added.)

To accept the shadow involves … the giving up of cherished ideals, … because the ideals were raised too high or based upon an illusion. Trying to live as better … people than we are involves us in endless hypocrisy … and imposes such a strain on us that we … become worse….[132]

Process learning is, therefore, also a crucial technique for *destroying Christian morality*.

Now, one can only get in touch with one's unconscious or shadow through occult trance. The occult connection between the shadow and getting in touch with one's unconscious through trance is explained by witch Starhawk.[133] Trance, she says, is used to "open up new sources of creativity. When the barriers between the unconscious and the conscious are crossed … solutions to problems arise freely." But trance can be dangerous

because it opens the gates to the unconscious mind. To pass through the gates, we must confront what has been called by occultists the Guardian, or the Shadow on the Threshold: the embodiment of all the impulses and qualities we have thrust into the unconscious because the conscious mind finds them unacceptable. All that we are and feel we should not be — sexual, angry, … guilty … — … refus[es] to let us pass until we have looked it in the face and acknowledged our own essential humanness. No fear is stronger than our fear of our own Shadow, and nothing is more destructive than the defenses we adopt in order to avoid the confrontation.

However, Starhawk demonstrates in an occult session that "confronting" the shadow can also be mentally destructive;

---

[132]Frieda Fordham, cited in Eady, ibid. Jung believed God also has a dark side. So he replaced the Trinity with a quarternity, the fourth person being Satan or Antichrist, "the other face of God" — the "dark side" or shadow of God. Thus, to know God one must experience both good and evil (the shadow), in the process deifying Satan. (Smith, ibid; cf. Thevathansan, ibid.) Eating (experiencing) the fruit of the Tree of Knowledge of good and evil was precisely what God forbade in Eden.

[133]Starhawk, *The Spiral Dance: A Rebirth of the Ancient Religion of the Great Goddess* (San Francisco: Harper & Row, 1979), pp. 139-40, 144-47.

but when successful, she claims, the personality is "inte-
grated" (union of grace and nature, or Jung's "wholeness"),
with a "flowering of personal and creative power," i.e., with
occult abilities. Recognizing the dangers, Denis and Green
tell adult faith process facilitators it is "critical" to "affirm the
learners and provide a secure learning environment" for
them.[134]

More Counterchurch "Sacraments"

Confirmation also involves the community. Community-building activities might even include "youth ministers"
preparing candidates for Confirmation or giving Confirmation "retreats." Further, in some dioceses it is mandatory for
children receiving the sacrament to do a social justice or "volunteer service" project, such as running a soup kitchen or
painting a parish hall.[135] This fits in with the new interpretation of Confirmation. Any militancy is anathema to the
peace-obsessed, so today it is not taught that Confirmation
makes one a soldier of Christ (in any case, fighting for Christ
is unnecessary in a universalist climate); instead, the teaching
is that Confirmation makes one a *full* member of the community. The membership dues are enforced volunteerism.

As for Holy Orders, a priest is increasingly not considered a priest unless the *community* empowers him. He is
only a priest in the community he serves. An article in the
October 1999 issue of *Eucharistic Minister*[136] describes a "eucharistic community" that takes away the pastor's stole and
"commissions" and "blesses" him when he moves elsewhere,
then gives the new pastor the stole and the keys to the
church. The author explains what it means to be a eucharistic

---

[134]Denis and Green, p. 49.
[135]Colleen Connors, "Youth Co-ordinator has an Impact on Halifax Project,"
Catholic Register, March 28, 2004, p. 7; "Kids in the Kitchen," ibid., April 23,
2001, p. 7; Maria Ruiz Scaperlanda, "Heart to Heart," *Columbia*, May 2004, photo
caption, p. 30.
[136]Pat Marrin, "Servants Worthy of the Name," p. 1. (Emphases added.)

community: "No individual member holds status or authority that ... is not derived from the community itself. The outgoing pastor did not take his role in the community with him as he left. Like the stole, that role resided in a *relationship to the community* ... *Every* minister [i.e., priest or lay "minister"] is empowered by the community s/he serves."

This condemned belief stems from the Protestant heresy that denies the ecclesiastical hierarchy by equating the royal priesthood of the faithful with the ordained priesthood. The error is manifested today in euphemisms like "shared leadership" and "the transfer of responsibility to all the baptized," and, as seen, is being openly encouraged by bishops. Pope Pius XII said this heresy leads to the belief that "the people possess the true priestly power, and that the priest acts only in virtue of a function delegated to him by the community." In practice, the people have "communal ownership of the liturgy," and so they limit the priest's liturgical function merely to consecrating by using many lay liturgical "ministers."[137]

The far-ranging effects of this heresy are evinced in the unsavoury case of an Ohio priest arrested for cultivating marijuana. His parishioners decided *they* were willing to forgive him and have him return. This stance is only possible in a community that authorizes a priest, because then it can fire or re-instate him as well. Until their pastor returns to "lead" their parish, parishioners are under a "lay ecclesial minister" or "parish life coordinator." He said the pastor "has given us a vision of what a caring community is supposed to be about, ... to be an adult faith community, to be in relationship with Jesus and one another."[138] Obviously, the faith derived from relationships cares neither about God's nor man's law.

The heresy that the people possess the true priestly power, and the priest acts only in virtue of a function dele-

---

[137]Ferreira, "Our Blessed Mother," ibid.; Ott, ibid.; Denzinger, ibid.; Marrin, ibid. Recall that Archbishop Meagher of Kingston said the priest is merely a facilitator and the *laity* is responsible for keeping the Church going.

[138]"Parish Behind Priest Facing Pot Charge," *Catholic Register*, February 15, 2004, p. 2.

gated to him by the community, also underlies the new interpretation of Penance. Instead of the priest taking the place of
Christ and absolving in His name, he takes the place of God
the Community. Hence, sacramental confession — which is
uncomfortably close to what New Agers consider the "sin" of
individualism — has been reinterpreted as confession to the
community, rather than to Christ. "Regarding the process of
reconciliation not taking place in isolation," Father Oakham
explains:

> By their nature, all sacraments are public celebrations and
> not private. So although one may go to confession to a
> priest (commonly referred to as private confession), it is not
> truly private, but rather individual. It is not private, be-
> cause the priest is *the community's representative. He sits in
> the place of the community as if they were all present.* It is *indi-
> vidual* in that the priest is praying with [Note: not forgiving
> the sins of] one individual and not the whole community.[139]

So confession is unavoidably individual, but also "communal"; this doublethink keeps everyone happy.

If faith is a relationship, and the community God and
alter Christus, then the explanation of the Counterchurch's
"sacrament" of Reconciliation is logical:

> Reconciliation is a breakthrough to a new relationship with
> the community of faith. As such, it is a breakthrough to a
> new relationship with God.... As the Body of Christ, we,
> the Church, are the presence of Christ and the revelation of
> God in our world today. Thus, a breakthrough to God is a
> breakthrough to the community and vice versa.[140]

Only offences against the community or its members
are "sins," so only the community need forgive. A middle-
man (the priest) is not needed as the community administers
the pseudo-sacrament. So a Regina church bulletin proclaims, "[W]hen we fall short, God and the community ex-

---

[139]Father Oakham, ibid. (Emphases added.)
[140]Ibid.

tend open arms of forgiveness and healing to us"; and at a service in Texas, attendants washed each other's hands in a basin of water, saying, "In the name of the community, *I* forgive you for your offences against the community."[141] In hospitals, where confession could be vital, a deacon's wife (acting as a community "minister" to the sick) assured us, "Because priests are hard to get, *we* are hearing confessions."[142]

Next, we come to the heretical interpretation of the Holy Eucharist. First, instead of part of the Mystical Body, the community considers itself the physical Body of Christ, thereby equating itself with the sacrament of Holy Eucharist. Eucharistic ministers are instructed: "Your life as a special minister of Holy Communion must be one of both *being* and *giving* the Body of Christ." They are also told that the *assembly* "is the Body of Christ made visible, audible and tangible."[143] This equating of the Real Presence — the Body and Blood, Soul and Divinity of Jesus — with the community, is implied in a question posed by Roger Cardinal Mahony of Los Angeles: "What does it mean when the Body of Christ comes forward to receive the Body of Christ?"[144]

Now, if the assembly is physically the Body of Christ, it must have undergone "transubstantiation." Father Charles Gallagher hints at this in his booklet *Being the Body of Christ*:

---

[141]Private communication with the author. Interestingly, Archbishop Marcel Gervais of Ottawa, one of the bishops who approved the *Adult Faith* report, "thanks the 12-step ... movement, especially Alcoholics Anonymous, for a new view of confession. In the fifth ... step, people are asked to seek forgiveness from others": Patrick Meagher, "In Terror of Holding God's Hand: The Sacrament of Penance is Being Remodelled," *Toronto Star*, October 25, 1997, p. L20.

[142]For the Church's condemnations and canonical penalties for the heretical act of lay people hearing confessions, see Ferreira, ibid.

[143]Father Michael Kwatera, OSB, *The Ministry of Communion* (Collegeville, MN: The Liturgical Press, 1983), pp. 16-17, 24. (Emphases in original.)

[144]Roger Cardinal Mahony, *Gather Faithfully Together — Guide for Sunday Mass*, as cited in "Liturgy '99 — The Real Absence," *The Catholic Advocate* (Jacksonville, FL), February 1999, p. 1. Note that believing one is the Body of Christ is an important tenet of religious feminism. In her 1983 book, *In Memory of Her*, Elizabeth Schussler Fiorenza said that because women's physical bodies constitute the Body of Christ and are the Church, then denying women autonomous control over their bodies as regards contraception, abortion and perverse sexuality is a "violent," "sacrilegious act": Cornelia R. Ferreira, *The Feminist Agenda Within the Catholic Church* (Toronto: Life Ethics Centre, 1987), p. 4.

When the priest holds up the Eucharist ... and says, "The Body of Christ," ... [he] is also pointing implicitly to the whole congregation and saying, "This too is the body of Christ. These people ... are incorporated into this body [the consecrated Host] of which Christ is the head."[145]

In other words, the Host is also the body of the *people*, i.e., *they* have been "transubstantiated." There's no doubt an heretical "transubstantiation" of the assembly is being promoted. Liturgical director Father Michael Kwatera instructs Eucharistic ministers that they, in particular, have a special "dignity and responsibility" to "become what they give":

You must *become* ... the Body of Christ that you give to your brothers and sisters. In you, as in the bread and wine of the Eucharist, God the Father starts with the *human* and brings out the *beyond-the-human....* the *divine*....[146]

Father Kwatera says "we become what we receive in the Eucharist: the Body of Christ," as expounded in the song, "To Be Your Bread." The song asks: "To be Your bread now, be Your wine now, Lord, come and *change* us.... *Blest and broken*, poured and flowing ... to be Your body *once again*."[147] The "once again" clearly refers to a repeatable event, namely, the requested "transubstantiation." Belief in the transubstantiation of man stems from Teilhard de Chardin and his disciple Karl Rahner.[148]

Thinking the community is the "sacrament" of the Holy Eucharist leads to the claims, "*we* are Eucharist people" or a "Eucharistic community." Adult Church Catholics also teach one should be "Eucharist to others — the body of Christ, in the world...."[149] This means we are gods because Christ is

[145]Father Charles A. Gallagher, SJ, *Being the Body of Christ* (Elizabeth, NJ: The Parish Renewal Weekend, 1978), pp. 30-31. This booklet, rife with heresy, bears the *Imprimatur* of Archbishop Dermot Ryan of Dublin, Primate of Ireland.
[146]Pages 12-13. (Emphases in original.)
[147]Page 13. (Emphasis added.)
[148]Father Wickens, pp. 14-15, 37.
[149]Mark McGowan, "Embracing Change in Our System," speech to Catholic educators in Ottawa, reported in the *Catholic Register*, March 13, 2005, p. 12.

God. Each of us is a god, and the community is collectively a reflection of the pantheistic, universal god. Of course, being divine, we cannot sin and we are all saved (the universalist religion). Further, if everyone is Christ, then there's no need to worship Him in the Blessed Eucharist, so out goes genuflection, Adoration and Benediction. Liturgy "experts" even teach the Eucharist is not "the thing in the box," because "I am Eucharist"; indeed, they say "*the tabernacle diminished our status as the Body of Christ and this was the reason for its removal to less visible locations.*"[150]

Now, it is Church teaching that every Catholic is a part of the *Mystical* Body of Christ. Therefore, the congregation cannot be the *physical* Body of Christ. Pius XII taught "the people in no way represents the person of the divine Redeemer." He condemned the "perverse" belief that Christ is physically one with His members because "while attributing divine properties to human beings, they make Christ Our Lord subject to error and human frailty."[151]

Of course, if the community is Christ, it possesses the priestly power, a condemned heresy which we saw earlier.[152] In the following gnostic piece from Fr. Ron Rolheiser,[153] note how believing one is Christ makes the priest, the Catholic Church and the sacrament of Penance redundant:

> … we are the Body of Christ — flesh, blood, tangible, visible, physical … clearly residing in nameable persons…. We are the ongoing incarnation of God….
>
> What are we given [in this incarnation]? The power, literally, to block death and hell. If we love someone, she [*sic*] cannot go to hell because Christ is loving her. If we for-

---

[150]"Liturgy '99" (emphasis added). This was the teaching at a workshop for catechists. (It should not surprise us that the focus of the Mass itself has changed from the unbloody enactment of the sacrifice of Calvary to a celebration of the community.)

[151]Pius XII, Encyclical letter The Mystical Body of Jesus Christ *Mystici Corporis Christi*, June 29, 1943, and Encyclical letter Christian Worship *Mediator Dei*, November 20, 1947 (Harrison, NY: Roman Catholic Books, n.d.), nos. 85 and 88, respectively.

[152]And see also Pius XII, *Mediator Dei*, nos. 86-88.

[153]"We're God's Incarnation," *Catholic Register*, September 25, 1993, p. 5.

give someone, he is forgiven because Christ is forgiving him.

If children of ours, or others we love, no longer go to church, our love for them and their love for us binds [*sic*] them solidly to the Body of Christ. They continue to touch the hem of Christ's garment as surely as did the woman in the gospels who suffered with a haemorrhage. Their end result, unless they reject their bond to us, will be like hers, namely, healing....

As Father Rolheiser said in a comment cited earlier, "[W]e can't go to hell if we stick close to family, community and parish."

Moving on, Matrimony is also said to concern the entire parish community. "The role of the parish is to help prepare the couple...." "A 'Church Wedding' has little to do with the building and everything to do with the parish church community." Each wedding "is a parish event, one that concerns the entire Church...." How does it involve the "entire Church" (i.e., the *local* parish community)? It's a bit of a stretch, but the priest does the paperwork; catechists (other couples) give the marriage preparation course; "[p]arish musicians offer a choice of music"; and other "parish ministers" (servers and "coordinators") play their part[154] — *ergo*, the "community" is involved.

Extreme Unction has been *restyled* Anointing of the Sick, and it too stresses community. All the following quotations on changes to the sacrament are from publications of the Toronto Archdiocese.[155]

The Sacrament of the Anointing of the Sick is especially intended to strengthen those who are suffering serious illness. For a long time, this sacrament was celebrated only with people who were dying .... It was meant to give them strength to face death. But today, it is offered to support,

---

[154]Catholic Office of Religious Education, Archdiocese of Toronto, *Preparing for Marriage*, 2004.

[155]Id., *Anointing of the Sick*, 2004; Office of Lay Ministry and Chaplaincy, Archdiocese of Toronto, *Understanding the Sacrament of the Anointing of the Sick*, 2000. (All emphases have been added.)

encourage and comfort all those who are seriously ill.

Since the emphasis is on healing, the condition of "seriously ill" has a wide interpretation. Anointing of the Sick is administered even to those suffering from chronic ailments like arthritis or diabetes. But "[i]n *'exceptional* circumstances' [imminent death, perhaps?], Anointing may be celebrated with *viaticum* and even combined with the Commendation of the Dying, but this is not the ideal."

The community aspect is emphasized when Anointing takes place "within the family, the smallest Christian community," or when "celebrated in larger groups, as the parish, hospital [or] nursing home … gathers for a communal celebration of the sacrament." The "communal form" used "at an extended Liturgy or during Mass" "allows the wider community to experience Anointing as a regular and inviting part of the Church's ministry to the sick. It shows clearly that the Anointing of the Sick is not a sacrament for the dying."[156] "Allowing the wider community to experience Anointing" means everyone in a group, *even the well,* can be anointed, a common occurrence today.

As with Baptism, in the bid to build community the emphasis has shifted from the primary effect and reason for Extreme Unction to the secondary. According to the Council of Trent,[157] Extreme Unction was instituted by Christ "to heal the maladies of the soul, rather than to cure the diseases of the body." "The salvation of his soul is to be the first object of the sick man's wishes, and after that the health of the body, with this qualification, *if it be for the good of his soul.*" The devil tries hardest to "deprive us of all hope of the divine mercy" at the time of death, but the sanctifying grace received through the sacrament supplies strength to fight him, encourages the

---

[156]The new emphasis on physical healing and community follows from Vatican II's *Sacrosanctum Concilium* and is the teaching of the *Catechism of the Catholic Church* (Washington, DC: United States Catholic Conference, 1994), nos. 1500 ff.

[157]*Catechism of the Council of Trent*, trans. with notes by Fr. John A. McHugh, OP, and Fr. Charles J. Callan, OP (South Bend, IN: Marian Publications, 1976; reprint ed., Rockford, IL: Tan Books and Publishers, 1982), pp. 311-15.

soul by the hope of divine goodness, and thus enables it to bear the burdens of sickness. It is to be received only by the Faithful who are in danger of death by serious illness.

However, today, highlighting the importance of community and the fact that one *doesn't* have to be in danger of death, the anointing and the giving of viaticum is ideally done at Mass or in the church, "with family and friends actively involved."[158] "Active involvement," as we have seen, means even healthy relatives or friends present receive the Anointing of the Sick. This completely disregards the whole basis of the sacrament: "Is any man sick amongst you? Let him bring in the priests of the church, and let them pray over him, anointing him with oil…" (James 5:14).

Another reason for receiving anointing and viaticum at Mass could be that priests are no longer expected to visit the sick and dying. Since "[d]eacons, religious and lay people are chaplains in hospitals …, *they* give *viaticum* and pray the Commendation of the Dying (including those rites when death has occurred)." "Extraordinary ministers of Communion" also give viaticum and "lead prayers for the sick *on behalf of the parish community*." (And as noted above, lay people also "hear confessions" in hospitals.)

Now, in Extreme Unction, the eyes, ears, nostrils, mouth and hands are anointed because they may have been involved in sin. Anointing of the Sick, however, only involves the forehead and the hands. The form of Extreme Unction asks God to pardon the sins committed by the sight, hearing, etc.; but the form of Anointing weakens the reality of sin: "May the Lord who frees you from sin save you and raise you up."[159]

Extreme Unction eradicates mortal sins still remaining if the sick person cannot receive the sacrament of Penance (provided he has contrition) or if he has forgotten them; it also remits venial sins and some or all of the temporal pun-

---

[158]Anointing at Mass is recommended in the *Catechism of the Catholic Church* (no. 1517) because it is "a liturgical and communal celebration."
[159]Ibid., no. 1513.

ishment due to sins. Hence, there is a serious obligation to receive or help a gravely ill person to receive the sacrament.[160] But forgiveness of sin is no longer the focus of Anointing of the Sick.[161] This is probably why reception of Anointing is not seen as necessary, but as a comfort in illness. For the dying, viaticum is considered more important than Anointing. So the Toronto Archdiocese says no one should take it upon himself to request Anointing for another:

> There is a need for those who are gravely ill to have expressed a desire, or by their lives to have demonstrated, that celebrating this sacrament would be important to them. *It is not enough for family members or hospital staff to desire it on the sick person's behalf.*
>
> It is important to try to ensure that those who are sick *and those around them* understand the significance of the Sacrament of the Anointing of the Sick as a sacrament of *healing* and are prepared to celebrate it *well* [otherwise — forget it?].

Finally, in the church of shared responsibility, lay people also give "blessings." Since it is Catholic teaching that only priests have the power to bless,[162] lay "blessings" are officious shams. Nevertheless, lay Eucharistic ministers or chaplains routinely "bless" the sick they visit; children have been known to "bless" and distribute ashes on Ash Wednesday; and even priests accept "blessings" from lay people today.

It would seem that in the adult Counterchurch the priest is the *extraordinary* minister of almost everything!

---

[160]*Catechism of the Council of Trent*, pp. 311-12, 314-15; Ott, pp. 448-49.

[161]The *Catechism of the Catholic Church* itself, in explaining Anointing of the Sick, besides quoting James 5:15 ("and if he be in sins, they shall be forgiven him"), makes only one general reference to "forgiveness of sins" if the person could not receive Penance (no. 1532).

[162]Cf. Pius XII, nos. 46-47.

Chapter 3
The Peter Pan Syndrome

The word "Youth" in World Youth Day is a major misnomer, considering large numbers of participants are adults up to age 35 (in Rome the age limit was 39), who should be married, raising families and steadily employed. Indeed, given today's prevalence of teenage pregnancies, whole families of parents and children could fit into the 16-35 "youth" category, as there are people who are *grandparents* by age 35 or earlier! This definition of "youth," insulting to many in this age group who rightfully consider themselves adults (including priests and religious), encourages extended adolescence, irresponsibility and immaturity — the Peter Pan lifestyle.

Humanized Catholic education has had the desired subversive effect on the generation of under-40s. Most of them find the Church "irrelevant" and are non-practising Catholics, but they're needed to keep the Counterchurch solvent and operational. So, they are being lured with adult faith principles that allow them a faith that reflects *their* values and is referred to as *their* faith, not the *Catholic* faith. Young people, especially those at World Youth Day, are described as being "excited about *their* faith." Sure. If *their* faith, *their* better world includes autonomy, raucous music, dancing and mixed-company travels, and the Church permits this because a faith journey meets the needs of the pilgrims, why wouldn't they be excited?

Following Dewey and Jung, today's youth are given "experiences" that foster *spirituality* — a "virtual-reality" Catholicism.[163] The rationale for virtual Catholicism was pro-

---

[163]As a marketing consultant from New York City told a meeting of Catholic adult educators in Ottawa some years ago, "Religion is out. Church is out. It's over. It's gone.... Spirituality is in." See Mary Jo Leddy, "Is it Enough to Leave a Bowl of Cat Food at the Garden Gate?", *Catholic New Times*, September 7, 1997, p. 6.

posed by a Canadian drama teacher, Edmond Dixon, in a speech to the (U. S.) National Catholic Education Association.[164] Teenagers, he said, are

> creatures who live by emotions and experiences. They are ... suspicious of any outright moralizing and generally turn right off if they feel they are being preached at.... for many, the church and religious life are irrelevant.

Rather, therefore, than teaching the absolute and revealed truths of Catholicism, catechesis must give youth a *feeling* of religion, a "religious experience" with which they can "identify." Dixon somehow concluded that *actors* "identify with the moral dilemmas the characters face and the Christian responses." Even if true, this is only values clarification with a Christian veneer, as in the absence of absolutes, both sides of the "dilemma" are equally valid.

The real value of drama-as-evangelization, however, revealed Dixon, is that preparing a performance provides "shared experiences" and *builds community*, thus fostering "Catholic education for a lifetime." That is, the actors will develop a hunger for community and will tend to gravitate towards adult faith programs like World Youth Day. Following Jung, many adult religious educators also use drama as an occult tool, "to help learners tap into their unconscious, where their creativity often lies. It is there ... that we frequently discover new insights into both God and ourselves."[165]

An Aberrant Society

Youth are being especially subjected to adult faith techniques at World Youth Day, an important tool for building the *world* community. A Holy Ghost missionary who

---

[164]"Translating Religious Belief Through Drama," *Catholic Register*, August 26, 1995, p. 15.

[165]See Parent, p. 14.

works with youth "cautions those embarking on ministry to youth that the older formation methods have lost their ability to attract young people." Hence, advocates his *confrère*, Fr. Michael Doyle, CSSp,

> There is need to develop programs in tune with the mentality of young people if we hope to accomplish lasting results.
>
> .... goals must come from the youth, as *their* goals and not those imposed by an "expert" [i.e., not the traditional goals of the Church]. They will be reached in a non-formal inductive process [i.e., no *Baltimore Catechism*] which will help [them] to move from a passive, cultural reception of the Faith to an "owned" Faith in which youth take responsibility for their beliefs, actions and life style, a journey that takes time.... This process may even involve criticism of some present structures and a desire to have more input....
>
> During WYD [2002] a youth workshop led by a young lady[166] ... met to produce a draft for a proposed Constitution for the Catholic Church. [The group's] stated purpose was to "encourage other believers to think critically[167] and creatively about the present state of the Church and about possible futures."... what came through in the proposals was the desire of young people for a Church in which they would be heard, and for a method of governance enabling responsible participation at all levels, geared ultimately to the creation of "a more respectful, compassionate and just world community."[168]

How many parents could have known that their chil-

---

[166]The catechesis sessions and other meetings were "all animated by young people": Maria Dalgarno, "A View From the Media Room," *Living City*, October 2002, p. 13.

[167]"Critical thinking," as practised in today's schools, means challenging moral absolutes and authority. It is a dialectical process for modifying behaviour through the "analysis" and discussion of selected information that leads students to a pre-determined conclusion. See Ferreira, "New Age Education."

[168]Father Michael Doyle, CSSp, "The Seventh Continent," *Spiritan Missionary News* (Toronto), February 2003, p. 4. (Emphasis in original.) The editorial (p. 2) betrayed the dissimulation of the applause and encomiums lavished upon the Pope. In it, Fr. Patrick Fitzpatrick, CSSp, wrote that for "many people," including himself, the Stations of the Cross "was the highlight of a memorable week. No Pope, no surrounding bishops with strange hats, no grey hairs."

dren would receive revolutionary training at World Youth Day to prepare them for a democratic Counterchurch and a new world order? World Youth Day is an exercise in adult religious education to *make sure* youth journey away from the Catholic Church. Youth can be conditioned in a few days if subjected to peer pressure in discussion groups (like the catechesis sessions) or to intense and emotional activity that leaves no room for thought.[169] (The incessant entertainment at World Youth Day also prevents serious thought.)

Father Doyle makes it clear that

> the older generation has *unreal* expectations of the emotional and spiritual maturity of their offspring [even though some may be as old as 35, according to the Church's current Peter Pan definition of "youth"!] together with the conviction that all will continue as it was before. In fact "the Seventh Continent" as youth has been labeled, has its own language, its own music and its own value system in which peer relationships play an enormous part.[170]

In other words, Father Doyle cooly informs us, *today's Church authorities do not intend to pass on the teachings of the Catholic Faith to the young*. Instead, they intend to perpetuate what clinical psychologist Gordon Neufeld and family therapist Gabor Maté call "peer-attachment disorder," "the greatest disorder of our times." According to these specialists, "Children have become attached to their peers and then *been given little incentive to break that bond*.... As a result, parents lose the power to direct their children.... If kids don't care what their parents think, why do what they want?"[171] The parallel between parents and the Church's hierarchy is obvious.

The two doctors explain that the peer-oriented syn-

---

[169]Song, dance, music, storytelling ("witnessing"), drama and mime are Jungian techniques for developing spirituality (cf. Likoudis, "Jung Replaces Jesus" and "Jungians Believe"). They are very much a part of WYD catechesis. "Catechesis" is another Catholic word with an un-Catholic meaning today. As already seen, catechesis passes on adult faith, not Catholicism.

[170]Father Doyle, ibid. (Emphasis added.)

[171]Alanna Mitchell, "Unglued," *Globe and Mail*, January 31, 2004, p. F1. (Emphasis added.)

drome leads to "the death of maturation, of proper develop-ment, with an aberrant society rising in its place."   Indeed, Father Doyle acknowledges that today's young Catholics *are* emotionally and spiritually immature. But the solution is not to *keep* them in this unnatural condition, which amounts to a *cult*, say Neufeld and Maté. Youth have to be reclaimed from the peer cult, they advise, by *removing* them from their peers. They must not be encouraged to gain their self-esteem from their peers. Parents "need to establish the hierarchy of the family and of the generations and 'embed' children in it."

Indulging the cult, as the institutional Church is doing, therefore, can only strengthen its anti-authoritarian attitude and guarantee its members will reject the Catholic Church, finding her "irrelevant," as drama teacher Edmond Dixon observed. The question then arises: Is this perpetuation of infantilism a mistaken pastoral policy or the furtherance of Masonry's plan to gain control of Catholics in their youth?

The Masonic Gospel of Pleasure

Pope Leo XIII warned that Freemasons sought control through promulgating "a gospel of pleasure." They had cal-culated that subjecting the multitude to the domination of the passions and satiating it with pleasure and "a boundless li-cence of vice" would so weaken wills that it would "easily come under their power." They contended that youth espe-cially should be instructed in a morality that is "free" of reli-gious belief. The evil fruit of this education was already evi-dent in Pope Leo's time, 120 years ago:

> For wherever, by removing Christian education, the sect has begun more completely to rule, there ... morals have begun quickly to perish, ... shameful opinions have grown up, and the audacity of evil deeds has risen to a high degree.[172]

---

[172]Leo XIII, Encyclical On Freemasonry *Humanum Genus*, April 20, 1884, nos. 19, 20.

The Masonic agenda has been carried out by its puppet, Communism.   Italian Communist Antonio Gramsci (1891-1937) devised a plan for Communism to win the West peaceably by corrupting morals and culture. Controlling the media would allow Communists to control the Western mind and destabilize society through corruption.   Furthermore, starting in the 1930s, thousands of Communist agents were sent into Catholic seminaries to train as false priests and future Church leaders. "Socialism," Gramsci had said, "is precisely the *religion* that must overwhelm Christianity."[173]

The Masonic/Communist plan to pervert Catholicism has been very successful. The moral code of Christianity is indeed "irrelevant" to most young Catholics today; that the post-conciliar Church approves of their attitude is illustrated by World Youth Days, at which no effort is made to ensure modesty and decorum. A participant in Rome's WYD happily noted, "Everyone was free to be themselves. No one cast judgment on another." At Rome, dubbed a "Catholic Woodstock," bare shoulders and midriffs and micro-minis were allowed in St. Peter's, and the Papal Mass featured dancing girls in wispy costumes. In Toronto, pilgrims "stripped down to bikini tops and frolicked in a fountain" at the main venue.[174]

A large poster hung in Toronto churches to advertise WYD depicted a scene in Rome that does resemble a Woodstock: a field full of thousands of bodies, male and female, packed together, some lying under tents, girls in bikini tops and shorts. They would have spent the previous night together, camped out for the Papal Mass in the morning. An older woman accompanying youth of the Neocatechumenal Way recalled, "There was absolutely no room to walk be-

---

[173]Cornelia R. Ferreira, "The Perestroika Deception Updated," *Catholic Family News*, December 2001, p. 1.

[174]Emanuel Pires, "I Was There to Get Closer to Christ," and "World Youth Day Gathering ...," *Catholic Register*, September 4, 2000, p. 6; Sabitri Ghosh, "Fifteenth World Youth Day ...," *Catholic New Times*, September 10, 2000, p. 13; Graeme Smith, "Playful Delegates Get Down to Some Fun," *Globe and Mail*, July 25, 2002, p. A8.

tween people and their sleeping bags."[175] The cover of this book cannot adequately portray the similarly degrading quarters of what can only be described as a hastily-erected refugee camp in a Toronto field. But given all the passion-stirring song, dance and music that accompany the cozy sleeping arrangements, what modern young adult wouldn't want to join the refugee party? It is the highlight of World Youth Day. It sure puts to scorn their grandparents' old religion of sin, guilt and hell fire!

Even the secular press, reporting sardonically on Toronto's overnight "Papal slumber party," recognized "some impure thoughts sparked by the close co-ed sleeping arrangements."[176] Stories abounded about the giddy kissing and other indecent games played at the slumber party.[177] But Church authorities (and seemingly most adult Catholics) are completely unperturbed by the massive challenge to purity posed by these co-ed dormitories, and by the sacrilegious Communions at the Papal Mass the next day of those youth who would have sinned mortally in thought or deed. Risking the loss of even one soul renders spurious the hierarchy's protestations of love for youth.

What good is the declaration by the Pontifical Council on the Family that "[t]he practice of decency and modesty in speech, action and dress is very important for creating an atmosphere suitable to the growth of chastity," and that for chastity, "self-control is necessary, which presupposes such virtues as modesty [and] temperance,"[178] when the hierarchy ignores the immodesty displayed all through World Youth Day? And how are parents to heed the Pontifical Council's admonition to be "watchful so that certain immoral fashions and attitudes do not violate the integrity of the home, especially through misuse of the mass media,"[179] when the hierar-

[175]Bettinelli, ibid.
[176]Siri Agrell, "'We're Keeping it Holy'," *National Post* (Toronto), July 29, 2002, p. A13.
[177]For one example, see Graeme Smith and Wallace Immen, "Good, Clean Fun at Muddy Mass Site," *Globe and Mail*, July 29, 2002, p. A5.
[178]*The Truth and Meaning of Human Sexuality*, December 8, 1995, nos. 55-56.
[179]Ibid., no. 56. WYD modesty being an oxymoron, a pamphlet condemning

chy upholds vulgar dress, unbecoming exuberance, wild rock music and immoral games as models for imitation? After all, WYD pilgrims were exalted by the hierarchy as the "light and salt of the world" and the "future of the Church." This pantheistic doublethink denotes the Jungian nature of the Counterchurch and its embrace of the shadow. It is also the triumph of Masonry's gospel of pleasure.

What about the scandal given to the world by such indecorous "Catholic" behaviour? If non-Catholics had expected attendees to act in a manner befitting their dignity as followers of Christ and tabernacles of the Living God, if they had expected to see noble and virtuous conduct, they would have been sadly mistaken.

One reporter honestly stated what anyone with an ordinary knowledge of human nature would expect: "It's hardly surprising that pheromones fill the air at an event for 16- to 35-year-olds, many of them far away from home and unsupervised." Yet, in some places the Church actually dangled the "singles" lure: "Advertisements for [Toronto's] World Youth Day even tease, 'Who in the world will you meet? God only knows.'" So some came "scouting for a husband," whilst "many others" admitted to salacious expectations.[180]

The "unchaste behavior" observed in Rome in 2000 by the correspondent of the *International Herald Tribune* prompted the paper to cite this eyewitness comment on the first page of its Italian edition: "I am sure in nine months we're going to see a huge population boom of babies named Jubilee."[181] In Toronto, "[c]ouples kissed in the dark edges of the field" during the Papal slumber party," discreetly commented one reporter. Another intimated that WYD's "week of prayer sessions, confession and communion" was meaningless in face of its wild finale, when pilgrims "let loose" and

---

immorality and immodest clothes that was handed out at WYD 2002 was "cheerfully ignored": Smith, "Playful Delegates."

[180]Smith, ibid.

[181]Robert Blair Kaiser, "Rome Diary 23/20 August 2000," justgoodcompany.org/RomeDiary/RomeDiary27.pdf, August 20, 2000.

"danced, sang, kissed and mingled the night away."[182]   Yet Fr. John Hibbard, coordinator of the Papal vigil earlier in the evening, attempted to portray the slumber party as an overnight vigil, following the "ancient tradition" of "praying from sundown to the following sunrise," prompting the headline, "Pilgrims to Pray all Night."[183]   Did he think the "Christian" Rock blasted from loudspeakers and the parade of "witnessing" groups on stage at ungodly hours of the night[184] qualified as all-night prayer?

These official attempts at making the overnight camping "Catholic" disturbed many exhausted pilgrims who were attempting to sleep, as John Vennari describes in Part II.   At the same time, "tens of thousands of Catholic youth burned their candles at both ends, proving pilgrims are blessed with the spirit to party," noted a journalist.   His diary of youth interviews conducted through the night reads as follows:

> **1 a.m.** — ....   [A 17-year-old youth says,] "It's all partying, all night," before he runs off toward one of the countless tribal drumming and dancing circles.   "It's like Mardi Gras here."
>
> **2 a.m.** — For the past hour and a half, [a pilgrim] has waved a cardboard sign that reads, "Kiss me, I'm American and it's my birthday."   He's earned 200 kisses, he estimates. Meanwhile [another pilgrim] has received 1,000 hugs in the four hours he's held up a sign urging people to hug him....
>
> **2:30 a.m.** — Anti-abortion activists put up a poster depicting a fetus with the words "Abortion exploits women and kills babies."   "That's a bit politically charged," says [a 20-year-old].   "I don't want anything to do with it."
>
> **5 a.m.** — ....   discussion turns to the Pope. [A 24-year-old who never went to sleep says,] "The crowd is hypnotized by him."
>
> And what did [he] gain from the Pope's address?
>
> A long pause.   Silence.
>
> "I don't know.   I can't think right because I'm so tired."[185]

[182]Agrell, ibid. Also see John Vennari's account of the party in Part II.

[183]Sarah Green, "Pilgrims to Pray all Night," *The Saturday Sun*, July 27, 2002, p. 4.

[184]Agrell, ibid.

[185]Brett Clarkson, "A Night to Stay Awake," *The Toronto Sun*, July 29, 2002, p. 25.

Is it any wonder that youth cheered a Pope who permitted such loose behaviour? An Australian priest who led a group of pilgrims to Toronto said, "They may not feel connected with their hierarchy at home, but with John Paul, they do.... They know he reached out to them."[186] This mutual admiration, as we shall see later, has been deliberately fostered to give the impression that the Church is thriving; however, nineteen World Youth Days have not arrested the decline of Catholicism. The attempts to build diocesan-wide communities are a testament to their failure.

A theologian familiar with youth religious movements explains why admiring John Paul II had little effect on behaviour: "Rather than accepting the Pope as the infallible teacher of God's word," the young "relate to him ... as an icon or symbol...."[187] In other words, they had no respect for the Pope's authority. He was just a "hero" to young people, either because of his world travels, or because he survived wars, promoted human rights, or "helped topple communism"; others saw him as "a martyr to his ailments." But this did not mean they were prepared to accept the teachings of the Church, such as the injunctions against fornication or contraception.[188] Pope John Paul's appeal also seems to have been strongly connected to what he did for this spoilt generation. A French pilgrim to Toronto insolently announced, "The next pope will need to do something to attract us.... Will he sing with us, will he mix in the crowd with us? He'll have to do something."[189] Almost certainly, if the Pope were to lecture youth on sin, hell, chastity, obedience to their parents, etc. — instruction totally missing at WYD — the adulation would quickly dry up.

One Toronto youth described WYD in terms that be-

---

[186] Crary, ibid.

[187] Alanna Mitchell, "Worldly Travel Aids Spiritual Journey," *Globe and Mail*, July 23, 2002, p. A3.

[188] Ibid.; Crary, ibid.; Smith, ibid.; cf. Father Doyle, ibid.; "The Festivities of John Paul II," *Globe and Mail*, July 27, 2002, p. A16. The myths that (a) Communism is dead, and (b) was toppled by the Pope, were exposed in Ferreira, "Perestroika Deception," and id., *New Age Movement*, pp. 12-16.

[189] Crary, ibid.

trayed the hollowness of this adulation:

> Pilgrims weren't getting their energy from a large wooden cross or an 82-year-old pontiff, but instead, they were being energized by each other's presence.
> Besides, it was never about seeing the Pope. As most pilgrims know, WYD is about being with a community that shares a common faith, not just a common religion. We share hope for a better sort of world....

Notice the distinction he made between faith and religion. That is because, in true adult faith style, by faith he meant one's personal "spirituality":

> World Youth Day was a "faith zone," a place you could feel confident that you weren't alone in your spirituality....
> Being cheerful and enthusiastic about faith is easy when a half-million others are there to join you....
> ... I left [the papal Mass] with a clearer understanding of my own faith....

This young man said he would not force his beliefs on others "while still travelling on my own spiritual journey."[190]

Meanwhile, Toronto has begun holding annual co-ed youth rallies "modeling the WYD experience." The weekend includes "sleeping under the stars," says an advertisement. Undoubtedly, other dioceses will follow suit, spreading the spirit of immorality and revolution.

They Beg to Differ

Not all young people are impressed with the shenanigans and pseudo-Catholicism of World Youth Day, but their voice is usually not heard. Two young people expressed their views to the author. One Torontonian, scandalized by the raucous behaviour of her peers, exclaimed: "If this is the

---

[190]Kazuo Oishi, "Life's Lessons," *Toronto Sun*, July 29, 2002, p. 28.

salt of the earth, I want to be on a low-sodium diet!"

Another Toronto woman who attended the Paris WYD at age 27, "in order to learn something about the Faith," made the following comments: "It was the worst thing I've ever done. I wasted my money. I spent $2,000 and got nothing out of it. I felt sick through the whole thing. I just wanted to get out, and I certainly wasn't going to the Toronto or any other World Youth Day."

When asked what about her Parisian experience she disliked so much, these were the reasons she gave:

- She learnt nothing about the true Faith.
- The group was taken to [the ecumenical community of] Taizé for a week and taught ecumenism.
- Youth were screaming, rowdy and unruly all day.
- They were completely devoted to "coupling" and "matchmaking." People were looking for husbands and wives; organizers excitedly announced engagements.
- Priests were having fun with the girls in the hotel swimming pool, "not behaving as priests."
- The washrooms at the overnight vigil were so filthy and unhygienic that women ran screaming from them. They had to resort to the bushes, while young men wandered all around.

Getting youth accustomed to sordidness belies the Counterchurch's obsession with the dignity of man.

The New "Evangelization"

This fawned-upon generation of younger Catholics seems not to have the faintest idea of why Christ set up His Church. They believe the Church should be grateful for their condescending presence, however fleeting and superficial. Sister Francine Guilmette, associate director of Toronto's World Youth Day, caters to this arrogance:

> If the young are to have time for a church, it must be one that accepts them [i.e., as they are], not one that treats them as a client [i.e., someone needing guidance to reach *heaven*] or an interloper....[191]

Speaking within the context of missionary activity, the European bishops have "committed themselves to 'evangelize youth and to *allow themselves to be evangelized by them*'"! Christian youth "are not just considered as [an] ... object of pastoral care," but are to be "recognized and received 'as a gift of Christ to his Church in all its mission.'" Hence, the bishops intend to "dialogue with them" and *collaborate* in "studying problems," "sharing quests and experiences" and "carrying out programs and initiatives."[192] This extraordinary statement, which inverts the Fourth Commandment, can only be understood in light of ecumenism and inculturation. These Counterchurch heresies arise from attempts to live peacefully with non-Catholic religions in view of the "greater good" of universal brotherhood and harmony.

Now, if Catholic youth, as Father Doyle has stated, live in a world of their own, a "Seventh Continent" with its own values, spirituality and faith, they can be considered as another *church*, estranged from the Catholic Church. Thus, following the principles of ecumenism, *youth must not be brought back to Catholicism*; this would be "an unreal expectation that all will continue as before," said Father Doyle. Instead, a friendly unity must be sought with them to ensure a future Counterchurch and world religion.

The first principle of ecumenism is universal salvation; its corollary is religious equality. Walter Cardinal Kasper, head of the Pontifical Council for Christian Unity, has said that Vatican II and Pope John Paul's encyclical *Ut Unum Sint*

> acknowledge explicitly that the Holy Spirit is operating in the other Churches and church communities. Consequently, there is no idea of an arrogant claim to a monopoly

[191]Mitchell, ibid.
[192]"European Bishops Decide." (Emphasis added.)

of salvation.[193]

Likewise, Father Raniero Cantalamessa, Preacher to the Papal Household, proclaimed at the Vatican's Good Friday service in 2002 that other religions "are not merely tolerated by God, but positively willed by Him" as a means of salvation.[194]   In line with this false teaching, the beliefs of the Seventh Continent are therefore just as salvific as those of Catholicism.

The second principle of ecumenism is dialogue and cooperation in solving problems.   As Cardinal Kasper describes it, "ecumenism is no one-way street, but a reciprocal learning process, or, as stated in *Ut Unum Sint*, an exchange of gifts."[195]   Following this rule, there is nothing abnormal about the European bishops' wishing to be evangelized by the youth of the Seventh Continent.   Their intention to dialogue, share experiences and collaborate as equals in solving problems is merely adult faith in action.

What might the bishops learn from their young "peers"?   Just what do the natives of the Seventh Continent believe that has earned them papal approbation and the designation of "gift" of light and salt to the Church and the world?   The following anthropological survey on youth morality, taken between 1999 and 2001 in Ireland, gives us an idea.   It shows, says Father Doyle, that the inhabitants of the Seventh Continent have "different priorities" and "think quite differently" from the Catholic Church; so the bishops have plenty to learn.   The survey questioned "young adults" aged 20-35.

> … in the area of morality the subjects were asked to evaluate the gravity of 28 behaviours [not *sins*] in terms of

---

[193]Cited in John Vennari, "Shrine Rector Confirms New Ecumenical Orientation at Fatima," *Catholic Family News*, February 2004, p. 13. Saying "there is no idea of an arrogant claim to a monopoly of salvation" defies the thrice-defined dogma of Faith that outside the Catholic Church there is no salvation.

[194]John Vennari, "From Pentecostalism to Apostasy," ibid., May 2002, p. 13. Father Cantalamessa was one of the speakers at Rome's WYD.

[195]Vennari, "Shrine Rector."

wrong-doing…. The five deemed "most serious" were:
1. Sexual abuse of children
2. Physical abuse in marriage
3. Constant verbal abuse in marriage
4. Abortion
5. Taking from another's rights and freedom

   At the other end of the scale, judged "not serious," were:
24. Casual [fornication]
25. Living with someone you didn't intend marrying
26. Missing Mass on Sunday
27. Contraception
28. Living with someone you intend to marry.[196]

These values are not atypical of most young Catholics. They do have different "priorities" from the Catholic Church, which follows the Commandments of God. Consider what they believe: Abuse is the highest form of immoral behaviour, worse than *murder* of an unborn child (this reflects the incessant abuse education in schools); fornication has differing social degrees of acceptability; contraception is a given; attending Sunday Mass — the minimum requirement for being considered a practising Catholic — is unnecessary. The three *mortal sins* committed widely by today's young Catholics ranked *lowest* in gravity as most do not think they are sins at all.

But following Dewey's dictum not to teach catechism or "adults'" values, no attempt is being made to teach youth the Truth. Catholic schools have failed to pass on the Faith.[197] Priests seem content with observing the lost inhabitants of the Seventh Continent like some exotic native culture, unconcerned with their eternal salvation. In a parish newspaper editorial, Fr. Patrick Fitzpatrick, CSSp, exhibited nonchalance towards the above anthropological survey. These WYD pilgrims, he breezily reported,[198]

---

[196]Father Doyle, ibid.
[197]See Cornelia R. Ferreira, "What is Catholic Education?", *Catholic Family News*, May and June 2003, and id., "New Age Education."
[198]"A Pilgrimage of Youth From Over 150 Countries," *The Steward* (Scarbor-

are in transition from where they have been to where they are heading, *perhaps* looking for *a* faith that makes a difference in their daily lives. *They have their own sense of morality.* A survey in Ireland named twenty-eight behaviours *generally* regarded [Note: no absolutes here] as in *some* way immoral and asked young adults to rank them in order of seriousness.

Father Fitzpatrick listed without comment the three "behaviours" at the top and bottom of the list, then continued:

> They are caring and irresponsible, serious and fun-loving, thoughtful and goofy, ready to reassure and in need of support, … eager and insecure, enthusiastic and moody….
>
> Relationships are at the heart of these young adults' life. Here, above all, they meet God.

Father Fitzpatrick is clearly stating that youth belong to Adult Church. They are on pilgrimage from "where they have been" to "where they are heading." They are searching for personal spirituality, "*a* faith that makes a difference in their lives." Their faith comes from their relationship with God the (youth) Community. Finally, they epitomize Jungian "wholeness," with pairs of opposing qualities acceptably merged in them.

That's why they inspire awe and reverence: *they are the first through-and-through adult faith generation.* Their parents and grandparents are like immigrants with memories and values of the "old country." But the under-35s are like the *children* of immigrants, born and raised in the new country, the post-conciliar Church, knowing or caring nothing about the "old" Catholic Church. As the European bishops recognize, youth consider the Catholic Church "as distant, foreign, not very credible."[199] After full immersion in Deweyite Catholic schools or parish religion courses[200], they *are* the

---

ough, ON), April 2002, p. 4. (Emphases added.)
[199]"European Bishops Decide."
[200]The religious teaching given in parishes to children who attend non-Catholic

Counterchurch; their spiritual nationality is Adult Faith. It has taken forty years of hard work to produce this first complete generation of counterfeit Catholics. It's no wonder all the stops are pulled out to make World Youth Day a party to "celebrate youth" (an oft-repeated phrase).

It is almost impossible for conscientious "old-Church" parents to overcome the destruction of Catholic teaching in the schools that is furthered by programs like World Youth Day. They do not realize that the present hierarchy is *content* to treat youth as another world, another religion.

And so, in the interests of world religious unity, the third principle of ecumenism is applied to youth. This principle, as stated by Cardinal Kasper, is: "The way to unity is therefore not the return of others into the fold of the Catholic Church."[201]   Or, as Joseph Cardinal Ratzinger, now Pope Benedict XVI, wrote in 1966 (and still holds):

> The Catholic Church has no right to absorb the other Churches…. [A] basic unity — of Churches that remain Churches, yet become one Church — *must replace the idea of conversion*….[202]

Having just succeeded in producing the first generation of the Counterchurch, it would make no sense to convert it to Catholicism. Hence, the European bishops, instead of converting, are applying the principles of ecumenism to youth. Meanwhile, meetings and programs give the *impression* of trying to "reach" youth to convert them.

The bishops are also practising inculturation, which is the extension of ecumenism to pagan practices. The Asian bishops have defined inculturation as the adoption of the "popular expressions of faith and piety" of indigenous relig-

---

schools is adult faith catechesis. For instance, see this report on a Wisconsin parish: Julianne Donlon, "Following the Light," *Africa* (Kiltegan, Co. Wicklow, Ireland), January/February 2004, p. 20.

[201]Vennari, ibid.

[202]Ibid. (Emphasis added.) Evangelizing for the purpose of converting people to Catholicism (cf. Matt. 28:19) is given the derogatory term "proselytization" today, and is frowned upon as the antithesis of ecumenical dialogue.

ions that pre-dated their evangelization. The Church must be "localized" to symbolize the universality of God's saving love, ceasing to be structured and governed in a way "foreign" to the native culture.[203] As their literature makes clear, this is what missionaries mean when speaking about being evangelized *by* the pagans. Similarly, the European bishops, by seeking to be evangelized by youth, are applying the principle of inculturation to the "indigenous" population of the Seventh Continent. Furthermore, since this population *is* the Counterchurch, what better group can teach adult faith principles to the world?

> "Youths are not only receivers of the proclamation, but they feel the vocation to be, themselves, protagonists of the mission to youths and any other person," the bishops continued. "Their contribution must be seen today as a necessary and irreplaceable good for Europe's evangelization."[204]

Having observed the first adult faith generation in action, Cardinal Ambrozic declared that after WYD 2002, he "learned to appreciate anew ... that it is the young people who are the main evangelizers of one another."[205]

Naturally, these evangelizers can only spread the errors and corruption of adult faith. Another reason WYD pilgrims appreciated Pope John Paul is because he empowered them to do precisely that by implicitly "giv[ing] them more clout in their local parishes":

> Some say they will use their elevated status as the "future" of the Church to do such things as introduce youth Masses and slip more modern music into the Church program.[206]

One smug Ontario teen recounted how her pastor had

---

[203]Cf. Cornelia R. Ferreira, "Mother Teresa 'Beatified' With Idolatrous Rites," *Catholic Family News*, January 2004, p. 13.

[204]"European Bishops Decide."

[205]Aloysius Cardinal Ambrozic, Pastoral Letter *After World Youth Day*, November 2002.

[206]Amy Carmichael, "Youth Prepare to Exercise New Influence," *National Post*, July 29, 2002, p. A13.

disallowed "exuberant music that appeals to young people" because he was "too afraid of upsetting the older members of the congregation."   These parishioners "thought it offended the sanctity of worship and wouldn't change for us, but they listen to the Pope."   When the priest heard that Toronto would host World Youth Day, he "did an about-face."

> "It was like almost overnight he must have heard the Pope's message that we are the future and they better pay attention to us."
> She said the priest helped her organize a youth mass that featured loud joyous singing and discussions about everything from drugs to sex ….   "Now lots of kids come out because it's fun…."[207]

Thus, Pope John Paul has not only endorsed young people's pilgrimage away from Catholicism, but through World Youth Day he has also empowered them to corrupt parishes they encounter on their journey.   That is why the most prestigious program for ensnaring people of all ages for the Counterchurch has become World Youth Day — change agent *par excellence*.

Now that youth are seen as the "key" to building community, dioceses "in the process of change" have a "big focus" on youth.   And youth are demanding to "hav[e] a voice that's not diluted by an adult agenda."   They accuse the Church of having "an oppressive structure, even at the parish level."   They complain, "There is no forum for them to speak and it's pretty disenfranchising for a kid."   They believe "it's important for youth to have a way to reach out and claim their faith and find their voice."   One 17-year old member of a newly-created Diocesan Youth Council in Prince Albert, Saskatchewan, sums up the importance of such Councils:

> If we want to be strong in our faith, it has to be us who are making the decisions….   When 50 of us … from differ-ent towns, different backgrounds, come together to make a

---

decision, chances are there's going to be another 300 kids that agree with what we decide.[208]

In Halifax, whose community-building we looked at earlier, parishes are being encouraged "to recognize the youth as necessary." Students from across Canada were to be trained in Halifax during the summer of 2004 in leadership: how to "do" evangelization and how to "do things like weekly church gatherings," drama camps and conferences. The goal of evangelization is the usual Unitarian Universalist social justice one of service: "The process [will not be] complete until they have been evangelized and serve."[209]

Note that volunteer or community service, a key New Age tenet, is an extension of the leftist social justice movement. Once exclusively a *punishment* for convicted criminals, community service is now enforced slave labour for the general public. "Volunteer" work is already compulsory for high school graduation, scholarships, college entrance, many jobs and even the sacrament of Confirmation; eventually it will be mandatory for all.[210] And, of course, "compulsory volunteering" is a brilliant example of doublethink!

---

[208]Connors, ibid; Karin Tate-Penna, "Council Gives Teens Voice," *Catholic Register*, March 20, 2005, p. 6.

[209]Connors, ibid.

[210]For more on community service as a New World Order requirement, see Ferreira, "New Age Education."

Chapter 4
Religion as Fun

World Youth Day was launched by Pope John Paul in 1985, "in collaboration" with the United Nations' International Youth Year.[211] Most people are only aware of the huge international extravaganzas usually held every two years, but World Youth Day is also held at the diocesan level in alternate years on Palm Sunday. This accounts for the way it is numbered. Thus, although WYD 2002 was only the ninth or tenth international celebration with the Pope (sources differ as to which of several youth gatherings was the first WYD), it was billed as the seventeenth. Rome 2000 was the fifteenth, and Cologne 2005 will be the twentieth.[212] At best, this is a confusing numbering system, being largely unexplained; at worst, a misrepresentation, giving the impression the enthusiastic international rallies have been going on for a long time, thus denoting a strong, vibrant Church.

Misleading Terminology

Besides the unclear numbering system, there are other areas of fuzziness connected with World Youth Day, starting with the name itself. The international gatherings span so many days they should be named World Youth Week. And, as seen in Chapter 3, the word "youth" is wrongly applied to

---

[211]"Persons of Faith: Pope John Paul II," *Oblates*, May-June 1994, p. 16. The meeting that year in Rome was not called World Youth Day, but led the Pope to call for an annual event on Palm Sunday. The first official World Youth Day was a diocesan celebration in Rome on Palm Sunday, 1986, and the first international one was in 1987 in Buenos Aires, after which the international WYD has been held approximately every two years. See "The History of World Youth Day," wyd.ie/history.html.
[212]"John Paul II Challenges Young People," Zenit.org, February 15, 2001; Carol Glatz, "Pope Marks 20 Years of WYD Cross," *Catholic Register*, April 18, 2004, p. 7. Note that in 2005, an unnumbered WYD was also held on Palm Sunday.

an age group made up mostly of adults.

Obviously, even the word "pilgrims," used to describe WYD youth, is a misrepresentation. It gives the impression of a pious group journeying to a sacred place as an act of devotion. But, of course, it is used in its humanistic sense. A pilgrim is a person on a journey away from an undesirable state of affairs. The WYD pilgrim is journeying from the Roman Catholic to the Adult Church. Even those *born* into the latter are on pilgrimage, as their faith has to keep up with a changing world. World Youth Day is unequivocally an adult faith program. It is a process of building community in the parishes from which pilgrims hail, the parishes of the host country, and amongst participants themselves (to build world community), through people united in working for a common goal: the success of WYD. And it has worked! A typical volunteer who billeted pilgrims in her home enthusiastically bubbled,[213]

> We experienced our own parish in a way we had never known it before. We became close with the person we see each week in the pews, but never spoke to; we learned to love in a way that was new to us.

And world community was built between her, the Honduran pilgrims she hosted and the parish:

> ... each evening when we had to pick them up again, they would keep hosting these big parties for our entire parish, where they entertained us and we all had lots of fun. We had a hard time getting them to come home....
>
> But they were so full of life and having so much fun.... So we danced and partied late each night.... We "Latino danced" and we praised the Lord in many new ways.... And as the emails [sic] and packages ... from our pilgrims continue to come, we are able to continue this friendship....

---

[213]Dianne Wood, "You're Never Too Old for World Youth Day," *Canadian Messenger of the Sacred Heart* (Toronto), July 2003, p. 16.

However, there were some perspicacious people who noticed the changed meaning of "pilgrim." The producers of the documentary *Unlikely Pilgrims* stated:

> There is a preconceived [i.e., traditional] notion of pilgrim.... You think of older people, very devout....
>
> At WYD, young people stood outside the perceived notion of pilgrims.... WYD changed the minds of a lot of people, in terms of who a pilgrim is and what their [*sic*] life is. .... young Catholics ... gave a new face to the popular perception of pilgrim as serious and devout seekers of faith.[214]

Indeed, rather than "devout," if there is one term used continually to describe World Youth Day, it is "fun." This reputation attracts participants. Many pilgrims to Toronto acknowledged they had come to have fun and "to party." And besides the official entertainment, there was lots of partying on the side. For a generation raised on education as fun, religion also has to be fun to be worthwhile.

Crucial to currying favour with the WYD crowd is providing it with its preferred style of music. The entertainment at WYD 2002 was so massive — 500 performances involving 150 groups — that it was officially called a "Youth Festival" and billed as "*the* entertainment event of this summer's celebration." Twenty-five stages were scattered around Toronto, five of them at the main venue, the Canadian National Exhibition.[215] Much of the wild rock was out of the public eye; but John Vennari recounts what he witnessed in Part II.

There are other facets to the entertainment mania. First, entertainment is a *democratizing* tool, as it "allows pilgrims to be co-producers of World Youth Day." It is also a chance for young adults to "evangelize," to "minister" to their peers by "shar[ing] their gifts of music, dance and thea-

---

[214]Gillian Girodat, "A Story of Youth and Faith," *Catholic Register*, November 30, 2003, p. 12.
[215]Paulina Ratajczak, "Performing Pilgrims," ibid., February 17, 2002, p. 7; "Performances," wyd2002.org.

tre." This enables them "to affect how their peers view the Christian faith" (i.e., to exert peer pressure).[216] Many Toronto youth acknowledged they wouldn't have attended WYD if they had not been performing, such as in the dance-and-drama production at its opening Mass.[217] Entertainment is such a fixture at World Youth Day and other rallies, giving birth to so many performing groups or individuals, that one might confidently assert that, if nothing else, *the future of the Counterchurch lies in the entertainment field!*[218]

And what is the result of twenty years of fun-filled World Youth Days? We are now into the second generation of WYD attendees. The youth who had been declared the "future" of the Church twenty years ago are now in their forties or fifties. Have they been a "gift" to Catholicism, arresting its decline, or are they populating the pews of Adult Church, if any religion at all? We actually have an official answer to this otherwise rhetorical question. In 2000, Abp. Louis-Marie Billé, then President of the French Bishops' Conference,

> was asked if the World Youth Days had brought more youth into the Church and if vocations to the Priesthood had increased as a result. He was obliged to reply "no" to both questions.[219]

Indeed, in recent years John Paul II expressed concern about France: its "grave crisis" in vocations, declining religious practice among youth, and the increasing belief that there is no objective right and wrong.[220] These problems are

---

[216]Ratajczak, ibid. In general, music is a "ministry" in today's Counterchurch.

[217]Valpy, ibid.

[218]The relatively recent surge of entertainment in the Catholic Church, even in the midst of religious services, coincides with the humanist agenda, set forth in *Humanist Manifesto II*, of "the cultivation of feeling and love," to balance rationalism and produce the "whole" person. "As science pushes back the boundary of the known, one's sense of wonder is continually renewed, and art, poetry, and music find their places, along with religion and ethics." See Kurtz, p. 18.

[219]Brother Ephraim (founder of the ecu-syncretic and Judaism-oriented Community of the Beatitudes), "Teaching, August 2000," beatitudes.us.

[220]"Pope Pushes French Bishops on Decline in Priestly Vocations," CWNews.com, December 9, 2003; "Pope Urges French Bishops to Evangelize Youth," ibid., February 13, 2004.

patently obvious in the universal Church, so why pick on France? Perhaps because the enthusiastic World Youth Day in Paris in 1997 generated false hopes of a "turning point" for the moribund Church in France (with Sunday Mass attendance as low as 8 percent in 2000). After WYD 1997, France started concentrating on "youth ministry" and attributed the "surprising" success of Rome's WYD 2000 to the 60,000-80,000 (estimates vary) French pilgrims, the second-largest contingent after the Italians.[221] Jean-Marie Cardinal Lustiger of Paris declared that World Youth Day was "a great gift of renewal" for the Church, and the large French contingent was "a measure of the fruitfulness of World Youth Day in Paris in 1997."[222] However, in February 2004, just three-and-a-half years later, he was forced to concede to the Pope that French Catholicism shows "a decline in religious practice, reduction in the number of active priests, the loss of Christian habits, and the secularization of morals."[223]

A New Age Cross

The travelling World Youth Day Cross, "entrusted to young people" by the Pope in 1984,[224] has several symbolic meanings, all unconnected with Christ's atoning death. First, the 12-foot cross is treated like the Olympic torch. The official schedule for WYD 2002 called the cross "the Olympic Flame of this great event." Like the Olympic torch, the cross is considered "a symbol of unity" because "it has been in many places ... *we* are all in the cross."[225] Not surprisingly, then,

[221]Sabrina Arena Ferrisi, "World Youth Day 1997 Bears Fruit for France in Rome," us.catholic.net/rcc/Periodicals/lgpress/2000-10/youth-97.html
[222]Bettinelli, ibid.
[223]"Evangelize Youth, Pope Tells French Bishops,"CWNews.com, February 20, 2004.
[224]Glatz, ibid.; Father Thomas M. Rosica, CSB, "Introduction," *Prayers for World Youth Day 2002* (Ottawa: Canadian Conference of Catholic Bishops, 2001), pp. 8-9.
[225]Susy Passos, "Pilgrims Catch World Youth Day Spirit," *Catholic Register*, April 14, 2002, p. 9 (emphasis added). Another "important symbol" was the "peace flame lit by John Paul II" in Toronto in 1984. It travelled through the

there is no Corpus on the cross, because it doesn't represent Christ's sacrifice on Calvary for our sins. This is an apt symbol of "a false church without a Redeemer," which doesn't believe in original sin and the need for redemption — the anti-Church seen by Bl. Anne Catherine Emmerich. The Jews taunted Christ that if He came down from the cross they would believe in Him.[226] The devil similarly tempts us: Why suffer? — join the world, have fun. Peter didn't want Jesus to suffer and die, and Jesus rebuked him for preferring a life of worldly comfort.[227] The World Youth Day Cross, in ignoring the redemptive nature of Christ's death, proclaims a false "Jesus" who has descended from the Cross and is one with the world[228]; this matches WYD's focus on fun.

The Canadian bishops' book, *Prayers for World Youth Day 2002*, makes quite clear that the "Pilgrim Cross" is *not* the crucifix, seen by the Old Age Catholic Church as symbolizing our redemption. World Youth Day, says the prayerbook's introduction, is an opportunity given by the Pope for youth "to herald the dawn of a new age."[229] Hence,

> The language of the Cross, if it is to speak to young people today, must be holistic and not just focused on the aspect of sacrifice and punishment reflecting the piety of previous generations. It is therefore essential to relate the Cross to the desire for life and the search for happiness.... The Cross ... helps young people in their quest for authentic human fulfillment and happiness.
>
> The Cross is intended to bring people of different backgrounds and experiences together to form community, and is not to be used for purposes that might jeopardize this goal[230] [like teaching about sin and redemption?].

---

streets in procession to the stage for the opening WYD Mass: Susan Fohr and Sandra Valenzuela, "The Pilgrimage of Youth Begins," ibid., August 11-18, 2002, p. 5.

[226] Cf. Matt. 27:39-42.

[227] Cf. Matt. 16:22-25.

[228] Jesus, however, intended His followers to be separate from the world and thus hated by it, observing that those *of* the world are loved by it (cf. Jn. 15:19).

[229] Father Rosica, ibid., p. 8.

[230] *Prayers for World Youth Day*, pp. 30-31.

Note the Jungian motif of the WYD Cross: it is "holistic." It unites the old idea of evil (sin) and the need for redemption to the new idea in which sin is an acceptable good, making redemption unnecessary. The pursuit of holiness (which involves mortification) is replaced by the pursuit of happiness.

The WYD Cross, therefore, also signifies the pantheistic New Age doctrine of wholeness, which teaches that "creedal religion," with its doctrine of sin, causes *guilt* or "brokenness," and, thus, unhappiness. Man frees himself from God's "oppression" by asserting the "centrality and sovereignty of the human person." This makes him *guilt-free* or *whole*, fulfilled and happy. Wholeness also refers to the pantheistic unity of races and religions in one humanity, which is also impeded by creedal religion. *Embracing the holistic doctrine represents one's "Luciferic initiation" into the New Age.*[231] The above bishops' pronouncement implies today's young Catholics are *already* initiated into wholeness; so *their* symbol, which apes the true Cross, represents pantheistic world unity and individual autonomy, with its acceptance of the shadow.

Another symbolic meaning of the WYD Cross is found in a report on the "massive celebration" (that included dancing girls) greeting its arrival in Canada for its own "pilgrimage" across the country. The cross, explains the report,

> ... symbolizes the faith that the church has in its young people and the flame that they must carry for the church....
>
> "... it symbolizes the hopes, joys, sorrows and dreams of the youth.... It is the symbol of the Pope's trust in us, God's trust."
>
> ... [it is] "the story of youth."[232]

The WYD Cross, then, does not represent Christ's sacrifice for the salvation of the world — it represents *youth*! It is, there-

---

[231]Ferreira, *The New Age Movement*, pp. 5-6.
[232]Emanuel Pires, "'Symbol of Hope' Makes its Canadian Debut ...," *Catholic Register*, April 23, 2001.

fore, an *idol*, the symbol of a *new faith*. A Toronto WYD official declared that the event and its cross was a chance for young Canadian Catholics "to become enthusiastic and believe in *their* faith."[233] This is a faith of song, dance, fun and "unity." Naturally, it is surrounded with merriment.

The WYD Cross also represents a universalist faith. As already noted, pilgrimage is a journey from the exclusivist Catholic Church to the universalist Counterchurch which will be part of the one-world religion. The bridge is culture. The Old Age — i.e., the true — Church was allegedly a construct of Western culture. The New Age one has to fit into a multicultural world, and so must be universalist. The following statement in the WYD prayerbook reveals that the significance of the Cross today is cultural and universalist:

> The Cross ... was publicly known in Jesus' own time as a symbol of cruel torture and death. After ... the spread of Christianity, the Cross took on new significance and marked the culture of the western world.... Today, in our cultural context we must be sensitive to those who do not share our faith; for whom the Cross has little or perhaps even negative significance. Special care should be taken to avoid any form of "triumphalism" and to clearly relate the Cross as a sign of God's self-giving love poured out for all people.... it is important to underline the "universal" significance of the Cross ... for the youth of the *world* [not just Catholics] today.[234]

All through the official prayerbook, the cross is tied to the *love of God* for suffering mankind rather than Christ's death to *redeem* us from sin and open Heaven to us (the heresy of Unitarian Universalism). The *crucifix* denotes Catholicism's "triumphalism" and exclusivity. However, since World Youth Day is becoming increasingly syncretic, *its* cross

---

[233]Ibid. (Emphasis added.)

[234]Page 32 (emphasis added). Reportedly, Vatican II rejected "triumphalism," which it defined as the Church's belief it is the Kingdom of God and the only means of salvation: Steve Tyson, "Vatican II Rejected Roman Catholic 'Triumphalism,'"*Catholic Register*, January 15, 2001, p. 10. This rejection contradicts the thrice-defined dogma that outside the Catholic Church there is no salvation.

must have a universalist meaning. Only a cross representing a *humanitarian* or social-justice *love*, instead of Christ's loving acceptance of *punishment* for the remission of sins, could have universal appeal. At the same time, it suits heretical Catholics who do not believe in original sin and the need for redemption. This brings us to the final significance of the World Youth Day Cross: it is the symbol of a social-justice church and the suffering caused by social evils.[235]

A social-justice cross does away with the "negative" Catholic religion of sin, contrition, penance, and the sacramental graces required for salvation, replacing it with the political Marxist religion described as "the preferential option for the poor," which teaches that "our salvation is directly linked to the suffering of the world." The only Lord who saves is the risen Lord "who walked in solidarity with the poor and the suffering." This new interpretation of the cross, the basis of liberation theology, is attributed to Lutheran minister Dietrich Bonhoeffer. [236] It has resulted in un-Catholic, Marxist meanings for the Catholic terms "Paschal Mystery," "following Jesus," "discipleship" and "carrying our cross." Even the whole reason for fasting has changed. No longer is it considered penance for our sins and a means to holiness; instead, it is taught from the pulpit that we fast in order that the money we save on food can be used to feed the hungry.

As seen earlier, Archbishop Sheen had predicted a future Catholicism that would be "religion without a Cross [i.e., without the *atoning Sacrifice* of Christ], a liturgy without a world to come, a religion to destroy a religion, a politics which is a religion, a church emptied of its divine content." Its only goal would be to better society. Blessed Anne Catherine Emmerich also saw the anti-Church without a Saviour, having only a temporal role and good works without faith.

Propagating the new "theology of the cross," *Gaudium et Spes*, the Vatican II document which Pope John Paul II

---

[235]For example, see *Prayers for World Youth* Day, pp. 23-27, 53.
[236]Ted Schmidt, "Cheap Grace ... Costly Grace," *Scarboro Missions* (Toronto), April 1996, p. 4. Schmidt was a television commentator for WYD 2002.

helped to draft,[237] teaches that, following (the humanitarian) Christ's example, we "must shoulder that cross which the world and the flesh inflict upon those who search after peace and justice." Perfectly in harmony with this theology, in the WYD prayerbook Father Rosica says, "Because we follow a crucified Christ, we enter into solidarity with the world's suffering masses...." The reason, says *Gaudium et Spes*, is "that the effort to establish a universal brotherhood [i.e., the Masonic world republic] will not be in vain."[238]

Now, since pantheism teaches we are all one with the universe, the Counterchurch logically proclaims, "the suffering body of christ [is] all creation."[239] It naturally follows that there cannot be the figure of Jesus on the WYD Cross; instead, since all creation is on the cross, it can symbolize *anything, anybody and any emotion*. It's a fill-in-the-blank cross. So, it is used to represent youth, as noted above. And in a pantheistic, Jungian way, the pilgrim cross can "symbolize the hopes, joys, sorrows and dreams of the youth." So the Disney-happy-ending type of Catholic, who cannot bear the thought of suffering anything in imitation of Christ, is perfectly free to negate His atrocious sufferings; every reference in the WYD prayer book to His death includes His resurrection in the same sentence. For example, in the section "Christ in Dance and Song: Creative Celebration in the Presence of the [pilgrim] Cross," we find: "... organize a feast of 'youth creativity' in the presence of the Cross as a sign of the resurrection of the Lord." Another example: the cross "is the symbol of the entire paschal mystery, the suffering, death and resurrection of Jesus."[240]

Hence, the cross representing the generation that is the hope of the Counterchurch was surrounded by entertainment as from April 2001 it rambled through Canada,

---

[237] George Weigel, *Witness to Hope* (New York: HarperCollins Publishers, 1999), pp. 166-69.

[238] Pastoral Constitution on the Church in the Modern World *Gaudium et Spes*, December 7, 1965, no. 38; Schmidt, ibid; *Prayers for World Youth Day*, p. 27.

[239] Schmidt, ibid.: see photo caption, p. 5.

[240] *Prayers for World Youth Day*, pp. 54, 89.

sponsored by the Knights of Columbus.[241] Even on Good Friday, the most serious and solemn day of the Church year, in 2002, the World Youth Day spirit was alive as the cross was exuberantly "body surfed" over a crowd in Quebec City to the chants of the WYD slogan, *"lumier [sic] du monde, sel de la terre"* — light of the world and salt of the earth. WYD director Fr. Tom Rosica complacently observed,

> World Youth Day is revamping the church and public adoration....   Young people don't have to have a quiet faith....
>
> The Catholic faith is being reborn in Canada and especially in Quebec....[242]

Nothing could be further from the truth.   This religion, which is being reborn with the help of World Youth Day, is a *perversion* of the Catholic faith. The great early twentieth-century spiritual writer, Fr. Reginald Garrigou-Lagrange, OP, comments that St. Paul tells us the soldier of Christ must be detached from things of this world (2 Tim. 2:3-4), meaning he must use them as though not using them; otherwise he will lose the spirit of Christ and be like *salt that has lost its savour* and "is good for nothing anymore but to be cast out, and to be trodden on by men."   Like Christ, the true Christian must also accept hardship, suffering and being despised and persecuted.[243] St. John of the Cross explains that to follow Christ crucified is to deny oneself every attachment, temporal, natural and *spiritual*. Experiential religion, which seeks agreeable spiritual feelings,[244] is not self-denial, but what he labels

---

[241]Pires, ibid.; Tim S. Hickey, "Bringing a Catholic Message to Canada," *Columbia*, March 2004, p. 13.

[242]Passos, ibid.

[243]Father Garrigou-Lagrange, *The Three Ages of the Interior Life*, 2 vols., trans. Sister M. Timothea Doyle, OP (St. Louis, MO: B. Herder Book Co., 1947), 1:295-98.

[244]Experiential religion can be based on one's own life experiences; on sampling the religious practices of other faiths; or on one's own feelings, emotional and physical. For instance, Susan Walker, in "Liturgy: A Feast for the Senses," *Eucharistic Minister*, November 1998, p. 1, instructs Catholics to pray with "our entire bodies," employing all five senses. Example: "Our senses of taste and smell are fed at the eucharistic table.... A bit of bread, changed by our prayer

"spiritual gluttony." Its followers are

> *enemies of the Cross of Christ*; for true spirituality seeks for God's sake that which is distasteful rather than that which is delectable; and inclines itself rather to suffering than to consolation...."[245]

St. Paul similarly teaches that those who mind earthly things and seek the pleasures of the senses are enemies of the Cross of Christ (cf. Phil. 3:18-19).

Idolatry and Occultism

Being a symbol of universalism and an idol itself, the World Youth Day Cross was the centrepiece of many pagan rituals on Canada's native reserves. The way it was handled vividly demonstrated that on the reserves the Counterchurch is fully merged with paganism. Father Robert Foliot, SJ, savoured how in one area it was assembled near the Sacred Fire; how it was smudged; how prayers and chants were offered to the Great Spirit in the four directions; and how "[i]t was an experience and a sign of respect, peace and mutual harmony between Christians and traditionalists...."[246]

"Traditionalists" in *this* context are not traditional Catholics but pagan natives; their ceremonies are referred to as "traditional prayer services." Here's another exemplification of the new meaning of "traditionalist": An Indian Chief "asked that a new cemetery, which had been smudged and blessed only by the traditionalists, be now blessed by the

---

and God's love, is placed in our hands, and we roll it around our tongues, feeling the texture, tasting the wheat. We smell the wine for a brief moment before sipping from the cup. The alcohol tingles ... and burns ever so slightly as we swallow. The taste lingers in the back of our throats, perhaps past the end of the liturgy, and reminds us of what we have done and who we are [we are Eucharist, of course]."

[245]*Ascent of Mount Carmel*, 3d rev. ed., trans. and ed. E. Allison Peers (Garden City, NY: Doubleday & Company, 1958), pp. 190-94. (Emphasis added.)

[246]Father Foliot, "Cross Brings Christ's Healing Message," *Mission Canada* (Toronto), Winter 2001, p. 14.

Catholics with the presence of the Cross."[247]

As a symbol of native inculturation, the cross even made its way into a Ukrainian-rite church in Ottawa in which Inuit youth venerated it with "traditional" drum dancing and throat-singing.[248] As a symbol of unity, the cross visited non-Catholic churches. As a symbol of the humanitarian "Christ," it put into practice the *Gaudium et Spes* teaching seen above, that, following Christ's example, we "must shoulder that cross which [is inflicted] upon those who search after peace and justice." The Stations of the Cross during Toronto's World Youth Day (written by Pope John Paul) had an unmistakable social-justice flavour.

Now, a generic "Christ" can be *anyone*; so the "Christ" in the Stations of the Cross enacted with the WYD Cross in the streets of Ottawa in 2001 was an Inuit *woman*.[249] Presumably she was depicting "shouldering the social problems devastating native people." The precedent for having a woman portray the social-justice "Christ" during the Stations at World Youth Day was set in Denver, Colorado, in 1993. Eduardo Cardinal Pironio, president of the Pontifical Council

---

[247]Ibid.

[248]Note that many older Indians consider drumming in church to be revolutionary. Tragically, they are being led away from Old Age (i.e., true) Catholicism by the consciousness-raising of *paganizing missionaries* about the "mistaken zeal of early missionaries" who vetoed the "sacred drum" and other "traditions" as devil worship. The propaganda is that the sacred drum was originally used as a "call to worship" (which was indeed devil worship, as St. Paul designates idolatry in 1 Cor. 10:20), so it can be used in Catholic services, (replacing church bells that were blessed in order to *dispel* demons by their ringing: cf. Father Michael Müller, CSSR, *The Holy Sacrifice of the Mass* [New York: Fr. Pustet & Co., 1874; reprint ed., Rockford, IL: Tan Books and Publishers, 1992], p. 554). *The Papal Mass at Toronto's World Youth Day was introduced by this demonic "call to worship"* (prompting John Vennari to flee, as recounted in Part II). See Deacon Bill Callaghan and Molly Callaghan, "The Sacred Drum: a Call to Worship," *Catholic Missions in Canada*, Summer 2003, p. 21.

The mind-altering and occult nature of native drumming and chanting, as recognized by the early Catholic missionaries, is confirmed by witch Starhawk. She says rhythmic motion, song, drumming and chanting can induce trance. Certain rhythms are used to produce emotional states like anger. Further, "Afro-American religions depend heavily on rhythmic drumming and dancing to induce a trance state in which worshippers become ... possessed....": Starhawk, p. 149.

[249]Lynne S. Rollin, "World Youth Day Cross Visits Nunavut!", *Catholic Missions in Canada*, Summer 2002, p. 8, with photo of the female "Christ" on p.12.

for the Laity, led the Stations whilst a troupe of mime per-
formers acted them on a stage. The use of mime was the justification for perverting the Way of the Cross. In response to
outraged criticism of the female "Christ" by "Old Age"
Catholics unaware that the historical God-Man had been replaced by His humanitarian counterfeit, officials declared:

> Mime is never an historical representation. The organizers
> never intended the portrayal of the Stations of the Cross to
> be an historical representation. *Anyone, even a child, could
> have played any of the roles.*

The Pope's spokesman, Joaquin Navarro-Valls, added that "a
woman can represent all humanity and all humanity was represented by the death of Christ."[250]

This is demoting Jesus' Passion and Death to a mere
icon or type of suffering, a completely futile act that was un-
able to end suffering in the world. It is the heresy of Unitarian Universalism, which denies Christ's atonement for sin.
Since the pantheistic cross represents the sufferings of humanity (and the cosmos), on one Canadian reserve, the Way
of the Cross with the WYD pilgrim cross had 24 stations —
"which represented all the families of that reserve as well as
the visitors from other villages"![251]

Perverting the significance of the Crucifixion — and of
the very nature of Jesus Himself — is one of the clearest indi-
cations of a deliberate attempt by Church officials *to use World
Youth Day to corrupt the foundations of Faith.* They have succeeded so well in deadening Catholic sensibilities that they no
longer need resort to the subterfuge of "non-historical" mime
to revise Catholic history and doctrine. At the Papal Good
Friday Stations in 2004, "[t]he cross was carried by witnesses

---

[250]"Group Outraged That Woman Depicted Christ," *Catholic New Times*, September 26, 1993, p. 2 (emphasis added). A former Jungian convert to Catholicism states that "body-prayer" and mime are part of the *Jungian* "approach to
liturgy" (Likoudis, "Jungians Believe"). These techniques are frequently used in
today's Catholic gatherings and services.

[251]Sister Joann Sutherland, MCR, "World Youth Day Cross Comes to Ana-
ham," *Mission Canada*, Fall 2001, p. 24.

of human suffering on various continents, including a young woman from Madrid ... and a nun from Burundi."[252]

The Canadian bishops' official prayer book for World Youth Day itself encourages idolatry and occultism. It contains "A service in the Aboriginal tradition" entitled "Praying in Six Directions." Besides prayers to East, South, West and North, there are prayers to Mother Earth ("We bow down and touch Mother Earth," which "provides all that is needed to sustain life") and to the sky. Each "direction" is treated as a god and each prayer ends, "We praise and thank you, Creator God."[253]

"Creator God" is another title for the all-inclusive Great Spirit of Native Americans, according to John Robinson of the Toronto Centre for Native Spirituality. At a recent Franciscan Celebration of World Peace, Robinson demonstrated that prayer to the four directions is a "traditional purification rite" that invokes the gods (also called spirits or winds) of each direction to bless and protect the "sacred space," the place of assembly. In his performance, he also added a prayer to the Earth goddess: "We greet you, Great Spirit of the Earth. It was from you we came as from a Mother; you nourish us still."[254]

Witch Starhawk explains that invoking the spirits of the four directions and saluting earth and sky is very important in witchcraft. Rituals must begin with "casting a circle," i.e., "creating a sacred space," through this ceremony. She says, "The concept of the quartered circle is basic to Witchcraft," adding that moving in a clockwise direction (as in the bishops' aboriginal prayer) calls down the energy and power of the elements earth, air, fire and water.[255]

Toronto's World Youth Day was "viewed as a vital opportunity to reconcile the traditional spiritual practices of

[252]"Suffering of Christ and the World Recalled at Stations of the Cross," Zenit.org, April 10, 2004.
[253]*Prayers for World Youth Day*, pp. 97-99.
[254]John Robinson, "Native Spirituality," *Companion* (Toronto), July/August 2001, p. 5.
[255]Starhawk, pp. 55-75.

native groups with the celebration of the Roman Catholic faith." Prominent native symbols at the main WYD site were a "towering teepee, a sacred fire and a sweat lodge." Pilgrims were led in a circle purification ceremony, and aboriginal groups from around the world held seminars, prayer sessions, music and dance performances.[256]

Besides native inculturation, there were many other ecu-syncretic activities, as befits the universalist nature of the Counterchurch. Indeed, *World Youth Day is now open to youth and volunteers of any or no religious persuasion.* Describing Toronto's volunteer training centre, Father Rosica, director of WYD 2002, stated:

> Through this volunteer centre and World Youth Day, Pope John Paul II invites volunteers of different religions and non-believers to put into effect interreligious and intercultural dialogue and collaboration.[257]

And so Muslims and Mormons volunteered, whilst pilgrims were hosted by Jewish families.[258]

The choice of Father Rosica as director of WYD is revealing. Long head of the liberal Newman Centre at the University of Toronto, in 2001 he told a meeting of priests and rabbis, "There is anti-Judaism in [the Gospel of] John." "John's bitterness against the Jews," expressed in his "passion narrative," "does not represent Jesus' message, nor ... the authentic teaching of the Church." Further, "The continuing validity of the Jewish covenant has to be affirmed."[259]

By painting St. John's Gospel — which highlights the divinity of Christ — as unreliable because it is "racist," Father Rosica casts doubt on the divinity of Jesus. Further, asserting that the Old Covenant was not replaced by the New denies

---

[256]Wallace Immen, "Festival to Have Native Flare [*sic*]," *Globe and Mail*, July 22, 2002, p. A5; "In Review," *Catholic Register*, August 11-18, 2002, pp. 14-15.

[257]"Training Centre for World Youth Day Volunteers Opens," Centre news release, April 26, 2002.

[258]"Toronto Still Abuzz."

[259]Michael Swan, "Biblical Potholes Trip up Both Catholics and Jews," *Catholic Register*, March 5, 2001, p. 8.

the reason for Christ's death and His founding of the Catholic Church. These errors provide the rationalization for an Arian social-justice "Christ." Father Rosica's speech also attacked the Church's infallibity. Her infallible inclusion of St. John's Gospel in the Canon of Sacred Scripture as the inspired Word of God and a vital part of her authentic teaching completely recognizes it as correctly presenting Jesus' message. Her infallible recognition of the sainthood of St. John precludes any possibility of his being racist. Father Rosica's beliefs are modernist errors condemned by Pope St. Pius X.[260]

Father Rosica moved from WYD to found and head the Salt+Light Television channel whose aim, he says, is to harness the "electricity and energy" unleashed at WYD by presenting "the message of a younger vibrant church to an older church." Station programming has been described as "the Catholic Church with nose-studs": "pop music, news, documentaries, talk shows, … theological instruction … and saint-food. All with a beat. Thumpa-thumpa-thumpa. All Catholic." (But also syncretic.) Musical talents showcased include folk-guitarist nun Sr. Maeve Heaney and rapping priest Fr. Stan Fortuna. As for the "saint-food" — that's a cooking show featuring the recipes of saints, prepared by chefs of classy restaurants and sampled by Father Rosica.[261]

Marxist New World Order Indoctrination

Father Garrigou-Lagrange explains how religion as fun *leads to* the social-justice church, Communism, a false world community and wars:

> Without God, the seriousness of life gets out of focus. If religion is no longer a grave matter but something to smile at, then the serious element in life must be sought

---

[260]See Syllabus Condemning the Errors of the Modernists *Lamentabili Sane*, July 3, 1907, nos. 9-18.
[261]Michael Valpy, "A New Station of the Cross," *Globe and Mail*, December 9, 2004, p. R1.

elsewhere. Some place it ... in social activity; they devote themselves religiously to ... the establishment of justice be-tween classes or peoples. After a while they are forced to perceive that ... relations between individuals and nations become more and more difficult.... the same land cannot simultaneously belong wholly to several men, nor the same territory to several nations. As a result, interests conflict when man feverishly makes these lesser goods his last end....

If the serious element in life is out of focus, if it no longer is concerned with our duties toward God, but with the scientific and social activities of man; if man continually seeks himself instead of God, ... then events are not slow in showing him that he has taken an impossible way, which leads ... to unbearable disorder and misery....

... religion can give [a] ... truly realistic answer to the great modern problems only if it is a religion that is pro-foundly lived, not simply a superficial and cheap religion made up of some vocal prayers and some ceremonies in which religious art [leave alone rock music and dancing!] has more place than true piety.[262]

Father Garrigou-Lagrange also delineates the dangers to the Church of its *hidden* enemy: humanitarianism, the ape of true charity. One of the dangers is ecumenism (and hence, world brotherhood):

There is also a false charity, made up of humanitarian sen-timentalism, which seeks to have itself approved by true charity and which, by its contact, often taints the true.

One of the chief conflicts of the present day is that which arises between true and false charity. The latter re-minds us of the false Christs spoken of in the Gospel; they are more dangerous before they are unmasked than when they make themselves known as the true enemies of the Church.... The worst of corruptions is that which attacks ... the highest of the theological virtues. The apparent good which attracts the sinner is, in fact, so much the more dan-gerous as it is the counterfeit of a higher good. Such, for

---

[262]Father Garrigou-Lagrange, pp. 7-8.

example, is the ideal of the pan-Christians, who seek the union of the Churches to the detriment of the faith, *which this union presupposes.* If, therefore, through stupidity or more or less conscious cowardice, those who should represent true charity approve here and there the dicta of the false, an incalculable evil may result. This evil is at times greater than that done by open persecutors, with whom evidently one can no longer have anything in common.[263]

Social justice/humanitarianism as practised today is not charity but politics. Charity involves the renunciation of *all* pride, vanity and *spiritual* sensuality (feel-good religion).[264] The justice and peace movement is political. It has accepted Satan's temptation of Christ in the desert to turn stones into bread, i.e., to make earthly prosperity the goal of religion.

The movement is a Marxist, anti-Catholic movement for social and structural change, including that of the Church. Its naturalistic rallying call of "human rights" and "equality" includes all the unjust "rights" demanded by Communism and feminism. Nevertheless, "human rights" is the mantra of today's Church and the fuel of the one-world religion. Cardinal Kasper has stated that religions show unity by "giv[ing] unanimous witness to the world for justice, reconciliation and peace."[265] This syncretic human rights agenda betrays the Arian nature of the Counterchurch and its complete negation of supernatural verities. As Father Garrigou-Lagrange reminds us,

> The Savior did not come upon earth to carry out a *human* work of philanthropy, but a *divine* work of charity. He accomplished it by speaking more to men of their *duties* than of their *rights*....

Not only is the social justice movement not charitable; it is not even just. True justice first gives to God the honour and worship due to Him as our Creator and Redeemer. It is

---

[263]Ibid., p. 151. (Emphasis added.)
[264]Cf. ibid., p. 240.
[265]Cited in "Vision of Christian Unity for the Next Generation," *Missions Today*, January/February 2004, p. 7.

united to true charity, which is first the love of God through following His Commandments, and then the love of neighbour. Love of neighbour means, above all, concern for his eternal happiness and the salvation of his soul. Thus, true Christian justice "ought to be less preoccupied with jealously defending [one's] temporal rights than with winning over to God the soul of [one's] irritated brother." Further, since sin is an offence against God, then true justice involves the virtue of penance. Inspired by love of God, penance involves mortification to destroy in us sin and its consequences.[266]

The social justice movement, however, does not acknowledge personal sin or the need for penance. It is thus a most *unjust*, unloving, anti-Christian movement, the child of Freemasonry. Pope Leo XIII said naturalists and Masons,

> exaggerating rather our natural virtue and excellence and placing therein alone the principle and rule of justice, ... cannot even imagine that there is any need at all of a constant struggle ... to overcome the ... rule of our passions.[267]

Nevertheless, World Youth Day is being used to mobilize the next generation of social-justice Catholics. In his first speech, on arriving at Toronto's airport, Pope John Paul made clear that social justice is the key agenda for WYD. He stated that "one of the *principle* [sic] reasons for the World Youth Day" is "[y]oung people coming together to commit themselves ... to the great cause of peace and human solidarity." Canada was congratulated for being "a champion of human rights and human dignity."[268]

In Rome, the social justice program was directed by Pax Romana ICMICA (International Catholic Movement for

---

[266]Father Garrigou-Lagrange, pp. 283, 285. Of course, all ecu-syncretic activities are a grave injustice towards God.

[267]*Humanum Genus*, no. 20.

[268]"Thank you, Toronto, Thank you, Canada," official text of speech, *Catholic Register*, August 11-18, 2002, p. 2 (emphasis added). The Pontiff clearly uses the word "solidarity" to denote the social justice and peace movement, and its work to destroy inequalities and "change ... the established structures of power which today govern societies." See his World Day of Peace message, January 1, 2001, nos. 17-18.

Intellectual and Cultural Affairs). Headquartered in Geneva, ICMICA has been engaged in human rights advocacy since 1947 and is perhaps the largest Catholic lay group dedicated to justice, peace and ecology. With branches in more than seventy countries in all continents, it has permanent representative status at the UN, UNESCO and the Council of Europe, and recognition by the Holy See. *It is also a member of the global coalition for an Earth Charter campaign*, and it promotes interfaith dialogue, inculturation and a democratic Church. It is "committed" to "the empowerment of women by promoting their leadership as a high priority at all levels in the Church." For Rome's WYD, Pax Romana youth groups worked with Church leaders and Pope John Paul to help plan events; were members of the World Youth Day Forum that "acted as the official representation of the world's young people and met and prayed with the Pope a number of times during the week"; and ran consciousness-raising workshops on combatting poverty. Pax Romana will also have a strong planning and leadership role at the 2005 World Youth Day in Cologne.[269]

Now, the Earth Charter was launched in 1994 by Mikhail Gorbachev and Maurice Strong, Canada's premier New Ager, occultist and religious environmentalist.[270] Gorbachev, who is using environmentalism to help implement Communist world government, has said, "Nature is my god," whilst Strong has written, "We are all gods now, gods in charge of our own destiny." Gorbachev has stated, "My hope is that this charter will be a kind of Ten Commandments, a 'Sermon on the Mount,' that provides a guide for human behavior toward the environment...." Strong, chairman of the UN's 1992 Earth Summit, has added that "the real goal of the Earth

---

[269]"Pax Romana MIIC/ICMICA"; *Pax Romana JubilE-News*, No. 23, September 1, 2000; "World Youth Day 2000 in Rome"; "Global Strategic Plan: 2002 to 2004"; *E-Update No. 21*, December 13, 2003; all posted at paxromana.org. See also Pax Romana's International Young Catholic Students (IYCS) News Page, at iycs-jeci.org, ca. September 2004.

[270]For more on Strong's spiritual activities see Dennis Laurence Cuddy, *Now is the Dawning of the New Age New World Order* (Oklahoma City: Hearthstone Publishing, 1991), pp. 319-20.

Charter is that it will in fact become like the Ten Commandments."[271]

To be adopted and implemented by the United Nations or the European Union, the Charter is a set of *commandments* for a global society based on respect for nature, universal human rights, economic justice and a "culture of peace." Pantheistic, occult interconnectedness is a key tenet, expressed in its Principles 1a ("Recognize that all beings are interdependent....") and 16f ("Recognize that peace is the wholeness created by right relationships with oneself, other persons, other cultures, other life, Earth, and the larger whole of which we are all a part"). Communism is couched in Principle 10A: "Promote the equitable distribution of wealth within nations and among nations." Principle 11 is the feminist agenda: "Affirm gender equality and equity as prerequisites to sustainable development...." Pax Romana has published a study book of "reflection for action" on the Earth Charter.[272]

Blasphemously signifying its status as the replacement for God's Ten Commandments, the Earth Charter, handwritten on papyrus, is travelling the world to raise consciousness in the Ark of Hope, a painted sycamore chest that mimics the Ark of the Covenant. The sycamore tree was sacred to most ancient Middle Eastern pagan religions. The carrying poles of the Ark of Hope are shaped like unicorn horns "to render evil ineffective." Painted by aboriginals, its four panels represent the occult elements earth, air, fire and water. Symbols of the world's religions surround the top panel whose painting portrays "Spirit." The Ark also contains books of "prayers and affirmations for Earth." Rooted in Jungian occultism, they are known as the Temenos Books.[273]

---

[271]Id., "Ten Commandments on Public Display ...," *The Times Leader* (Princeton, KY), October 29, 2003, p. A7; Gary H. Kah, "The 'Ark of Hope' Comes to Indianapolis," *Hope for the World Update* (Noblesville, IN), Fall 2003, p. 7.

[272]earthcharter.org; "Earth Charter Book Issued ...," March 11, 2002, News and Events for 2002, ibid.

[273]arkofhope.org; Kah, ibid; Terry Melanson, "The Earth Charter & the Ark of the Gaia Covenant," *Despatch Magazine* (Australia), March 2002, p. 58.

Now, in Canada, the Marxist Canadian Catholic Organization for Development and Peace (CCODP), an official agency of the Canadian bishops, took the WYD social justice agenda a step further than Rome's program.   Whereas Rome's initiative was one of discussion and reflection, Canada's involved actual voluntary work.

A CCODP newsletter defined World Youth Day as "a spiritual *pilgrimage* involving prayer, reflection, *social service*, *celebration* and *community-building.*"[274]   (What WYD *celebrates* is "the life and faith of young people"[275] — call it building egoism and narcissism.)   "Youth," blared the newsletter, are "the light of the world by shining as advocates for change.... leading efforts to create a just world."   Hence, social justice was to be a special focus of World Youth Day, and Development and Peace offered "training in 'faith and action for justice' in the months leading up to July 2002," and various activities during WYD.   Additionally, for three or four days prior to World Youth Day, interested pilgrims volunteered across Canada in a program called "Days in the Dioceses."[276] Of course, like the Church in general, the CCODP has an "aging membership" and is "attempting to attract more young people."[277]   World Youth Day provided it with a great recruitment opportunity.

As an example of the type of service training before WYD, students in Hamilton, Ontario, were to engender solidarity with sweatshop workers.   Supported by CCODP, they lobbied diocesan schools, parishes and agencies to adopt a purchasing policy that "demanded" their suppliers "comply with fundamental labour rights...."[278]

As Father Garrigou-Lagrange indicated, false charity involves both humanitarianism and pan-religious activity. Not surprisingly, therefore, service projects during WYD 2002

---

[274]*Development and Peace*, ibid. (Emphases added.)

[275]This was, allegedly, why John Paul II instituted WYD: "Pilgrims for Jubilee Year," *Oblates*, August 2000, p. 9.

[276]"Young People Acting for Justice," *Development and Peace*, ibid.; Michael Swan, "Youth Ministers Meet to Prepare for WYD," *Catholic Register*, January 8, 2001, p. 3.

[277]"CCODP Remains Vital ...," *Catholic Register*, November 3, 2002, p. 11.

[278]*Development and Peace*, ibid.

were *designed* to "express an ecumenical spirit." Following Cardinal Kasper, pilgrims showed their unity with people of any or no faith by "working in solidarity with all people" to "express [their] common love for God." Projects included visiting nursing homes and AIDS hospices, environmental work, assisting at food banks, building homes for the ecumenical organization Habitat for Humanity, etc.[279]

The next step for World Youth Days will be to make "volunteer" service mandatory, as it already is for school graduation and other events.

YouthPride

The festivities for WYD 2002 started a year earlier with a kickoff celebration whose performances included "an in-your-face, brash rap" rendition of the Gospels, co-written by charismatic priest Fr. Stan Fortuna and performed by students. Justin Trudeau, 29, a drama teacher and son of the late prime minister Pierre Trudeau, struck the note of revolution, garnering loud cheers. In the presence of Cardinal Ambrozic, he "ministered" to his peers by sharing his faith experience, which was nothing else but an invitation to join the adult church, where they can do as they please.

Trudeau "recounted his childhood struggles with the strict tenets of Catholicism," after which, he said, "I started to rediscover my *own* religion." And what does his personal religion teach? "Church isn't about rules. It's about guidance." Glorying in World Youth Day's self-aggrandizing theme, "You are the salt of the earth and light of the world," Trudeau boasted, "... *we* are the flavour, the combustible element, the light of hope in what is becoming a darkened world." He professed that WYD 2002 would "empower the young people," and "he urged them to reject 'old men with

---

[279]wyd2002.org; Sabitri Ghosh, "Countdown to World Youth Day ...," *Catholic New Times*, September 9, 2001, p. 1. Habitat is a member of the occult New Group of World Servers organization that follows Alice Bailey's plan for enabling "volunteer" slave labour in the new world order. See "Groups, Human Services," at ngws.org.

old ideas. It's time to change our world and it starts to-night.'"[280]

Trudeau's mutinous rhetoric sounded the keynote of World Youth Day. That keynote is *inordinate self-love*, on full public display in 2002. Shortly before WYD, the Toronto archdiocese stoked the pride of youth volunteers by hosting "a tribute to their leadership." Cardinal Ambrozic confirmed *youth* as the "main evangelizers" at WYD. Grabbing the torch thrown by Trudeau a year earlier, a 20-year-old evangelizer declared, to wild cheers, "We are not just the future leaders of the church. We are the present leaders of the church." He illustrated the calibre of peer ministry when he told the crowd they were "Jesus in the world today." Further, they were "models of Christian behaviour not just to their younger siblings and friends, but also to their parents, teachers ... and elders." They were also "beacons of hope and love."[281] Clearly, the most important requirement for the job of youth evangelizer is pride.

Father Garrigou-Lagrange warns that inordinate self-love leads to spiritual death, as Jesus said, "He that loveth his life (in an egotistical manner) shall lose it; and he that hateth (or sacrifices) his life in this world, keepeth it unto life eternal."[282] So, says Father Garrigou-Lagrange, "From inordinate self-love, the root of every sin, spring the three concupiscences which St. John speaks of, ... 'the concupiscence of the flesh and the concupiscence of the eyes and the pride of life, which is not of the Father, but is of the world' (1 Jn. 2:16)."

Father Garrigou-Lagrange explains the pride of life:

> The pride of life is the inordinate love of our own excellence, of all that can emphasize it.... He who yields more and more to pride ends by becoming his own god, as Lucifer did. From this vice all sin and perdition may spring....

---

[280]Christian Cotroneo, "Catholic Teens Wowed by Justin Trudeau," *Toronto Star*, July 29, 2001, p. A2; "Countdown to WYD 2002," *Catholic Register*, August 6-13, 2001, p. 13 (emphases added).
[281]"Youthful Presence in Church Celebrated," *Catholic Register*, June 30, 2002, p. 6.
[282]Jn. 12:25.

According to St. Gregory and St. Thomas, pride or arrogance is *more* than a capital sin; it is the root from which proceed especially four capital sins: vanity or vainglory, spiritual sloth ..., envy, and anger.

The serious consequences of vainglory are notable characteristics of adult faith. Vainglory, says Father Garrigou-Lagrange, "engenders disobedience, boasting, hypocrisy, ... discord, *love of novelties*.... It is a vice that may lead to ... *apostasy*." He cites St. Augustine: "Two loves built two cities: the love of self even to contempt of God built the city of Babylon, that is, that of the world and of immorality; the love of God even to contempt of self built the city of God."[283]

The city of Babylon, mentioned in the Apocalypse, represents all the wicked, blinded with pride, vanity and sensuality. It is the city of the devil. It opposes Jerusalem, the city of those who follow Christ in humility and penance, the city of God, the Catholic Church. The people of God are told to avoid and detest Babylon and her wicked ways, as she will be destroyed by God.[284] However, World Youth Day *cultivates* vainglory, sensuality, disobedience and revolution; i.e., it is constructing the city of Babylon, guided by the pastors of the Catholic Church. For all their touted love of youth, they are leading them to spiritual death and a possible eternity in hell.

Although there *are* some priests and laity who try to spread Catholicism at these gatherings, handing out rosaries, scapulars and good literature, this doesn't change the fact that World Youth Day embodies the Deweyite agenda for journeying out of the Catholic Church through community-building and pilgrimage. As seen above, Toronto's Cardinal Ambrozic himself stated WYD is "a pilgrimage, a journey creating a community of its own."

---

[283]Father Garrigou-Lagrange, pp. 300-303. (Emphases added.)
[284]Cf. Apoc. 14:8, 17:5, 18:4-5, 8, and explanations in Father Geo. Leo Haydock's Commentary on the Douay-Rheims New Testament (New York: Edward Dunigan and Brother, 1859; reprint ed., Monrovia, CA: Catholic Treasures, 1991). See also his introduction to the Apocalypse and commentary on Apoc. 17:15.

If any good comes out of WYD, it is in spite of, not because of, the program. World Youth Day is process learning and a mortal danger to faith and morals. It should be placed on an "Index" of forbidden activities.

Chapter 5
Sects and the Civilization of Love

How did the idea of World Youth Day come about? Ex-Focolare member Gordon Urquhart answers that question in his exposé of the new ecclesial movements, which he calls sects because of their hold over their members and their sense of being elected to save the Church and the world. Urquhart states that World Youth Day is the "brainchild" of these community-building sects, especially Focolare. The format of WYD closely follows Focolare's large "showbizzy" youth festivals or "Genfests," which began in 1971. Pope John Paul attended Focolare's massive 1980 rally, as well as a similar event held by Communion and Liberation in 1982. After an International Youth Meeting organized by the sects on Palm Sunday in Rome in 1984 to mark the Extraordinary Jubilee Year, which was attended by over 300,000 youth, he instituted World Youth Day, with the help of the movements.[285]

Vast numbers of WYD attendees actually belong to the movements, says Urquhart, with the Neocatechumenal Way or Neocatechumenate (NC) seemingly leading the pack. In 1991, in Poland, there were 50,000 NC members from Italy alone, whilst in Denver, there were 40,000, more than a fifth of the registered participants. As Urquhart notes, "The presence of the movements at that gathering was out of all proportion to their numbers in the wider ecclesiastical community...." The movements also hold their own assemblies at World Youth Day.[286] This helps their recruiting and exten-

---

[285]Gordon Urquhart, *The Pope's Armada: Unlocking the Secrets of Mysterious and Powerful New Sects in the Church* (London: Bantam Press, 1995), pp. 22-23, 189-94; "History of World Youth Day," ibid. A French bishop confirmed, "During the first World Youth Days, it was [the] new communities *above all* who brought the young," one of the main groups being Focolare: Ferrisi, ibid. (Emphasis added.)

[286]Urquhart, pp. 190, 192-94, 196-97. Flyers in churches advertised Focolare's gathering during Toronto's WYD. The event was entitled "Interfaith Dialogue to Build the Universal Family."

sion, as attested to by Abp. Charles Chaput of Denver, who remarked that Denver's 1993 WYD led to the establishment or expansion of the movements — including erection of their own seminaries — in his archdiocese.[287] Focolare's large, spirited WYD "Genfests," full of dance, rock music, song, mime, flags and testimonies, are syncretic, to express "unity." They are open to youth of any religion, some of whom address (i.e., "evangelize") the participants.[288]

Perhaps the low turnout of young Torontonians (about 18,000) at Toronto's WYD reflected an insignificant influence of the movements in Canada's largest archdiocese. Volunteers outnumbered local registrants by about 5,000. Some parishes lowered the age limit of attendees from 16 to 14 "to meet their quota." Even then, the turnout was dismal, with some youth admitting, as noted earlier, they would not have gone if they had not been part of the liturgical entertainment.[289] This apathy is more normal for a generation indifferent towards the Church than is the emotionalism that is put on show for the world during World Youth Days.

The world is led to believe that the huge outpouring of enthusiasm for the Pope is spontaneous and sincere. In reality, it is largely the result of *a calculated and systematic manipulation behind the scenes*. Chiara Lubich, founder and head of Focolare, described the "very important role" played by the ecclesial movements and new communities[290] in what one could call the "selling of the Pope." At the same time, the first Adult Church generation is "sold" to the Pope. Bernard

---

[287]Archbishop Charles Chaput, OFM Cap., "World Youth Day: Promise of a Bountiful Harvest," archden.org/archbishop/docs/7_24_02_wyd.htm.

[288]Urquhart, pp. 193-94; "Youths of Various Religions Participate in World Youth Day," Zenit.org, July 28, 2000.

[289]Valpy, "Volunteers Outnumber Local Registrants." Overall, this WYD had the lowest number of registrants (187,000) in the 16-year history of WYD and a $38-million (Canadian) deficit. Paying off its bills was one of the chief causes of a major downsizing of the Canadian Conference of Catholic Bishops' bureaucracy two years later. See Art Babych, "Parishes Reaping the Spiritual Fruit of WYD," *Catholic Register*, November 3, 2002, p. 10; id., "Bishops' Deficit Skyrockets," ibid., November 7, 2004, p. 3; Deborah Gyapong, "$800,000 in Cuts Made as Bishops 'Economize,'" ibid., November 21, 2004, p. 3.

[290]"Made for Great Ideals," *Living City*, December 2000, p. 4.

Cardinal Law of Boston continually reminded the pilgrims he accompanied to Rome that "World Youth Day was not for the pilgrims to see the Pope. Instead, the purpose was for the Pope to see them and be encouraged...."[291]

The movements' tightly-controlled members[292] provide a reliable workforce. Lubich says they labour together with associations, parishes and church leaders to drum up support for the impending World Youth Day; work with youth "of *every faith*"; "encourage the hesitant and the undecided"; arrange transportation; and "accompany them throughout their stay." They get young people "ready to hear the pope's message," and "instill in them an appreciation of his love for them." Lubich remarks that this patent conditioning "[makes] the meeting with the Holy Father even more effective."

Discussing Rome's WYD, she proudly illustrates the effect of the sects' marketing techniques:

> Let me give you an example of what their contribution can be: one Cardinal said that 2,200 young people attended the World Youth Day from his town. For the most part they were brought by people of the Movements. Otherwise, he felt, only about *200* youth would have come.[293]

Observing the crowds at World Youth Day, one has to wonder how many of them are sect members, how many have been enticed by them, and how many are *non*-Catholics.

The main events at World Youth Day, says Urquhart, follow *Focolare's* "formula" (which is obviously Jungian): bands, dances, mime, personal testimonies, and processions with national costumes and flags that draw loud cheers. Further, he notes, even the delirious emotion exhibited towards the Pope parallels the "manipulated mass hysteria" surrounding Lubich at Focolare's youth events.[294]

---

[291]Bettinelli, ibid.
[292]See, for instance, Urquhart, pp. 47, 52.
[293]"Great Ideals." (Emphases added.)
[294]Pages 190, 194, 196-98.

The Very Model of the Counterchurch

Chiara Lubich, perhaps the most influential "Catholic" syncretist and promoter of Masonic world religion and government,[295] is revered by religious leaders, the UN and heads of state. She is a worthy recipient of the Templeton Prize for *Progress* in Religion, the religious equivalent of the Nobel Prize. Her influence is felt in politics, economics and world governance as, using high-flown rhetoric, she propagates the absolute equality taught by Masonry and Communism.

It is Lubich who developed the *prototype* of the adult faith community or Counterchurch: the "new parish." Her New Parish Movement has been turning parishes into democratic communities by promoting *co-responsibility*. In a new parish, says Father Joseph Arruano, a member of Focolare's Priests Branch, "it is normal now to see pastors, priests and laymen form an *authentic* community, so that the parish does not become a bureaucratic [i.e., hierarchical] institution." Within these parishes, "the people are *united* with one another and to their pastors, and consider themselves to be co-responsible for the entire spiritual and social life of the parish." That is because "*each neighbor is Jesus* and ... in his presence, not even the pastor can set himself above the others as teacher and judge…. Before God, it is not important whether we are men or women, rich or poor, Jew or Greek, nor does it matter whether we are priest [*sic*] or laymen" (this is a famous misinterpretation of Gal. 3:28, used also to justify feminism and indifferentism). This egalitarian parish community develops "fraternity" and "one body" (in which non-Catholics are welcome). "Father Joe" calls it "a real evangelical revolution."[296] *Note that "united" and "authentic" are code for equal.*

In Focolare's inner circles, its anticlericalism and con-

---

[295]Lubich says she dreams "that the moment of the one church may appear close at hand"; that "an expanding sense of brotherhood" may "become a universal accomplishment"; and "of a world ... joined under one rotating authority": Chiara Lubich, "A New Millennium has Started," *Living City*, February 2000, p. 4.

[296]Cf. S. C. Lorit and N. Grimaldi, *Focolare After 30 Years* (Brooklyn, NY: New City Press, 1976), pp.93-99 (emphasis added); cf. Caterina Ruggiu, "The Parish: A Community in Dialogue," *Living City*, July 2002, p. 16.

tempt of priests with a "priestly mentality" (i.e., a lack of submission to Focolare's egalitarianism) is undisguised. Its public obeisance towards and "love bombing" of the hierarchy, especially the Pope, is just public relations. Gaining episcopal members or protectors silences critics and helps expansion.[297] But in 1966, at the opening of a school in Rome for the formation of priests in Focolare's spirituality of unity, Chiara boldly proposed the dismantling of priestly authority:

> If priests could learn how to set aside everything, *even their very priesthood*, to ensure the presence of Jesus amongst them [each person in the community, and the community as a whole, thus being *alter Christus*], ... then ultimately Jesus will transform them into "new" priests, with a "new" pastoral approach, and there will be "new" seminaries.... And if they are also *united* [as equals] to the lay section of the Movement, this will give rise to what I would call the "Church-City" or "Church-Society".... *We* can offer the world "new priests" who are "new" because they live the New Commandment [of equality]....[298]

Focolare was founded in 1943 in Trent, Italy, as a small Christian community. Almost from its founding, when ecumenism was forbidden for Catholics, Focolare was non-denominational. Starting in 1949, it held large annual ecumenical gatherings in temporary "cities" termed "Mariapolises." (Thirty-three Mariapolises are now permanent towns, prototypes of the world community.)[299] Focolare thus operated as the indifferentist Counterchurch long before the Council. It was championed by the pro-Marxist Monsignor Montini and officially approved by John XXIII. Later Montini, as Pope Paul VI, commented, "May God bless this new form of communitarian life, this new Christian life and fervor

---

[297]Neocatechumenate and Communion and Liberation have the same mentality. See Urquhart, pp. 136-44.

[298]"The Priests Movement," focolare.org/en/sacerdoti_e.htm, 1998 (emphases added). According to this article, the priestly communion called for by the 1965 Conciliar Decree *Presbyterorum Ordinis* was that being lived by *Focolare* priests with each other and the laity.

[299]Lorit and Grimaldi, pp. 11, 156, 160-80; *Living City*, October 2004, p. 31.

which is blossoming in the *bosom* of the Church,"[300] thus institutionalizing Communism and Masonic indifferentism as an exalted form of Catholicism.

Focolare's "quiet" ecumenism became publicly structured with the inauguration by Augustin Cardinal Bea, President of the Secretariat for Christian Unity, of its ecumenical village with Lutherans in Ottmaring, Germany, in 1968. With Church approval, praying together in this village that was living Focolare's spirit of unity was standard practice. Ottmaring became the model for ecumenical communities around the world.[301]

Focolare's rapidly expanding *interdenominational* priest and bishop branches have been approved as "Catholic" by Pope John Paul.[302] Each year the Bishops Friends of the Focolare Movement meets for Catholic and non-Catholic bishops to study how to apply Focolare's spirituality of unity or communion in their lives. Begun in 1977, the group became ecumenical in 1982 and received canonical approval in 1998. For many years, the meetings have been organized by Miloslav Cardinal Vlk of Prague, a *focolarino* since 1964, who was shaped "far more " by Focolare "than the seminary."[303] Pope John Paul promoted this Lubich apostle through the ranks to Cardinal, and appointed him to head the Council of European Bishops' Conferences in 1993. Before his term expired in 2001, Cardinal Vlk signed an Ecumenical Charter with the Conference of [non-Catholic] European Churches, which includes gnostic Old Catholic Churches. The Charter commits Catholic and non-Catholic bishops to work for a

---

[300]Lorit and Grimaldi, pp. 182, 185-86. (Emphasis added).

[301]Ibid., pp. 139-42, 150-51. Note that Focolare helped with the organization of the 1986 papal interfaith World Day of Prayer for Peace at Assisi (Weigel, p. 513).

[302]Cf. "The Priests Movement."   John Paul called the bishops "Venerable Brothers in the Episcopate" who exhibit "the bond of ecclesial communion between yourselves and with the Successor of Peter."   See his message to the convention of the Bishops Friends of the Focolare Movement (its theme: "Towards the unity of nations and the unity of peoples"), *Living City*, June 1998, p. 11.

[303]"Ottmaring's Twenty Years," ibid., March 1989, p. 16; Michele Zanzucchi, "At Home with John Paul II," ibid., June 2002, p. 10; "Christian Unity is Urgent Challenge, Pope Says," Zenit.org., December 3, 2000; Desmond O'Grady, "Wolf in Cardinal's Robes," *Catholic Register*, December 3, 1994, p. 14; Urquhart, p. 455.

Europe united in government and religion and for all the usual leftist demands of the New World Order.[304]

The "spirituality of unity," or "collective spirituality," as it's termed, is based on changing Jesus' words, "Where two or three are gathered in My name..." (Matt. 18:20) to "Where two or three are united in My name." This is then interpreted to mean that "individualism is banned" in ideas, possessions, friendships and piety. This enforced conformity is called charity or love. In Focolare, "all differences vanished in the fire of charity."[305] This spirituality is cultish and Communistic. It is also Jewish. Lubich says[306] it is based on the Talmud, the Jewish body of man-made beliefs considered higher than the Bible.[307] The Talmud contains occult teachings[308] and has

---

[304]"Miloslav Vlk," nieuwsbronner.com/katholieke/pausmakers/vlk.html; "7th European Ecumenical Encounter ...," ccee.ch/english/press/2001_1.htm; Conference of European Churches, *Charta Oecumenica*, cec-kek.org. Lubich gave the keynote address to the Second European Ecumenical Assembly in Graz, Austria, in 1997, which was presided over by Cardinal Vlk and his Protestant counterpart: Urquhart, pp. 453-54; "Cardinal Martini and Chiara Lubich to Address European Church Gathering," June 13, 1997, catholic-ew.org.uk/cn/97/970613a.htm.

[305]Lorit and Grimaldi, pp. 57-58, 87-88, 167; Urquhart, pp. 33, 41, 47-48.

[306]In her speech at the Buenos Aires B'nai B'rith headquarters: "To Embark on a Common Journey," *Living City*, October 1998, p. 10. The B'nai B'rith is Jewish Freemasonry: Father Denis Fahey, CSSp, *The Kingship of Christ and the Conversion of the Jewish Nation* (n.p.: 1953; reprint ed., Hawthorne, CA: The Christian Book Club of America, 1987), p. 75.

[307]According to *Archives Israélites*, "the absolute superiority of the Talmud over the Bible of Moses must be recognized by all"; whilst the Talmud itself states, "One who studies the Bible does something indifferent; one who studies the Mischna deserves a recompense; one who studies the Ghemara performs the most meritorious of all actions": Father Fahey, pp. 92, 95. (The Mishnah is the first book of the Talmud, the Gemara the commentary on the Mishnah. Spellings vary for both words.) A leading American Jewish scholar, Orthodox Rabbi Jacob Neusner, says the Talmud is "the alpha and the omega of truth"; yet the introduction to the Yale University translation of the Talmud admits the Mishnah "is a document of imagination and fantasy," "remarkably indifferent to the Hebrew Scriptures," and a compilation of the sayings of authorities of the late first and second century: Michael A. Hoffman II, *Judaism's Strange Gods* (Coeur d'Alene, ID: The Independent History and Research Co., 2000), pp. 26, 34-35, 80, 118.

Jesus Himself proclaimed that the oral form of the Talmud that existed in His time as "the tradition of the elders or ancients" (later written down as the Mishnah), nullified the Word of God. The Pharisees and Scribes asked Him, "Why do your disciples not live according to the traditions of the ancients?" He called them hypocrites for teaching the doctrines of men and rejecting the commandment of God. He added, "Well do you make void the commandment of God, that you may keep your own tradition" (Cf. Mark 7:1-13, Matt. 15:1-9, and Father Haydock's commentary on the latter.)

been condemned in many Papal Decrees.[309]

Although Jesus clearly condemned the Talmudic teachings of the Pharisees,[310] Chiara claims that His words, "Where two or three are gathered together in My name, there am I in the midst of them," are *based* on the Talmudic teaching, "If two sit together and the words between them are of Torah then the Shekinah (the divine dwelling) is in their midst (Misnhá Avot, 3,2)."[311] In Judaism, Torah can symbolize either the Old Testament (which has been very distorted) or the Talmud (the false "Oral" Torah).[312] One wonders if Lubich realizes this verse from the Babylonian Talmud is predicated on the belief that each Jew is God,[313] so in any gathering of Jews, God is present. And does she know that in the kabbalistic beliefs of Orthodox Judaism, Shekinah is a *goddess* at the centre of a whole sexual mythology?[314]

Now, according to SS. Cyprian and John Chrysostom,

---

[308]According to Neusner, the Mishnah was allegedly secretly given to Moses at Sinai and passed down orally through the ages to the authorities of the first and second centuries A.D. *through* the Kabbalah. The Kabbalah, thus also claiming to be part of the tradition of the elders given to Moses, is a collection of books of black magic, "which arose in Babylon, as did the initial texts of the Talmud and both are heavily influenced by the … occult practices and superstitions of Bablyon." See Hoffman, pp. 36, 83. Cf. Father Haydock's commentary on Matt. 15:3.

[309]Father Fahey, p. 89. Focolare's spirituality can be both Communistic and Talmudic because, as noted by Jewish historian B. Lazare, Karl Marx was "a clear and lucid Talmudist" who "was full of that old Hebrew materialism which ever dreams of a paradise on earth…." According to Marx's correspondent Baruch Levy, "who formulated the Marxian thesis in striking fashion," the One-World Republic would be ruled by the Jews, "thanks to the victory of the proletariat," thus fulfilling "the promise of the Talmud" in what the Jews call "the Messianic Age": ibid., pp. 98, 100. Not surprisingly, Lenin, Trotsky and other Communist leaders were Jews: Hoffman, p. 107.

[310]Mark 7:1-13, Matt. 15:1-9.

[311]"To Embark on a Common Journey."

[312]Father Fahey, pp. 94-95; Hoffman, pp. 6, 9, 18, 120.

[313]Rabbi Adin Steinsaltz, *Opening the Tanya: Discovering the Moral and Mystical Teachings of a Classic Work of Kabbalah* (San Francisco: Jossey-Bass, 2003), p. 85; Hoffman, pp. 8, 58; Father Joseph Sievers, "Espiritualidades Judia y Cristiana …," talk given on June 27, 2001, sinectis.com.ar. Jews believe their bodies are created in the image of God, i.e., they are each God, whereas Catholic teaching is that man's likeness to God is chiefly in his soul, i.e., it is spiritual.

[314]This mythology, and its effect on Jewish piety and even the politics of the Middle East, are recounted in Israel Shahak, *Jewish History, Jewish Religion: The Weight of Three Thousand Years* (London: Pluto Press, 1994), Chap. 3, published at biblebelievers.org.au/jewhis7.htm.

Jesus' words, "In My name," and "There am I in the midst of them" are understood only of assemblies gathered in the name of Christ, assembled by authority received from Him, in the manner appointed by Him, for His sake, and seeking only His glory. These conditions apply to lawful ecumenical councils.[315] But Lubich heretically interprets this Gospel passage to teach that it is in a community (as opposed to in the tabernacle) that Jesus is present, so that the community is His Body, i.e., God. As seen earlier, such thinking has infected the rest of the Counterchurch.

Focolarini (Focolare members) seek Jesus *only* in unity with each other and claim they "can *generate* the presence of Christ" amongst themselves. As with Unitarian Universalism, they translate "God is Love," into "love is God," where "love" denotes a unity stemming from *complete equality and unanimity*. From this they seem to conclude that the community that is united "loves," and is therefore God. Hence, a Counterchurch community like Focolare that "loves" by living unity, sees itself — including its *non*-Catholic members — *as* God, Jesus enfleshed, the Church. Focolare's New Parish spokesman Father Joe elaborates: "… when a community accepts Jesus, he dwells there and the parishioners become his members, his Body. I have found the Church." Whether talking, working or resting, *everything* this community does automatically "becomes an expression of the supernatural, a manifestation of the divine in human activities." As with Unitarians, God for Lubich and her co-founders was an abstract power, an "*ideal* worth living for and as a result they focused their lives on the Gospel" — their falsified Gospel.[316]

The "Trinitarian" Model of Masonic Brotherhood

Focolare sees "the Trinitarian family" as "the model

---

[315]See Father Haydock's commentary on Matt. 18:20.

[316]Lorit and Grimaldi, pp. 14-15, 55, 57, 104-6; Sharry Silvi, "Antonio: Larger than Life," *Living City*, October 2001, pp. 12; ibid., p. 31; Urquhart, p. 65. (Emphases added.)

and goal" for its unity. Chiara says *focolarini* are "called to be a reflection of the Holy Trinity," to whom she attributes a sort of pantheistic brotherhood (a heresy also circulating in other Counterchurch communities). The three divine Persons are "eternally one and eternally distinct" (from the New Age perspective, a model of "unity in diversity" or brotherhood). Most importantly, Chiara claims, they are "eternally in dialogue." How? Well, as the Focolare magazine's cartoon strip proclaims, "to dialogue you have to be on the same level," meaning both parties are equal. Since the three Divine Persons *are* equal, Chiara concludes they are eternally in dialogue, conveniently ignoring the fact that They do not disagree on anything, so have no need of dialogue! Dialogue is the process of smoothing out differences in order to attain unity. Nevertheless, Chiara tells her followers that because they must reflect the Holy Trinity, "ours is a life of unending dialogue."[317]

This pantheistic interpretation of the Holy Trinity has started circulating in the adult church in order to justify equality and syncretism. This is how the Trinitarian model "justifies" equality within the Church:

> Our communion is to reflect the very communion of Trinity: utterly one, yet utterly different, and all equal.
> Shared leadership is the practical consequence of this theological insight. Shared leadership of the pope with the bishops, ... the priests and people with their bishop.... of the pastor and his people....[318]

Marc Cardinal Ouellet of Quebec City, Primate of Canada and coordinator of the January 2002 Papal interfaith Assisi meeting, explains how the Trinity "justifies" dialogue; but going further than Lubich, he asserts man was *created* for dialogue:

---

[317]Lorit and Grimaldi, pp. 104, 89; Walter Kostner, cartoon strip "B.J. and Double U.," *Living City*, October 2001, p. 30; Chiara Lubich, "Builders of Unity at All Times," ibid., May 2004, p. 13.

[318]Father Barry McGrory, "The Parish Council Empowers People," *Catholic New Times*, June 20, 2004, p. 12.

> Because if God Himself is Trinitarian and is so dialogi-
> cal [sic], and He created the whole humanity in His image,
> we are created to be in dialogue…. for unity, for reconcilia-
> tion, for peace, for justice.[319]

If *we* achieve unity through dialogue, and we are a reflection of the Holy Trinity, then what the Cardinal implies is that the *Trinity* has achieved and sustains Its unity through eternal dialogue!

For man, to be in unending dialogue means working continuously to build community. Thus Lubich recommends doing everything for the *glory of the community*. St. Paul teaches that the honour and glory of God should be the motive of all our actions: "Whether you eat or drink, or whatsoever else you do; do all things for the glory of God" (1 Cor. 10:31). But Chiara teaches, "And if … I must devote time to myself (eating, resting, … and so forth), this too should be done in function of my brothers and sisters, with them in mind." Her reason for this bold perversion of Catholic teaching is that "only in this way, by continually living the 'spirituality of unity' or 'of communion,' can I effectively contribute towards … building … ever vaster spaces of universal brotherhood."[320] *"Communion" signifies or is a synonym for unity, equality, community, syncretic brotherhood[321] and now, Trinity.*

Although working to destroy hierarchical authority, Focolare, however, does not practise equality within its own ranks. Its authoritarian hierarchy enforces unity of thought and controls every detail of its members' lives, down to arranging marriages between them and demanding that members smile at all times. Chiara herself is accorded near-divine status, not least because Focolare's founding, doctrine and actions are based on her many private "revelations." These revelations have binding authority as they are seen as the product of "Jesus in the midst." Hence, *focolarini* are told belief in God is

---

[319]Sabitri Ghosh, "Bringing Jesus to a New Generation," *Catholic Register*, December 12, 2004, p. 11.
[320]Lubich, ibid.
[321]Lubich makes this clear in "Our Jewish Roots," *Living City*, May 1998, p. 13.

not needed if one believes in Chiara.   Practising collective spirituality means all must think and act in unison with Lubich, forming "one soul" of which she is the centre.[322]

Focolare acknowledges its spirituality of unity is a novelty:

> The great novelty which has turned the old spiritual patterns upside down is the discovery ... of the "collective Christ." In other words, the novelty is a collective spirituality, the "building" of Christ within the community.... It is a new kind of asceticism, in a way, able to fulfill the desire for unity felt by many.

This new asceticism is the sacrifice of one's individuality to the collective. In line with pilgrimage doctrine, Focolare's collective spirituality is considered superior to an individual journey towards holiness. For Lubich and her co-founders,

> the way of understanding sanctity changed. No longer could they consider an individualistic way of going to God through one's own separate practices of piety. They wanted first of all to seek the kingdom of God in their midst through charity, through mutual love.[323]

Notice that love of God, Jesus, the Catholic Church and the Blessed Virgin Mary are superseded by love of community. This description of the spirituality of unity also highlights two heresies associated with it. The first is gnosticism, as it is practised independently of the Catholic Church, the kingdom of God on earth; Focolare allegedly generates the kingdom within the movement. The second is the pantheistic heresy of *monopsychism*, meaning one soul or mind for all, which does away with individual conscience and personal responsibility. New Agers refer to the one-world brain as *global consciousness* and believe unity of conscience will create

---

[322]Urquhart, pp. 30-34, 44, 54-55, 153-54, 232, 336-40; Lorit and Grimaldi, pp. 10-11.

[323]Lorit and Grimaldi, pp. 15-16, 18, 27, 160-61; cf. Tomasso Sorgi, "Igino Giordani's Multifaceted Life," *Living City*, March 2004, p. 14.

a healthy community.[324]

Lubich's revolutionary spirituality of unity was commended by Pope John Paul II. At the 2003 conference of Bishops Friends of Focolare, whose openly Masonic theme was "Spirituality of Communion: Ecclesial Unity and Universal Brotherhood," the Pope recalled his "invitation expressed in the Apostolic Letter *Novo Millennio Ineunte* to promote a spirituality of communion … (no. 43)." He told the conference that the spirituality of communion has been "enriched by the contribution made … by the Focolare Movement." He emphasized that it was necessary "to overcome every difficulty" in building this spirituality, and to "continue without pausing on the path undertaken, confident of the support of divine grace to give life to … a solid 'universal brotherhood.'"[325]

The Civilization of Love Realized

Focolare's spirituality of unity naturally leads to *living* ecu-syncretic world brotherhood. Spanning every continent, with over four and a half million adherents of different races, religions and social backgrounds, it considers itself a small "people," the "seed" of a "new humanity" and new world order.[326] With its mystical humanistic spirituality practised by thousands of Catholic laity, clergy and religious, and its members living together in interfaith houses and towns, *Focolare is a working model of community, of the Counterchurch*, praised by conciliar popes for its spirituality of "love." Paul VI, who coined the phrase, "civilization of love," probably had Focolare in mind as he believed they were living "the Gospel of Love."[327] Pope John Paul was well-known for his yearning for the civilization of love. States Focolare, his hope "that all

---

[324]Ferreira, *New Age Movement*, p. 10.

[325]"Towards Unity, Without Respite," *Living City*, May 2003, p. 22.

[326]"The Focolare Movement," focolare.org/en/sif/Press19990423e_a.html, January 28, 2000.

[327]"In Rome They Said," *Living City*, March 1989, p. 11; Lorit and Grimaldi, p. 155.

may be one" (based on a new interpretation of John 17:21) is also "the ideal that inspires the Movement."[328]

Because Focolare "aspires to win everyone to God" (i.e., to the ideal of love), it believes it must unite agnostics and atheists within Focolare. Its spirituality of love and unity "values all that is positive in every individual and every group,"[329] i.e., it is nothing else but Masonic tolerance of error. It is in line with Alice Bailey's dictum that the illuminized Church *must* show "a wide tolerance." Lubich openly admits she is producing a new doctrine, which "develops and renews the theological tradition. It is a new theology and ... a new philosophy." "The spirituality of unity carries a revolutionary message about breaking with the old...." Focolare believes its spread will unite "the profane and the sacred, the world and the Church."[330] This is identical with Dewey's goal of uniting nature and grace, and Jung's of uniting the evil shadow with good.

The spirituality of unity is directly anti-Christian. First of all, Jesus said the true practice of His religion would provoke the hatred of non-followers, causing dissensions and wars, with Christians even being handed over to persecutors by their own family members (Matt. 10:21-22 and 34-36). Second, He absolutely condemned striving for the pantheistic unity of the human race, as St. Paul tells us:

> Bear not the yoke together with unbelievers. For what participation hath justice with injustice? Or what fellowship hath light with darkness? And what concord hath Christ with Belial? Or what part hath the faithful with the unbeliever?... Wherefore, go out from among them, and be ye separate, saith the Lord, and touch not the unclean thing.[331]

---

[328]Lorit and Grimaldi, p. 76. At the ecumenical meeting of Bishops Friends of Focolare in 2004, Cardinal Kasper praised Focolare's community model. "We must live together to get to know one another.... I am most grateful to the Focolare for offering a model for this kind of ecumenism of life and friendship": Peter Parmense, "Bishops Without Borders," *Living City*, March 2004, p. 18.

[329]Lorit and Grimaldi, pp. 57, 76.

[330]Ibid., p. 57; "On to Mexico," *Living City*, September 1997, p. 14; "Dialogue on Family Life," ibid., November 2001, p. 10.

[331]2 Cor. 6:14-17.

The civilization of love is a humanistic, gnostic, anti-Christ utopia, so it isn't surprising to find Lubich equating the spirituality of unity with the pantheistic *Talmudic* teaching that God is one with the world.[332] She is also promoting it to heal so-called "divisions" in the Church, i.e., differences between religious orders. Focolare has been working to efface these differences by forming religious in *Focolare's* spirituality, building community between them. Focolare boasts that if its spirituality spreads through parishes and orders, building communities of love and unity that "generate Christ in their midst" (i.e., become Christ), the Church will survive.[333] Of course, this is the Arian New Age "Christ" and the illuminized Adult or Counterchurch.

The whole idea of the Counterchurch is to fold Catholicism into the Masonic one-world religion and community by modifying it to make it palatable to non-Catholics. That one-world religion is now here, institutionalized as the United Religions, the one-world church and religious arm of the United Nations. Lubich is an honorary president, and Focolare a member, of the World Conference on Religion and Peace, the syncretic organization that co-founded with Gorbachev the United Religions.[334] Pope John Paul said that Focolare is making the Church "a school of communion," and the *focolarini* are "apostles of dialogue" who are "in harmony with the Magisterium."[335] So, on October 16, 2002, he commissioned Focolare to promote his "ecumenical Rosary for peace" and its new Luminous Mysteries.[336]

---

[332]"Embark on a Common Journey"; Sievers, ibid.

[333]Lorit and Grimaldi, pp. 105-24.

[334]Cornelia R. Ferreira, "One-World Church Expected Next Year," *Catholic Family News*, October 1996, p. 1; id., "One-World Church Starts Up," ibid., November 1997, p. 1.

[335]Papal message on the 60th anniversary of Focolare, *Living City*, February 2004, p. 6. The pontiff had such high regard for Focolare that he gave it the audience hall in Castelgandolfo, his summer residence, for its exclusive use. Its principal international meetings are held there. Pope Paul VI, for his part, allowed Chiara to see him privately and immediately any time she wished. See Urquhart, pp. 177-78.

[336]Cornelia R. Ferreira, "Focolare and the Ecumenical Rosary of the Counter-Church," *Catholic Family News*, January 2003, p. 3.

The personal faith Lubich has concocted from her experiences — her so-called visions and revelations — reinterprets the Blessed Virgin Mary, perverting the Hail Mary and the Rosary to aid the cause of brotherhood. The Year of the Rosary (October 2002-October 2003) provided Focolare with a papally-approved opportunity to spread her Marian heresies. The *syncretic* International Marian Congress it organized for all the movements at its Castelgandolfo centre in April 2003 "to propagate the Rosary" was attended by 1,500 people, including cardinals, bishops, priests and religious, and broadcast live all over the world by three satellite television networks and the Internet. With Muslim, Jewish and Protestant contributions, the International Marian Congress presented *Mary as a model for dialogue and communion.*[337]

In her address to this Congress,[338] Lubich shared her interpretation of the Rosary and other Marian doctrines. Based on her revelations, the Hail Mary and the Rosary were no longer to be prayers of praise and intercession because Chiara saw herself and her first women members as *each* Mary, each a bead of a "living rosary." Praising Mary was fine, "[b]ut the 'Hail Mary' *I* wished to say had to be made up of living words, of people, who, almost like other little Marys, would give Love to the world. For us, this was the only way that saying the rosary would take on its full value...."

To help Chiara sell these Marys to Protestants (to aid brotherhood), God gave Chiara another disclosure in the "'illuminative' period" of Focolare, which enabled her to perform a sleight of hand in which Our Lady and the little Marys each became *Jesus,* became *God.* Of course, the *focolarini* were already God, but now Mary was revealed as part of the Holy Trinity, "set like a jewel *in* the Most Holy Trinity." She is "*all word of God,*" — i.e., she is *Jesus*, the Word of God. Since Scripture is also the Word of God, Mary — as Christ — became the "'personification' of Sacred Scriptures," and thus acceptable to Protestants who joined Focolare. Chiara admits this is a

---

[337]Michele Zanzucchi, "Mary, a Pure Reflection," *Living City*, July 2003, p. 6.
[338]Chiara Lubich, "Mary's Presence," ibid., p. 12. (Emphases added.)

"new understanding" of Mary. As a Focolare journalist reported,

> While the role of Mary in revelation has been the unfortu-
> nate cause of disagreements and divisions, all could appre-
> ciate how an image of Mary as "completely clothed in the
> word of God," as Chiara Lubich explained, could open
> paths of true dialogue based on Scripture and on mutual
> understanding.[339]

Jesus' most stunning "revelation" to Chiara is that she
— and Focolare through her — is the mother of the
(Counter)church and all mankind. One day she had asked
Him why He remains on earth in the Holy Eucharist, but had
"not found a way to have his mother here" to help humanity.
Now, as St. Louis de Montfort teaches, Our Lady is never
separated from Jesus, being in a "necessary union" with Him:

> Thou, Lord, art always with Mary, and Mary is always with
> Thee, and she cannot be without Thee.... She is so inti-
> mately united with Thee that it were easier to separate the
> light from the sun, the heat from the fire; nay, it were easier
> to separate from Thee all the angels and saints than the di-
> vine Mary, because she loves Thee more ardently and glori-
> fies Thee more perfectly than all the creatures put to-
> gether.[340]

But intent on her own agenda, Chiara imagined this answer
from Jesus in the tabernacle, as she told the Marian Congress:

> I didn't leave her [on earth] because I want to *see her again
> in you* (in all of you) [i.e., in the movement]. Even though
> you are not immaculate, my love will purify you, it will vir-
> ginize you. Your arms and your hearts will be open to hu-
> manity *as those of a mother*, this humanity which now, just as
> then, is thirsty for God and for his mother. Now it is up to
> you to soothe the sufferings....

---

[339] Zanzucchi, ibid.

[340] *True Devotion to Mary*, trans. Father Frederick Faber (Rockford, IL: Tan
Books and Publishers, 1985), p. 39.

Focolare's "new understanding of Mary" also sees her as "only a creature," equal to us, with no extraordinary privileges or right to be venerated. One leader scornfully says, "We [i.e., the pre-Vatican II Church] have often made of Mary a distorted cliché, a little statue, or a series of special devotions."[341] One "distorted cliché" is obviously the Litany invocation, "Virgin Most Powerful." At another 2003 ecumenical conference on Mary, theologian Joan Back, from Focolare's Centre of Ecumenism in Rome, explained Lubich's "new understanding," formulated in 1947. "The Blessed Virgin is nothing, emptiness…." She is merely an empty void, an open "door" which leads to God, who is unity.[342]

Contrast this quietist, Buddhist-type Mary to the Church's teaching on her constant *advocacy*, as explained by many saints. Mary "is most powerful with her Son." She obtains everything she requests of Him, and is "omnipotent" in saving sinners who invoke her intercession. "[L]ike a queen, she sends the angels to enlighten, to purify, and to perfect her servants." Jesus, "in a certain manner," regards her prayers as *commands*.[343]

The "empty" Mary who is merely "one among many," however, is "the model that everyone can follow," an ecumenical Mary for non-Catholics. She is also acceptable for her "silent way of service" that influenced "the early Christian community," and so the social-justice focus of Foclare is continuing the work of Mary and hopefully, "a vital reality which changes things from within."[344] In other words, humanism is cloaked in the Catholic-sounding name, "Work of Mary," which is the official designation of the Focolare movement. Building up the Catholic Church and saving souls, in imitation of the true Mary, is definitely not what "The Work of Mary" is about.

---

[341]Lorit and Grimaldi, p. 31.

[342]Patrice Goddard, "Focus on Ecumenism," *Living City*, October 2003, p. 13.

[343]St. Alphonsus Liguori, *Preparation for Death*, ed. Father Eugene Grimm, CSSR (Brooklyn, NY: Redemptorist Fathers, 1926), pp. 326-37. Quietism is discussed in Chapter 6.

[344]Lorit and Grimaldi, pp. 28-29, 31.

Yet Focolare's Statutes, approved in 1990, state that the Work of Mary, "wishes to be, in as far as possible, a presence of Mary in the world and, as it were, a *continuation* of her." And based on her visions, Focolare is seen as the "mystical body" of Mary in the Church, and Lubich as the mediatrix of all graces for the Masonic world order. "In me," she has stated, "are all the graces for those who wish to join together in unity."[345]

"Salt and Light": The Original

Light and luminosity are words frequently found in connection with Focolare. Lubich describes her gnostic doctrine as "a Light from on high," another private revelation. Terming this Light "the Ideal," she describes it *as* "Jesus in the midst," and the Ideal hence has binding authority for Focolare, with Chiara's words totally identified with God's. Much is also made of the fact that Chiara's name means "light."[346]

Now, the World Youth Day theme in 2002 proclaimed that youth are the light of the world and salt of the earth. It just so happens that Focolare describes itself as "light and salt" because "[i]t is made up of members of the most varied social classes, nationalities and races [not to mention religions], bearing witness to the universality of the Movement."[347] This suggests that *practising Masonic brotherhood is being salt and light*. After all, Masons describe Freemasonry as a "search after Light."[348]

In a pantheistic meditation, Lubich describes the "great attraction" of being "points of light" in the crowd.[349] This is

---

[345]Lubich, ibid.; Urquhart, pp. 34, 339.

[346]Urquhart, pp. 336, 338, 31. Lubich changed her baptismal name of Silvia to Chiara (Clare) when she joined the Third Order of St. Francis in her youth (p. 31).

[347]Lorit and Grimaldi, p. 20.

[348]According to Albert Pike, father of modern Freemasonry, the light sought is Lucifer, the Lightbearer. He added that the search leads back to the Kabbalah. See Craig Heimbichner, "The Ordo Templi Orientis (OTO) and the New Gnostic Springtime," *Catholic Family News*, October 2004, p. 13.

[349]"The Great Attraction Today," focolare.org. Lubich claims Focolare Centres "are the points of greatest warmth and light" within the movement: Urquhart, p. 152.

occult terminology used by occultists and New Age leader Alice Bailey to describe the volunteer slaves of the new world order. Persons or groups who experience higher consciousness, an awareness of global oneness and the need to solve global problems by serving the common good, are points of light. To facilitate the divine unity of the universe and the open rule of the Illuminati and the Antichrist, such groups and individuals must be united through conscious cooperation.[350]

Recalling the Luminous Mysteries entrusted to Focolare, it is intriguing to read why Focolare claims its youth festivals or Genfests are luminous. Keep in mind ecclesiastical enthusiasm for WYD and the significance of its social-justice cross whilst reading it:

> Simple and joyous expressions of Christianity by the youth, often expressed in songs and music by the Gen [Focolare youth] bands and by the cordiality of their solidarity, are the luminous note of life in the *deadly night of disunity*. It is no wonder that the great majority of this family … is made up of young people. With them, we older ones, after being rescued from our depressing solitude, are compelled to experience a daily rebirth of our spirits and youthfully overcome boredom and death. These young people do not turn away from life by escaping into … drugs, but heroically embrace the Cross and accept the 'gift of suffering' in order to serve humanity.[351]

This statement by "co-founder" Igino Giordani reveals the illuminized nature of Focolare. According to a former Rosicrucian chief, the illuminized subject, who ceases to think for himself, "becomes a vessel of light" (point of light), hypnotically controlled to serve "'humanity,' or more correctly, [work] against humanity," by spreading the Masonic World Revolution. The overpowering sound, light, music, dance and ceremonies of Genfests and World Youth Day are equivalent to the mind-altering tools used by Illuminism.[352]

---

[350]Ferreira, "New Age Education, Part II."

[351]Lorit and Grimaldi, p. 62. (Emphasis added.)

[352]*Light-bearers*, pp. 65-66, 74, 105, 108-10.

Giordani's canonization process has been initiated, even though he disobediently fostered ecumenism in the 1920s, when it was unequivocally forbidden, and promoted a democratic Church. Termed "a forerunner of ecumenical initiatives within the Catholic Church" and "of certain guiding principles characteristic of John XXIII," in 1961 he headed Focolare's *centre for ecumenism* in Rome.[353] Giordani did not believe one's cross consists of the sufferings sent by God; he scorned this Catholic teaching as "passivity." His was the new theology of the cross, discussed earlier, in which the cross represents the sufferings of the world. He preached that only service to humanity is carrying one's cross.[354]

As for "the deadly night of disunity," Focolare tells its members that *disunity originated with the Council of Trent.* But, fortunately for all, since Lubich was born in Trent, her baptism in the church where the Council met "commenced the dawn of unity." Similarly, another sect mentioned earlier, the Neocatechumenal Way, believes the Church founded by Christ ended with Constantine and was then resurrected by Vatican II. In between, everything the Church did was illegitimate, the Council of Trent being the low point of this travesty. It "paralyzed" the Church because it was "determined to fix formulae of faith, liturgical rites...."[355] These two Protestantizing sects are the inspiration for and the mainstay of World Youth Day!

A Pope of Their Own

Like Focolare, other syncretic sects have received, or

---

[353]Lorit and Grimaldi, pp. 53-54, 56-58; Chiara Lubich, "Igino Giordani," and Claire Zanzucchi, "Highlights of a Life," *Living City*, March 2004, pp. 10 and 12, respectively; Sorgi, ibid.

[354]Sorgi, ibid. Pope John Paul said he used his illnesses to "serve all of humanity." Jean-Marie Cardinal Lustiger of Paris explains that the Pope was a "sign of a compassionate Christ who carries all the suffering in the world ... for the good of humanity." See John Thavis, "Prayer Taking Precedence," *Catholic Register*, February 27, 2005, p. 11.

[355]Urquhart, p. 340; Father Enrico Zoffoli, "The Neocatechumenals ...," *Christian Order*, April 1995, p. 193.

are in the process of receiving, canonical status, allowing them to masquerade as Catholic *religious orders*, complete with Statutes, community life, vows, and even seminaries. The Neocatechumenate alone, founded by a lay man and ex-nun, has produced 196 priests from its Redemptoris Mater diocesan seminary in Rome and more than 1,000 from its 50 seminaries across the world. Besides the priests being developed by this and other sects, many other clergy live their spirituality. Bishops have already come from their heretical ranks, ordained by John Paul II and favoured with privileged positions, some within the Roman Curia and on Pontifical Councils. It is only logical to assume that they could produce a pope, loyal only to his particular "church" or movement. The ecclesial movements comprise priests, religious, single and married laity — each movement a parallel or anti-Church within the bosom of the Catholic Church.[356]

But we don't have to look to the future for a pope produced by a lay movement. Pope John Paul himself was the "*product* and progenitor of dynamic lay groups." In 1940, Karol Wojtyla, aged 19, fell under the sway of a Polish rationalist and self-taught psychologist, Jan Tyranowski, who had "developed his own spirituality" and had the reputation of a "mystic." Quite in line with Deweyite and Jungian adult church principles, Tyranowski preached a gnostic experiential religion; "inner *liberation* from *the* faith," i.e., from Catholicism; and "transformation of personality from within," i.e., spiritual growth, through the "friendship" of a community. He also preached a life of service, especially to those of one's community, as the fruit of the "practice of the presence of God." "To bring young people into this same faith" — not Catholicism — he led weekly discussion meetings for young men he recruited, "in which theological questions were argued."[357]

[356]Urquhart, pp. 28, 141-44, 147, 149-52, 155, 160-61, 163-68, 454-55; "Pope Thanks Neocatechumenal Way for Vocations it Inspires," Zenit.org, March 18, 2003. Urquhart notes that the movements pick members for ordination based on administrative and spiritual needs, not because they have a vocation. This would be consonant with their anticlericalism.

[357]Tom Hoopes, "Groundswell: The Pope, the New Movements, and the Church," *Crisis*, December 2004, p. 32; Alicia Mosier, "Letter from Poland,"

(Questioning the Faith is called "critical thinking" today.)

> Tyranowski formed the Living Rosary, which shared many
> of the characteristics of modern lay movements. Its weekly
> meetings were run by lay people in homes, not by priests in
> parish halls. By 1943, there were 60 "animators" who re-
> ported to Tyranowksi. One of those group leaders was
> Karol Wojtyla.[358]

It is strange that Chiara Lubich also termed her group
"the living Rosary." Did she get the idea from Bishop Wojtyla, whom Focolare got to know in Poland?[359] "The Living
Rosary as created by Jan Tyranowski consisted of groups of
fifteen young men, each of which was led by a more mature
youngster who received personal spiritual direction ... from
the mystically gifted tailor."[360] The difference between the
two "living" Rosaries is that Tyranowski's groups represented the decades of the Rosary,[361] whilst Lubich's members
were Hail Marys.

The inner transformation taught by Tyranowski is
what New Agers today call a change in consciousness or
paradigm shift, in which one synthesizes two opposing ideas,
such as believing one is a good Catholic even if holding superstitious or occult beliefs. It is similar to Dewey's merger of
nature and grace or Jung's "wholeness." It is an occult, gnostic, kabbalistic method of producing a personal shift in values

---

firstthings.com, April 1999; Helen Whitney, "John Paul II: The Millennial Pope.
Interview with Bill Blakemore," *Frontline*, pbs.org, September 1999; Weigel, pp.
59-61; Rocco Buttiglione, *Karol Wojtyla: The Thought of the Man who Became
Pope John Paul II*, trans. Paolo Guietti and Francesca Murphy (Grand Rapids,
MI: Wm. B. Eerdmans Publishing Co., 1997), pp. 28-29. (All emphases added.)
    Weigel is a member of the Council on Foreign Relations ("Pope's Biographer
Received Honorary Degree at Seminary Commencement," benedic-
tine.stvincent.edu/seminary/newsevents/events/commence2000.html, April 13,
2000). He is also a signatory to the Statement of Principles for the Project for a
New American Century (newamericancentury.org). Buttiglione is a leading
member of Communion and Liberation and was an advisor to John Paul II, including on his encyclical *Veritatis Splendor* (1993): Urquhart, pp. 121, 188, 252.
    [358]Hoopes, ibid.
    [359]Urquhart, p. 173.
    [360]Weigel, p. 60.
    [361]Mosier, ibid.

that engenders social transformation. Inner transformation led to religious orders abandoning the supernatural focus of Catholicism for naturalistic social activism after Vatican II.[362]

Pope John Paul II's acceptance of the gnostic philosophy of the sects is also the product of the theatrical experiences of his youth. Theatre for Karol was "an experience of community"; but more than that, it was a serious training in gnostic transformation by Mieczyslaw Kotlarczyk, director of the Rhapsodic Theatre, which he co-founded with Karol. This Theatre, with its "theme of consciousness," provided Wojtyla's "initiation to phenomenology." Kotlarczyk, who lived for some time in the Wojtyla home, tutored Karol in his method from the time Karol was sixteen until he joined the seminary six years later. He created a "theater of the inner word" to present "universal truths and universal moral values, which ... offered the world the possibility of authentic transformation." Plot, costumes and props were not important. Instead, speech — the "word" — was his focus, the goal being to use it to transform the consciousness of the audience (and actor). Hence Kotlarczyk insisted on every word being pronounced just so.[363]

That this was a training in the kabbalistic, occult use of words became clear when Kotlarczyk's book, *The Art of the Living Word: Diction, Expression, Magic*, was published in 1975 by the Papal Gregorian University in Rome. Cardinal Wojtyla penned the preface to this book in which Kotlarczyk listed the sources of his ideas. They included the writings of

---

[362]Marilyn Ferguson, *The Aquarian Conspiracy: Personal and Social Transformation in Our Time* (Los Angeles: J. P. Tarcher, 1987), pp. 18, 46, 72; Sister Rosalie Bertell, GNSH, "Christology and Cosmology," *Catholic New Times*, November 21, 2004, p. 10.

[363]Karol Wojtyla, *The Jeweller's Shop*, trans. Boleslaw Taborski (New York: Random House, 1980), p. xi; George Huntston Williams, *The Mind of John Paul II: Origins of his Thought and Action* (New York: Seabury Press, 1981), pp. 53-54, 64-65, 71-72; Weigel, pp. 37-38, 64-66, 70; Buttiglione, pp. 21-22, 27-28. Williams (d. 2000), a Unitarian, was Hollis Professor of Divinity at Harvard and an observer at Vatican II. He was made a Knight of the Order of St. Gregory the Great by John Paul II. See Forrest Church, "George Huntston Williams ...," harvardsquarelibrary.org/unitarians/williams.html; "George H. Williams ...," bostontheological.org, October 11, 2000.

several occultists and theosophists, amongst them some of the foremost kabbalists and occultists of modern times: Russian Mason Helena Blavatsky, founder of the Theosophical Society and the New Age Movement; French occultist Eliphas Levi (who influenced Blavatsky, Albert Pike, Grand Commander of Scottish Rite Masonry, and sorcerer Aleister Crowley, long-time head of the high Masonic Ordo Templi Orientis or OTO); and Rudolf Steiner, Illuminatus, Rosicrucian, theosophist, OTO member, Communist and founder of the Anthroposophical Society and Waldorf Schools.[364]   Theosophy had been condemned by the Church in 1919, the Holy Office stating one could not "read [theosophists'] books, daily papers, journals, and writings."[365]

Kotlarczyk believed he was an "'archpriest' of drama," his living word method being a religion and "vocation," with the actor as priest. As with theosophists who use the title "Master" for highly evolved humans who guide humanity, he called himself "Master of the Word." He saw theatre "as ritual" and "understood *the liturgical character of theatrical action*, ... offering the possibility of entering into a new dimension...." Theatre could be "a way of perfection" if "'the word' had absolute priority" over "externals and spectacle."[366]

Compare Kotlarczyk's ideas with Anthroposophy or "Christian Illuminism," which is a "Luciferian initiation" that forms the enlightened or "deified" man with occult abilities. Anthroposophy teaches that occult knowledge, or the "inner meaning" of realities can be obtained through a "disciplined"

---

[364]Williams, pp. 54, 60, 64-65, 72, 357-59; Buttiglione, p. 21; Craig Heimbichner, *Blood on the Altar* (Coeur d'Alene, ID: Independent History & Research, 2005), pp. 147-48, 47; "Steiner, Rudolf," themystica.com; Inquire Within, *Trail of the Serpent*, pp. 5, 178, 206, 213, 211; id., *Light-Bearers*, pp. 60-61, 78-80. Amongst the works cited by Kotlarczyk was Blavatsky's *Isis Unveiled* (1877), which has a "vicious anti-Christian bias" (James Webb, *The Occult Underground* [La Salle, IL: Open Court Publishing Co., 1974], p. 82), and for which she received "a high Masonic degree" (Joseph Head and S. L. Cranston, eds., *Reincarnation* [New York: Causeway Books, 1967], p. 166).

[365]Denzinger, no. 2189.

[366]Williams, p. 65; Buttiglione, p. 22; Weigel, pp. 37, 65; Father Mieczyslaw Malinski, *Pope John Paul II*, trans. P. S. Falla (New York: The Seabury Press, 1979), p. 14; Ferreira, *New Age Movement*, pp. 3-4; Webb, pp. 83-84.

use of the arts, words, colour, music and eurythmy ("universal harmony"), a way of dance that Steiner (1861-1925) created to express the inner meanings of sound. The explosion in the Church today of theatrics, "creative liturgy," and eurythmic-style "liturgical dance" (even at Papal Masses) as an experiential means of teaching the Faith, denotes both a Jungian and Steinerian influence. (Steiner's techniques are actually a "subversive" form of hypnosis applied to religious, political and educational groups to make them tools for effecting the Masonic Universal Republic. Destroying rational thought, they produce the "false idealist" and "soft peace-monger" who lives by feelings, finds goodness and beauty in ugliness and evil, does not criticize error, gives up his personality and blends with another. He is then easily controlled and even obsessed.[367])

Karol and his friends committed themselves to "the dramatic exploration of the interior life" under Kotlarczyk. Amongst his many roles, Karol was the "Seer John" in Steiner's arrangement of the Apocalypse. Other esoteric works in which he acted or which had "significance in his spiritual formation" included productions by Juliusz Slowacki (1809-49) and Adam Mickiewicz (1798-1855). Slowacki was an evolutionist and reincarnationist who believed Poland's political sufferings were "karma." Mickiewicz was a kabbalist and Martinist (a form of occultism). Both men subscribed to Polish Messianism, which was intertwined with Jewish Messianism and occultism. Their ideas were incorporated into their plays. To "rebuke" Pius IX, who did not support Polish nationalism and the Masonic revolution in Italy, Slowacki also composed a poem about a future "Slavic Pope" who would head a "reformed papacy," and would be tough, but "a brother of the people." As Pope John Paul II, Karol would

---

[367]"Anthroposophy," themystica.com; "Steiner, Rudolf"; "Erich Mendelsohn's Expressionism and Rudolf Steiner's Theosophy ...," tulane.edu/~swacsa/abstracts/27; Tarjei Straume, "Scientology vs. Anthroposophy," uncletaz.com/hubbstein.html; *Trail of the Serpent*, pp. 103, 41, 208, 220-21, 252-54; *Light-bearers*, pp. 15, 20-22, 61, 64-69, 72-77, 109-10, 201.

later apply this poem to himself.[368]

The following comment by Father Wojtyla (under a pseudonym) in 1958 shows how the Rhapsodic Theatre solidified his rejection of individualism in favour of the one mind enforced in the new ecclesial sects:

> This theater ... defends the young actors against developing a destructive individualism, because it will not let them impose on the text anything of their own; it gives them inner discipline. A group of people, collectively, somehow unanimously, subordinated to the great poetic word, evoke ethical associations; this solidarity of people in the word reveals particularly strongly and accentuates the reverence that is the point of departure for the rhapsodists' word and the secret of their style.[369]

After his ordination, Father Wojtyla created his own youth group, "Little Family," whose members called him "Uncle." Little Family became the core of a larger community known as Środowisko or "milieu," which he led until elected Pope. The seeds for World Youth Day lay in the co-ed hiking and kayakking groups Father Wojtyla led. They travelled across Poland, sleeping in barns, discussing anything, singing, praying, and attending his outdoor Masses. His good friend, Fr. Mieczyslaw Malinski, another Tyranowski graduate, admiringly referred to him as "Wojtyla the revolutionary," who shocked "the entire Cracow diocese." He was also the type of priest Focolare likes, "wholly devoid of clericalism." Tyranowski's training taught him to highly value the laity, and he tested his philosophical ideas on Środowisko friends and his Lublin University doctoral students, encouraging a "mutual exchange" of ideas, happy to learn from them.[370]

---

[368]Weigel, p. 63; Williams, pp. 44-45, 56-57, 60, 65-68, 356-57; Buttiglione, pp. 19-20; Webb, pp. 246-51, 253.

[369]Buttiglione, p. 27. Cf. Williams, p. 72.

[370]Hoopes, ibid; Elżbieta Pawelek, "Lolek's World," www2.warsawvoice.pl, June 15, 1997; Weigel, pp. 493, 61, 102-6, 108, 138-39, 331. A former female member of Father Wojtyla's first youth groups recalled how he acquired the name "Uncle." In 1952, he took five young girls on an overnight trip to see crocuses. "... at that time it was almost unheard-of for a priest in lay clothes ... to

Having gone from lay leader to Pope, it is no surprise that John Paul became the greatest promoter and protector of the lay movements, starting with gaining them official recognition at Vatican II. Furthermore, Focolare, Neocatechumenal Way, Communion and Liberation and Light-Life (or Oasis) were well established in *Communist* Poland, where Karol Wojtyla got to know them; and he championed them since his days as Archbishop of Cracow. He saw the movements as crucial "for achieving his vision": they are "privileged channels for the formation and promotion of an active laity...."[371] The following statement he made to Communion and Liberation in 1979 encapsulates the continuity of thought between his Tyranowski days and the modern sects: "the true *liberation* of man comes about, therefore, in the experience of *ecclesial communion*...."[372]

Pope John Paul's Apostolic Letter for the Year of the Eucharist (October 2004-October 2005) shows that Vatican II was a bridge for this continuity. Citing Vatican II's *Lumen Gentium*, Pope John Paul says the Eucharist is a sign and instrument of "the unity of the whole human race" — i.e., it is meant to bring about the pantheistic Masonic one-world community! Hence, the Eucharist is "a *project of solidarity* for all of humanity." It should inspire Christians to "become promotors [*sic*] of dialogue and communion," and communities to "*building a more just and fraternal society.*"[373]

Shepherds for the New Springtime

The explosion of gnostic sects, each considering itself as messianic, as God, as the Church, and as "authentically Christian," with authority equal or superior to that of the

---

be taking a party of girls on an overnight excursion.... It was on that trip that we decided, with his permission, to call him 'Uncle' in public, as it would have caused a sensation if we had addressed him as a priest." See Father Malinski, p. 247.

[371]Hoopes, ibid.; Urquhart, pp. viii, 77, 173-88. Cf. Weigel, p. 331.

[372]Urquhart, p. 174. (Emphases added.)

[373]*Mane Nobiscum Domine*, October 7, 2004, nos. 27, 28. (Italics in original.)

hierarchy, had been fracturing the Catholic Church. Until recently, the groups had not sought unity with each other or with "ordinary" Catholics.[374] Following the Illuminist principle of "destruction and reconstruction" seen earlier, now the time has come for these parallel churches to be combined and moved towards the global community. In 1998, Pope John Paul called together the movements and "expressed the wish" that they "be more in communion with each other." Focolare was standing by: "Given that the charism of the Focolare … is all about unity, Chiara pledged to work for the unity of the movements…. This has been going on since then."[375] It would seem that Focolare is positioning itself as leader of the expanding Counterchurch.

The expansion includes merging diocesan associations through get-acquainted conferences and other events featuring high-ranking Church officials. The Pontifical Council for the Laity is very involved. (New Agers call this technique for building community between different sectors of society "networking.") Jubilee 2000 provided Toronto with the opening for launching a community-building process. All its lay groups were invited to a day of "celebrating" their "charisms," organized by Focolare, Neocatechumenal Way, the Charismatic Movement and other communities. The archdiocesan paper whooped on its front page: "Move Over Father, the Laity are Here." Its publisher/editor reported:

> For this crowd there was a realization that the clerical church of the past is history. Faced with a diminishing number of priests … these lay groups recognize their role has expanded to include prayer and evangelization, social justice, service….[376]

As noted earlier, laymen are being instructed they are

---

[374]Urquhart, pp. 10, 22, 65, 74, 407-10; Father Zoffoli, ibid.

[375]Celia Blackden, "Background" to "Dare to Share Conference," catholic-ew.org.uk, July 13, 2003.

[376]Joseph Sinasac, "Celebrating the Lifeblood of the Church," *Catholic Register*, June 12, 2000, p. 9. Note that the crowd was re-educated and illuminized to accept the restructuring of the Church, as described in Chapter 1.

responsible for the future of the Church — i.e., the Counter-church — and there is a concerted effort to have them do the work of the clergy. But in this church, *the sects will be the "religious orders" and provide the shepherds for the flock,* accountable only to their leaders and the Pope.

The bishops of the world were officially put on notice that this is the emerging reality by Bishop Paul-Josef Cordes, then-Vice President of the Pontifical Council for the Laity, at the Synod on the Laity in October 1987: "He appeared to place movements and bishops on the same level...." Don Luigi Giussani, founder of Communion and Liberation, Fr. Franciszeck Blachnickij, founder of Light-Life, and Fr. Tom Forrest of Catholic Charismatic Renewal, had convinced Pope John Paul to hold the Synod, with the hidden agenda of promoting the movements to the world's bishops. Sure of papal support, at a Convention of the movements in March 1987, Don Giussani crowed that the pontiff's recognition "represents a point of no return for our future in the Church." In his speech to the Convention, the Pope himself seemed to equate them with the bishops. He proclaimed them "indispensable and co-essential [with the hierarchy]."[377]

Not only does this elevation of the sects reduce the role of the bishops, but since they are seen as "essential" to the life of a Christian, those not belonging to one are considered second-class citizens, even "pagans" or "atheists" (because they do not believe in God the Movement or God the Community.) The movements themselves seem to have coined the term "new springtime," used at their March 1987 Convention to describe their aim for the Church. Once the Pope began using the slogan, they could claim that the Church sees *them* as the awaited new springtime.[378]

Not surprisingly, the Papal report on the Synod of the Laity, *Christifideles Laici*, strongly promotes the movements. The entire Adult Church (termed "mature ecclesial communi-

---

[377]Urquhart, pp. 66, 71-72, 77-80.
[378]Ibid., pp. viii, 70, 79, 23, 185, 407, 409.

ties"[379]) agenda is also proposed for implementation in this post-synodal Apostolic Exhortation.

The get-acquainted networking and collaborative action of the sects and diocesan groups follow Dewey's formula for effecting an illuminized democratic society (for "society," substitute community or Counterchurch):

> A society, he reasoned, "is a number of people held together because they are working ... with reference to common aims. The common needs and aims demand a growing interchange of thought and growing unity of sympathetic feeling."
>
> .... For Dewey, democracy was ... a way of living which ... pervade[d] all aspects of society. Dewey recognized that every social group, even a band of thieves, is held together by certain common interests ... and he knew that every such group also comes into contact with other groups. He believed, however, that the extent to which democracy has been attained in any society can be measured by the extent to which differing groups share similar values, goals, and interests and interact freely ... with each other.
>
> A democratic society, therefore, is one in which barriers ... among groups are minimized, and numerous meanings, values, interests, and goals are held in common.... "The emphasis must be put upon whatever binds people together in cooperative human pursuits...."[380]

In the Old Age Catholic Church, common belief and practice bound Catholics together, regardless of nationality, culture or age. But in the illuminized democratic New Age

---

[379]Vocation and Mission of the Lay Faithful *Christifideles Laici*, December 30, 1988, no. 36.

[380]*Encyclopedia of Education*, ibid. Note the similarity of Dewey's goal of spreading democracy to that of Grand Orient Freemasonry, stated in 1922: "An active propaganda is urgent, so that Freemasonry shall again become the inspirer, the sovereign mistress of the ideas through which democracy is to be brought to perfection...." (*Light-bearers*, p. 17). Note also that Lenin equated democracy with socialism and Communism (Ferreira, "Perestroika Deception"). Democracy was condemned by several popes, and St. Pius X immediately stopped the first attempt to penetrate Masonic democracy into the Church through the Sillonist movement (see Yves Dupont's Introduction to Pius X, *Our Apostolic Mandate*, pp. 6-7).

church, there is no unity in belief or practice; the only unifying thread is "cooperative human pursuits."

Chapter 6
Teilhard and the Sillon Triumph

As noted earlier, the Church's pilgrimage to the Counterchurch started at Vatican II. The Council was actually a coup against the Catholic Church, utilizing the combined forces of Masonry, Communism, humanism and modernism. These naturalistic enemies, which had lain underground for decades due to papal condemnations, burst forth at the Council to become official policy.

In Europe, very high Masons of the Ordo Templi Orientis publicly celebrated the opening of the Second Vatican Council. The OTO carried its occult symbol of the New Age, an icon of the "Stele of Revealing," in fervent pilgrimage from Hamburg to Zurich, and thence for a ceremony in its Gnostic chapel in Stein, with all the chapel bells ringing. This suggested that Masonry had advance information about the progressive nature of the Council and the gnostic path upon which it would set the Church: the exaltation of Man.[381]

As for the Masonic puppet, Communism, the Church gave up the fight against this foe with the 1962 Vatican-Moscow Agreement in which, in order to have Russian Orthodox observers at the Council, the Holy See promised not to attack Communism.[382] This agreement, still in force, has silenced the Church and allowed the errors of Russia to spread unchallenged. Archbishop Sheen predicted that the Counterchurch would follow orders from Moscow.[383] Indeed, the Communist influence over the Church is so strong today

---

[381]Heimbichner, "Ordo Templi Orientis." The celebratory pilgrimage, notes Heimbichner, was described in the Masonic journal *Oriflamme*. The OTO's stele is also called Stele 666 after the original Egyptian stele or funerary tablet which was so numbered in the catalogue of the Egyptian (formerly Boulak) Museum in Cairo.

[382]See Atila Sinke Guimarães, "The Pact of Metz," *Catholic Family News*, September 2001, p. 13.

[383]Cf. Archbishop Sheen, p. 25.

that one can say the Red flag flies over it.[384] Only the Collegial Consecration of Russia to the Immaculate Heart of Mary, as requested by Our Lady of Fatima, will destroy the growing Counterchurch.

In the religious sphere, Communism is manifested as pantheism. Pantheism is atheism as it denies the existence of God by identifying Him with the universe. The world, therefore, becomes the only reality, and God-centred religion man-centred. So naturalism flows from pantheism. Both doctrines underpin the social-justice church, interested only in temporal good, and both aid the spread of political collectivism, giving it "theological" justification. In pantheism and collectivism the individual and private property are absorbed in the collective. Now, if God and we are one with the universe, then the worship of God is self-worship, but it masquerades as "universal love, to which individuals are to be pitilessly sacrificed." Pantheism and collectivism are the two prongs of both Illuminism and Communism.[385]

One of the people responsible for infiltrating Communist ideas into the Church was the condemned modernist, pantheist and evolutionist, Fr. Teilhard de Chardin, SJ (1881-1955), the darling of Marxists and New Agers. He too wanted to found a Counterchurch, a "human faith, one that combined 'the rational force of Marxism' with the 'human warmth of Christianity.'"[386] Henri Rambaud, in *The Strange Faith of Teilhard de Chardin*, said Teilhard

was not prepared to receive the words of life from the Church, but to offer them to Her. His whole dream [was] to act as the Church's midwife and to help the old Mother to bring to birth the new faith She is unwittingly carrying in her womb and which tomorrow will be the religion of all Mankind.[387]

---

[384]See Ferreira, "Red Flag Over the Vatican."
[385]Cf. Father Clarence Kelly, *Conspiracy Against God and Man* (Belmont, MA: Western Islands, 1974), pp. 179-81, 185, 195.
[386]Father Wickens, pp. 47-48.
[387]Ibid., p. 49.

It was Teilhard who "produced a new Faith ... which masquerades as the Catholic Faith because it uses Catholic terminology" with un-Catholic meanings; Teilhard who promoted personal experience (spirituality) rather than external religion[388]; and Teilhard, who, as seen, is one of the inspirations for the RCIA and Adult Church. The Church's pilgrimage was initiated at Vatican II by Teilhardian bishops and *periti*.[389] The methodology of humanist John Dewey was conveniently available for implementing Teilhard's Illuminist dream and the Masonic/Communist goals set forth in the *Humanist Manifestos*: a one-world government, religion and community with every form of immorality a human right.[390]

That the Catholic Church knowingly undertook a humanist pilgrimage was made clear by Pope Paul VI on the day the Council issued its document upholding the Masonic principles of religious indifferentism and tolerance, the "Declaration on Religious Liberty," *Dignitatis Humanae*. Pope Paul affirmed for the Council:

> The Church of the Council ... is much occupied with Man, ... Man entirely occupied with himself, Man ... who dares pretend to be the beginning and the ultimate reason of all reality.... Humanism, profane and worldly, finally has appeared in its terrible stature and has, in a certain sense, defied the Council. The religion of God-made-man meets ... the religion of man-made-God. What has happened? A clash? A fight? An anathema? *That could happen, but it didn't.*

The Pontiff then exhorted "modern humanists" to "recognize

---

[388]Ibid., pp. 12-14, 48-49.

[389]Cardinal Ratzinger approvingly acknowledged that Teilhard's "daring vision" of the evolution of man and Christianity towards a "divine world" strongly influenced the Council, especially the document *Gaudium et Spes*: Joseph Cardinal Ratzinger, *Principles of Catholic Theology*, trans. Sister Mary Frances McCarthy, SND (San Francisco: Ignatius Press, 1987), p. 334. According to Father Wickens (p. 17), during the Council, "all the [George] Tyrell, [Teilhard] de Chardin, and [Karl] Rahner rhetoric came out of the mouths of the left-wing faction of Vatican II...." Tyrell was Chardin's mentor, Rahner his disciple.

[390]Cf. Kurtz, especially pp. 18-23.

our new humanism," i.e., the new humanistic orientation of the Church, and continued, "we too have, *more than anyone else*, the cult of man."[391]   And forty years later, former Soviet president Mikhail Gorbachev would hail Pope John Paul II as "the No. 1 humanist on the planet."[392]

Dignitatis Humanae, to which then-Abp. Karol Wojtyla made significant contributions, was used by the Vatican to press Catholic States, including Italy, to revise their constitutions to separate Church and State,[393] thus effectively laicizing or "atheizing" them.   This victory for Masonry was effected by Vatican II in contemptuous opposition to Bl. Pius IX's *Syllabus of Errors*, which condemned separation of Church and State, as well as pantheism, indifferentism, religious liberty and all the other errors of naturalism found in the Counterchurch.[394]   Interestingly though, in 1982, Cardinal Ratzinger, the future Pope Benedict XVI, unabashedly affirmed that Vatican II's *Dignitatis* (on religious liberty), *Gaudium et Spes* (relationship to the modern world) and *Nostra Aetate* (world religions) are a "revision of the *Syllabus* of Pius IX, a kind of counter syllabus."   He further said that *Gaudium* represents the Church's "attempt at an official reconciliation with the new era inaugurated in 1789"[395] — i.e., with the Masonic world order inaugurated by the French Revolution!

Remi de Roo, arguably Canada's most progressive bishop, who attended Vatican II, recently said he still gets "shivers up my spine" recalling that "when Paul VI came out to celebrate the Eucharist, ... there with him, all in red, were all those theologians who had been marginalized before the Council."[396]

One "marginalized" modernist theologian "who had

---

[391]Cited in Abbé Daniel Le Roux, *Peter, Lovest Thou Me?* (Gladysdale, Victoria, Australia: Instauratio Press, 1989), p. 13.   (Emphases added.)   The "religion of man-made-God," i.e., deified Man, is the goal of Illuminism.

[392]"World Mourns Great Humanist," *Catholic Register*, April 17, 2005, p. 2.

[393]Weigel, pp. 163-66; Abbé Le Roux, pp. 23-25.

[394]Denzinger, nos. 1701-80.

[395]Cardinal Ratzinger, pp. 381-82.

[396]Rosemary Ganley, "Remi De Roo at *CNT* ...," *Catholic New Times*, July 4, 2004, p. 12.

perhaps the greatest influence" on the Council was Fr. Yves Congar, OP. In a recent lecture at Toronto's St. Michael's College, marking the 100th birthday of Congar, theologian Fr. Thomas O'Meara "recalled the revolution in church thinking which Congar oversaw at Vatican II." Although "his books were still banned" and "he was forbidden to teach seminarians," Congar was "invited to advise the Council" on ecclesiology and ecumenism. "He wrote substantial portions of *Gaudium et Spes*, the church's pastoral constitution, and other documents," and his heresies are "now the most orthodox theology of the church, taught in every seminary and assumed by almost all Catholics."[397] Among Congar's partners in drafting *Gaudium* were Archbishop Wojtyla and another "marginalized" theologian, Fr. Henri de Lubac, SJ. Both theologians were highly impressed by the young bishop,[398] who as Pope later elevated them to the Cardinalate.

The Masons had every reason to celebrate the opening of the Second Vatican Council because it "generated the new Pentecost."[399] Now, just as the original Pentecost was the birth of the Catholic Church two thousand years ago, so the *new* Pentecost signifies the birth of a *new* church: the Counterchurch, the "Church of the People of God."[400]

Founded on Naturalism

The foundation of the anti-Church is naturalism. Practical naturalism, Father Garrigou-Lagrange tells us, is the

---

[397]Michael Swan, "Remembering Congar," *Catholic Register*, February 6, 2005, p. 5. Ecumenism was a new word for the Council, but Congar had written a book on the topic in 1937: Bishop Aloysius J. Wycislo, *Vatican II Revisited: Reflections by One who was There* (New York: Alba House, 1987), p. 109. The bishop served on various Vatican II Commissions.

[398]Weigel, pp. 167-68. For his part, Archbishop Wojtyla proclaimed Congar, de Lubac, Hans Küng and Karl Rahner to be "eminent theologians" of the Council: Father Malinski, p. 184.

[399]The Council "was a work of the Spirit, and the new Pentecost it generated, like the first, will need the prayers of all the People of God": Bishop Wycislo, p. 180.

[400]Ibid., pp. 165, 168.

"negation of the spirit of faith in the conduct of life." It has given rise to three condemned heresies: Americanism, modernism and quietism.[401] All the errors of adult faith that are also being propagated at World Youth Day and by the new movements fall into one or more of these heretical camps.

Americanism and modernism disparage mortification and obedience as passive virtues for negative people, better suited for the past; what is needed in modern times are active virtues that help human society. One is not to scorn the world but to ameliorate it. The "most serious offense" for modernists is "abstention from social works; consequently the purely contemplative life [is] considered quite useless...."[402] These errors have produced today's social-justice Church, "orientated to the outside world" by the Council,[403] which dovetails nicely with New Age humanitarianism and development.

Americanism also fuels ecumenism, syncretism and inculturation, "contend[ing] that it is opportune to win over those who are in disagreement" by ignoring or so "softening" doctrines that cause disagreement "that they do not retain the same sense as the Church has always held."[404] Further, the natural virtues are extolled over the supernatural, and it is believed that in our advanced civilization, the faithful should be given more liberty in thinking for themselves. Indeed, the entire external teaching office of the Church is rejected as "useless"; instead, the Holy Ghost is seen as teaching the faithful without any intermediary, "by a kind of hidden in-

---

[401]Father Garrigou-Lagrange, pp. 275, 277-78.

[402]Ibid., pp. 275-78. Cf. Pope Leo XIII, Americanism *Testem Benevolentiae*, January 22, 1899, Denzinger, nos. 1972-73; Pope St. Pius X, The False Doctrines of the Modernists *Pascendi Dominici Gregis*, September 8, 1907, ibid., no. 2104.

[403]Bishop Wycislo, pp. 51, 144-52.

[404]Leo XIII, Denzinger, no. 1967. Altering the deposit of faith to suit the new times was anathematized by Vatican I: ibid., nos. 1800, 1818. Note that the very *act* of trying to reconcile differences between religions is defined by the dictionary as syncretism (cf. *The Concise Oxford Dictionary*, 5th ed., 1964). Ecumenism itself is thus also syncretism and, indeed, is seen today as pertaining to the unity of mankind and the whole universe (cf. Bishop George Appleton, "Faiths in Fellowship," *World Faiths* [London], Spring 1977, p.3).

stinct."[405] We recognize in this gnostic error the Charismatic Movement and the policy of encouraging ignorant laity and youth to "evangelize."   We also recognize the liberty of thought promoted by Jan Tyranowski and imbibed and passed on by Pope John Paul II.   Decades of discussion groups have cemented Americanism in the Counterchurch.

Expanding the Americanist idea of liberty, modernism promulgates a democratic Church. It is "to be brought in harmony with the modern conscience, ... which tends entirely towards democracy."   Centralized authority must be "dispersed," and the laity given a share in governing. External devotions are to be reduced. Modernism also demands revisionism in history; dogma then has to be harmonized with revised history and changing times. Catechesis can only be concerned with dogmas "which have been reformed, and are within the capacity of the masses."[406]   Today's "faith-updating" adult catechumenate, the RCIA, and World Youth Day catechesis clearly follow this modernist principle. And since modernism is "the synthesis of all heresies,"[407] every heresy is found in the Counterchurch.

Whereas Americanism exalts action, quietism promotes the practical naturalism of *spiritual* inaction and sloth. Quietism preaches the "interior way": the mind must be shut off. "To wish to act offends God, who wishes to be the only one to act in us." By not acting, God alone lives and reigns in the soul. Also, "[t]he soul no longer needs to offer positive resistance to temptations, of which it no longer has to take account." Thus, there is no need to examine one's conscience or think of heaven or hell. One should not desire perfection or salvation. Further, "the voluntary cross of mortification is a heavy and useless burden which one must get rid of." Asceticism and the practice of the virtues are suppressed, setting the stage for great immorality. Molinos, the promulgator of quietism in the seventeenth century, went as far as declaring

---

[405]Leo XIII, ibid., nos. 1967-71.
[406]Pius X, ibid.
[407]Ibid., no. 2105.

that temptations are always useful, even when they lead to sinful acts; in fact, he "claimed to reach impeccability" — as Father Garrigou-Lagrange comments, "strange impeccability, reconcilable with all disorders." Impeccability underpins the Jungian notion of merging good and evil tendencies to reach "wholeness," as also the Dewyite dictum that nature and grace be combined. Quietist "prayer" is never intercessory, but consists in emptying the mind to gain an *acquired* passivity that *apes* infused contemplation. (Asceticism, the practice of the virtues, and being in the state of grace are the dispositions required for the *gift* of true contemplation and union with God, i.e., for holiness and perfection.) The "interior soul" scorns feasts and holy days, seeing all days as equal. Similarly, no place is holier than another.[408]

Chiara Lubich openly tells her devotees, "Jesus wants *the complete void of our minds* so that he can illuminate us...." In practice, the superiors of Focolare, especially Lubich, "illuminate" the void. All outside knowledge is rejected, including all the spiritual and doctrinal teachings of the Church. In problematic situations, *focolarini* are convinced that if they "empty themselves," i.e., let their minds go blank, the Holy Spirit will provide the solution.[409]

The Neocatechumenal Way is also quietist, repudiating mortification, the practice of virtue, and religious life. It maintains man is an unchangeable sinner, thus justifying moral licence. God forgives everything, so hell should not exist and one should not speak of Purgatory, indulgences or prayers for the dead.[410] Most Catholics are of the same mind today, thanks to John Dewey, as seen in Chapter 2. Even Pope John Paul II, in his book *Crossing the Threshold of Hope*, casts doubt on the existence of hell and purgatory.[411] Our Lady of Fatima, foreseeing this spreading disbelief in the reality of eternal damnation, showed the three children a terrify-

[408]Father Garrigou-Lagrange, pp. 277-79; Denzinger, nos. 1221 ff.

[409]Urquhart, pp. 267-68, 233.

[410]Father Zoffoli, ibid.

[411]*Crossing the Threshold of Hope*, ed. Vittorio Messori (New York: Alfred A. Knopf, 1995), pp. 185-86.

ing glimpse of hell, later noting, "[M]any souls go to hell, because there are none to sacrifice themselves and to pray for them."[412]

Quietism is running rampant in the Counterchurch, accounting for its complete disregard of the next world and of the Ten Commandments. In order to "find meaning" in a depressing life without God and the goal of eternal happiness, its members grasp at the creation of a worldly utopia, following the blueprint set forth in the *Humanist Manifestos*. Social justice work is more appealing to slothful souls than work for the salvation of souls because the latter requires us to use the means Jesus has indicated: a hatred of evil and error (rather than a desire to unite oneself with it), and progressive death to sin through mortification and the practice of the virtues.[413]

The quietist tenet on prayer is reflected in the explosion of Eastern and occult meditation. Its indifference towards feast days has resulted in the shredding of the traditional Calendar of Saints. And since no place is holier than another, then it's perfectly fine to have pagan rituals in a Catholic church; indeed, our churches and shrines should be *interfaith* places of worship. Finally, the quietist attitude towards impeccability and the next world seems to account for the otherwise incomprehensible apathy shown by most Catholics towards possible moral temptations at World Youth Days, especially at their sleepovers.

Sillonism Rebounds

Now, a hundred years ago, an attempt was made to demote the Catholic Church to a social-justice institution working for peace, harmony and world brotherhood. The naturalistic, modernist Sillon youth movement of France developed false democratic ideals based on Freemasonry's tenet

---

[412]Sister Lucia, pp. 167, 171.
[413]Cf. Father Garrigou-Lagrange, pp. 306-7.

of absolute equality, and these ideas then moved from the socio-political arena into the Church. In 1910, Pope St. Pius X condemned and shut down the Masonic Sillonist movement,[414] but its ideas, like modernism, spread underground, to re-surface at Vatican II. Its beliefs today form the backbone of ecu-syncretism and the democratic adult church.

The traditional Catholic Church was just as abhorrent to the Sillon — which was "regarded as the nucleus of the Future City" (as separate from the existent City of God, the Catholic Church) — as to today's adult church. As Pope Pius explained to the French bishops:

> You are the past; they are the pioneers of the civilization of the future. You represent the hierarchy, social inequalities, authority and obedience, worn out institutions to which their hearts, captured by another ideal, can no longer submit.[415]

The modern belief that only after Vatican II did the Church begin to understand how to work for justice and peace matches pre-conciliar Sillonist teaching:

> Distrust of the Church ... is being instilled into the minds of Catholic youth; they are being taught that after nineteen centuries She has not yet been able to build up in this world a society on true foundations ... they are told that the great Bishops and Kings, who have ... governed so gloriously, have not been able to give their people true justice and true happiness because they did not possess the Sillonist Ideal![416]

Do we not see this audacious claim that only the Sillonist Ideal is the solution to the world's ills repeated by Focolare with respect to its own "Ideal" and spirituality of unity? Indeed, the contention by the new ecclesial sects that non-members are pagans echoes the Sillon:

---

[414]Pius X, *Our Apostolic Mandate*. The Pope considered the movement a descendant of the Masonic French Revolution (no. 29).
[415]Ibid., no. 28.
[416]Ibid.

What are we to think of a movement so punctilious in its brand of Catholicism that, unless you embrace its cause you would almost be regarded as an internal enemy of the Church, and you would understand nothing of the Gospel and of Jesus Christ!

St. Pius X sternly rebuked this belief: "The Sillon does not give satisfaction to the Church." He "deemed it necessary to insist on that point because it is precisely its Catholic ardor which has secured for the Sillon … valuable encouragements and the support of distinguished persons."[417]   Just like the support of today's hierarchy for the sects and adult church!

The clearest "reincarnation" of Sillonism today is Focolare, the prototype of the Counterchurch and inspiration for World Youth Day. Sillonism was mainly a youth movement, like Focolare. Focolare's goal of world brotherhood, which Chiara Lubich herself says is the last plank of the (Masonic) French Revolution needing implementation, was the Sillonist goal. Also like Focolare, in order to construct the world community, the Sillon became interdenominational at a time when interfaith collaboration was officially forbidden.[418]

Sillonist ideas not only migrated from France to Italy and Focolare — they seem also to have made their way to Poland. Jan Tyranowski's Living Rosary, of which the future Pope John Paul II was a trained leader, seems Sillonist. As seen earlier, the Living Rosary consisted of discussion groups whose goal was spiritual growth, achieved through "friendship." Discussion groups, we noted in Chapter 1, are used to build community. Note also that "friendship" was the *Sillonist* term for what is called "community" today, and compare the Living Rosary with Pope Pius' description of the Sillon:

> The *study groups* are really intellectual pools in which each member is at once both master and student. The most complete fellowship prevails amongst its members, and

---

[417]Ibid, no. 30.

[418]Ibid., nos. 33, 34, 36. Note also the similarity between the Sillon's attempt to construct a New or Future City and the title of Focolare's magazine, *Living City*, a compendium of its successes in constructing a new civilization.

draws their souls into close *communion*; hence the *common soul* of the Sillon. It has been called a "*friendship*."[419]

Now, whereas Pius X condemned the Sillon and its syncretistic collaboration, John XXIII — who convoked the Second Vatican Council — supported both Sillonism and Focolare; and his encyclical *Pacem in Terris* rallied Catholics to work with non-Catholics, non-Christians and *unbelievers* for the common good. In *Pacem* he envisaged a world community, a new world order based on liberty, equality and brotherhood. Its "driving force" would be "Love." Although advising Catholics not to correct religious and moral errors so as to respect the human dignity of the person in error, he nevertheless believed the new order would be "founded on truth." Not the Catholic Church, but the world community, would be the Kingdom of God on earth and every believer in this new world was to be a "spark of light," i.e., *point of light*, and "center of love."[420] Sillonism, now officially resurrected, was openly promoted by Vatican II documents (like *Gaudium et Spes* which, as we have seen, had the input of Tyranowski's pupil, Karol Wojtyla), Pontifical Councils (such as the one for Interreligious Dialogue), and the ecu-syncretic movement.

Pope John XXIII's restoration of Sillonism, in defiance of St. Pius X's condemnation, is not surprising, given that he was an admirer of Marc Sangnier, the founder of the Sillon. The following is his testimony to Sangnier's widow after Sangnier's death in 1950, as quoted on the Sillon website, which concludes that John XXIII considered Sangnier "as, in effect, a saint":

I first heard Marc Sangnier speak at a meeting of

---

[419]Pius X, no. 27 (emphases added); cf. Buttiglione, p. 29. Recall the common soul sought by Focolare.

[420]Peace on Earth *Pacem in Terris*, April 11, 1963, nos. 7, 125, 149, 157-58, 163, 167-68, 171. *Pacem* was lauded by Communists, including Krushchev: Daniel Mason, "Gus Hall Greets Pope's Message as Aid to World Peace," *Christian Beacon* (Collingswood, NJ), April 25, 1963, p. 8; "Krushchev Applauds Pope's Statements on Peace in Encyclical," ibid. Undoubtedly the encyclical was lauded because of its Illuminist agenda.

Catholic youth in 1903 or 1904. The wonderful charm of his words and soul exhilarated me. The most vibrant memory of my whole young priesthood is of his personality as well as his political and social action.

His noble and frank humility in accepting late in 1910 the admonishment of [the] saintly Pius X — as affectionate and benevolent as it was — was to my mind the true measure of his greatness.

Souls like his with such a capacity to remain faithful and respectful to both the Gospel and the Holy Church are destined for the highest ascents which ensure glory: the glory of Christ who knows how to exalt the humble, even the glory of the present life before his contemporaries and posterity for whom the example of Marc Sangnier will remain as an example and as an encouragement.[421]

In Pope Pius X's condemnation of the Sillon's interfaith social justice movement, we see that the New Age philosophy of unity in diversity, used to promote religious harmony today, is exactly that of the Sillon:

> … alarming and saddening at the same time, are the audacity and frivolity of men who call themselves Catholics and dream of reshaping society … and of establishing on earth, over and beyond the pale of the Catholic Church, "the reign of love and justice" with workers … of all religions and of no religion, … so long as they forego what might divide them … and so long as they share what unites them.…[422]

Pope Pius forecast the evil results of "the reign of love and justice" (or what Paul VI and John Paul II have termed the "civilization of love," based on Focolare ideology):

> What is to come out of this collaboration? A mere verbal and chimerical construction in which we see, glowing … in seductive confusion, the words of Liberty, Justice, Fraternity, Love, Equality and human exaltation, all resting upon an ill-understood *human dignity*. It will be a tumultuous

---

[421]"Founder of the Sillon," sillon.net, 2001.
[422]Pius X, no. 38.

agitation, sterile for the end proposed, but which will benefit the less Utopian *exploiters* of the people…. the Sillon, its
eyes fixed on a chimera, brings *Socialism* in its train.

The end result, he continued, would be a Democracy that
would be a *religion* which is "more universal than the Catholic Church, uniting all men to become brothers … in the
'Kingdom of God' — 'We do not work for the Church, we
work for mankind.'"[423] The precise goal of Focolare and adult
church! We are reminded that Archbishop Sheen described
world brotherhood as "a religion to destroy a religion, or a
politics which is a religion — one that renders unto Caesar
even the things that are God's."

The Sillonists wished to "reconstruct society upon
new foundations," new conceptions of "human dignity, freedom, justice and brotherhood." They claimed to base their
social dreams on the Gospel, "but interpreted in their own
way," with "a diminished and distorted Christ." Like the
Counterchurch, theirs was an Arian "distortion of the Gospel
and the sacred character" of Jesus. They promoted a social-
justice Christ, overlooking His sacrifice for the salvation of
men. However, Pius X said Jesus "did not announce for future society the reign of an ideal happiness from which suffering would be banished." He did not preach a classless
equality. He did not tolerate error and sin, but instructed in
order to convert and save. He taught that happiness on earth
and in heaven is obtained *only* through membership in His
Church, obedience to His doctrine, carrying one's cross and
practising virtue. These teachings show in Jesus "something
quite different from an inconsistent and impotent humanitarianism."[424]

The role reversal that is turning the Fourth Commandment upside down today, with bishops seeking to learn
from youth, and laity performing priestly duties, was also a
practice of Sillonism. Its concept of *absolute equality* led it to

---

[423]Ibid., nos. 38-39. (Emphases added.)
[424]Ibid., nos. 7, 42.

the Communist notion of suppression of class differences, as all differences were seen as injustice (equality is the meaning of "justice" even today). Sillonism practised such "complete fellowship" that

> [e]ven the priest on entering, lowers the eminent dignity of his priesthood, and by a strange reversal of roles, becomes a student, placing himself on a level with his young friends, and is no more than a comrade.[425]

The young Sillonists drew away "a large number" of seminarians and priests from the authority or guidance of the bishops,[426] becoming in effect the new Shepherds. Had Pius X not shut down the Sillon, the clericalization of the laity would have occurred a century ago! Foreseeing this possibility, he commanded that whilst priests and seminarians might help lay Catholic groups,

> they shall *abstain from joining them as members*; for it is fitting that the priestly phalanx should remain *above* lay associations, even when these are … inspired by the best spirit.[427]

And so the priests and bishops who join lay ecclesial sects, and the men trained in their seminaries, directly violate this command. Clergy and the Bishops Friends of Focolare, who study and live its spirituality of unity under the tutoring of Chiara Lubich, have, as she desired, "set aside their priest-hood."

The true work of priests, said Pope St. Pius, is to "zealously devote their efforts to the sanctification of souls, to the defense of the Church, and also to works of charity in the strict sense," i.e., not to politically motivated humanitarianism. The bishops could select and place "at the *helm* of works of *Catholic* action" a few "level-headed" priests, knowledgeable about the history of civilizations and properly educated

---

[425]Ibid., no. 27.
[426]Ibid., no. 5.
[427]Ibid., no. 46. (Emphases added.)

in social questions. But, regarding these priests, he warned, in terms that also condemn Marxist social justice activities:

> However, let not these priests be misled ... by the miracles of a false Democracy. Let them not borrow from the rhetoric of the worst enemies of the Church ... the high-flown phrases, full of promises, which are ... unattainable. Let them be convinced that the social question and social science did not arise only yesterday; that the Church and the State, at all times and in happy concert, have raised up fruitful organizations to this end; that the Church, which has never betrayed the happiness of the people by consenting to dubious alliances, does not have to free herself from the past; that all that is needed is to take up again, with the help of the true workers for a social restoration, the organisms which the [Masonic French] Revolution shattered, and to adapt them, in the same Christian spirit that inspired them, to the new environment arising from the material development of today's society. Indeed, *the true friends of the people are neither revolutionaries, nor innovators; they are traditionalists.*"[428]

Now, as adult faith proselytizers have realized, freedom — *liberty* — from authority could disintegrate into individualism, and so love of community is substituted for obedience to authority. The Sillon, with its lessening of authority, similarly taught that community welfare is superior to personal and family interests, where the Sillon's community was the *world* community, said Pope Pius, noting this is the meaning of *fraternity*. Equality and fraternity signified, for Sillonists, that authority and power "reside in the people" and governments do not have their own authority, but it is delegated to them by the people, who can also revoke it. This idea was completely condemned by both Pope Pius and Pope Leo XIII as contrary to Catholic teaching that "the right of governing comes from God."[429] But, as we have seen, this democratic *political* Sillonist error is in full bloom in the Counterchurch, in which the priest gets his authority and his pow-

---

[428]Ibid., no. 44. (Emphases added.)
[429]Ibid., nos. 17, 21.

ers from the community, acting in its name.

Liberty, Equality, Fraternity, the pillars of what is called Democracy (said Pope Pius) — Sillonism was leading the Church into the Great Apostasy and the Masonic socialist world republic, with its one-world church, a hundred years ago:

> … [Sillonism] has been harnessed in its course by the modern enemies of the Church, and is now no more than a miserable affluent of the *great movement of apostasy being organized in every country for the establishment of a One-World Church which shall have neither dogmas, nor hierarchy; neither discipline for the mind, nor curb for the passions,* and which, under the pretext of freedom and human dignity, would bring back to the world (if such a [false] Church could overcome) the reign of legalized cunning and force, and the oppression of the weak, and of those who toil and suffer.[430]

In other words, Pope Pius foresaw that if most of the Catholic Church fell into apostasy, joining Satan's one-world religion, far from a civilization of love and peace, we would experience the reign of totalitarianism. The power of this last canonized Pope kept the Great Apostasy at bay for fifty years; then the Church, led by Sillonists and modernists, commenced its pilgrimage to apostasy at Vatican II. The brotherhood religion, the Masonic church planned by New Age leader Alice Bailey for the end of the twentieth century is now a reality (the United Religions), and the Counterchurch at least philosophically "a miserable affluent" of it.

Defeating the Counterchurch

Pope Leo XIII, on October 13, 1884, was made aware by God that Satan would be given free rein over the Church for one hundred years. We don't know when that period began or whether we're still in it, but quite clearly, we are still

---

[430]Ibid., nos. 13, 40. (Emphasis added.)

experiencing the events foreseen by Pope Leo. So terrified was the Pope, that he composed a long prayer to St. Michael, which contains a vivid description of what seems to be the Counterchurch.[431]

He describes a vision he must have had of the devils "prowling about among men, striving to blot out the name of God and of His Christ," and "to capture and destroy" the souls of the elect (as illuminized adult faith educators are doing). He saw the dragon

> pouring ... into the souls of men of ruined intellect and corrupt heart the poison of his wickedness, the spirit of lying, of impiety and blasphemy, the pestilent breath of impurity and of all vice and iniquity.

This describes the gnostic adult church, also seen by Bl. Anne Catherine Emmerich, which has blasphemously made itself equal to God, and is exhibiting the impurity and vice that Masonry engenders.[432] Further,

> Most cunning enemies have filled with bitterness and drenched with gall the Church ... and have lifted impious hands against all that is most sacred in it. Even in the holy place where the See of Blessed Peter and the chair of truth was set up to enlighten the world, they have raised the abominable throne of their impiety with the iniquitous hope that the Shepherd may be stricken and the flock scattered abroad.[433]

By usurping the authority and powers of the Catholic Church, the Counterchurch has raised its throne in the holy place where the chair of Peter was established. The flock "scattered abroad" means the sheep have been let out of the sheepfold, the Catholic Church. The Shepherd, the Pope, allows them to roam a perilous countryside, lost and prey to the wolves of passion.

---

[431] This prayer can be found on p. 228.
[432] Leo XIII, *Humanum Genus*, nos. 19-24.
[433] Cf. Mk. 14:27 and Zach. 13:7.

This prayer, which calls on St. Michael for help, has long been suppressed, as also the short St. Michael prayer that was formerly recited after Mass.   If vast numbers of Catholics say both prayers, it would hopefully vanquish the demons that are preventing the Collegial Consecration of Russia, the consequent restoration of the Holy Faith, and world peace, as promised by Our Lady of Fatima.[434]

The hour is very late, but Our Lady of Fatima will help us if we obey her requests. She has at Her command all the hosts of the heavenly army, led by St. Michael. So let us follow *Her* program of prayer and penance and also join Pope Leo in begging St. Michael to *"defend the people of God against the assaults of the reprobate spirits, and give them the victory."*

---

[434]Cf. Sister Lucia, pp. 198-99.

The predominant atmosphere of World Youth Day is not Catholicism; it is the rock 'n' roll culture.

(JMJ is the French short form for World Youth Day.)

World Youth Day during the Papal address on Thursday.

After the bishop's catechesis session at St. Rose of Lima Church, the youngsters were invited to stand and stretch before Mass. In the presence of the Blessed Sacrament, those in the crowd stood in the church chatting with each other in full voice; some were scratching each other's backs (above). They milled in and out of the pews, and wandered around the church.

At the Kiss of Peace at the bishop's Mass (above) there was lots of noise, handshakes and hugs. Young people wandered around the church to hug friends and strangers.

World
Youth Day:
The party
atmosphere
prevails.

The freaky punk band dAYZ wAGE performed a riotous rock concert at World Youth Day on Friday, in a hall adjacent to the "Vocations" room.

The crowd of youngsters goes wild as the band plays "YMCA," a rock song made popular by the homosexual band The Village People.

Young men and young women were "body-surfed" through the crowd during the concert. The crowd went wild in a rock 'n' roll frenzy. Above, a young girl jumps up on stage.

A Toronto policeman threatens to close the concert unless the crowd settles down.

And yes, the dAYZ wAGE concert was a scheduled WYD event.

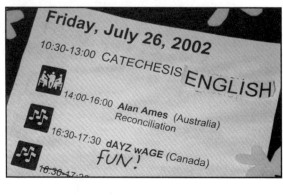

Friday, July 26, 2002
10:30-13:00 CATECHESIS ENGLISH
14:00-16:00 Alan Ames (Australia) Reconciliation
16:30-17:30 dAYZ wAGE (Canada) FUN!
16:30-17:30

Top: "Front-to-front-to-front" dance done by young people at the WYD Saturday night "vigil." Note, this is how they will be dressed for the Papal Sunday Mass the next day.
Middle: Crowd-dancing went long into the night.
Bottom: Girls and boys bunk together at the World Youth Day sleepover.

World Youth Day:
Showcase of Liturgical Abuse

An all-girl "liturgical dance" routine was performed after the First Reading at the WYD Papal Mass on Sunday.

Rock 'n' Roll and Eucharistic Sacrileges

One of the many lay Eucharistic ministers
at the WYD Sunday Mass

"Long-reach" Communion in the hand

Papal Mass
LIVE from Downsview Lands

Canada's Vision Television broadcast a total of 35 people receiving Communion from Pope John Paul II; 25 of these received Communion in the hand. This was contrary to the traditional teaching and practice of the Church, which regards this as sacrilege. It was also contrary to John Paul's own 1980 teaching against Communion in the hand.

Papal Mass
LIVE from Downsview Lands

Rock 'n' pop band on stage providing hip "hymns" for the WYD Papal Sunday Mass. This was in defiance of pre-Vatican II papal teaching on sacred music. Pope St. Pius X said that music for church or liturgical functions "may contain nothing profane."

Catholic event or refugee camp?
World Youth Day at 12:45 a.m. on Sunday, July 28, 2002.

Part II

World Youth Day:
An Eyewitness Account

By John Vennari

Chapter 7
Upon This Rock 'n' Roll
I Will Build My Church

World Youth Day should actually be called World Youth *Days* or World Youth *Week,* since its proceedings stretch for more than one day. I travelled to Toronto to cover World Youth Day, which took place from July 18 to 28, 2002. The following analogy will help explain what I found.

Imagine that you hear of a momentous youth congress to be held in Toronto for young people of the world who want to learn the Italian language. When the countless busloads of youth arrive, the party spirit is permeated not by an Italian atmosphere, but by American rock 'n' roll culture. The world's most famous Italian facilitator, who is the main attraction, comes to the Congress and gives vague lectures about the goodness of Italian: "Let Italian be your light"; "Choose Italian"; and "Italian is the way." The crowd cheers after every fourth or fifth sentence of the facilitator's speech. They even spend a great deal of time chanting the facilitator's name to the beat of hand-clapping rhythms.

Throughout the week, the crowd sings numerous cutesy songs, accompanied by pre-school-style choreographed hand-waving. They lock arms, sway and sing, "I love my Italian"; "Italian rules!"; and "Italian is awesome." They are also overdosed with "Italian Rock."

Yet the youth at this festival are taught nothing about Italian grammar, syntax and sentence structure, nor anything about the richness of the Italian culture of the centuries. Most of them have never heard of Dante or Puccini, and leave the congress as ignorant as when they arrived. In fact, the festival delivers a mutilated version of the Italian language and history that is permeated by some of the worst aspects of popular culture, and this pop-version of Italian contradicts fundamental rules of the language.

The news media, who know practically nothing about Italian tradition anyway, go to the conference and report to the world via radio, television, Internet and the press, that 300,000 young people converged on Toronto to learn and celebrate Italian. Here's a picture of them cheering the Italian facilitator on Wednesday. Here's another picture of them cheering the Italian facilitator on Thursday. Now here's a photo from Saturday in which the crowd is cheering the facilitator's name for the umpteenth time. O look! Here's a snapshot of them cheering the facilitator on Sunday.

According to the press, these young people, thanks to this festival, will now be "teachers" and "evangelizers" of Italian, despite the fact that the vast majority of these defrauded youngsters are clueless as to what truly constitutes the language and culture of Italy. Nonetheless, the youth leave this week-long pep rally charged with the belief that *they* are the hope of the future in regard to the transmission of the Italian language to the modern world.

Now take this description, remove the word "Italian," replace it with "Catholicism," and you will begin to understand what World Youth Day truly is.

Yet in many ways it is worse. As I will explain in these chapters, World Youth Day is a revolution against the Papal teachings of the centuries, especially regarding liturgy, reverence, modesty, sacred music and many other fundamental Catholic principles. Sure, there were minuscule dosages of traditional Catholicism here and there during WYD, but these smidgens were eclipsed by the rock 'n' roll culture that permeated the week. Papal ceremonies were no exception.

The Sunday Mass at World Youth Day implicitly placed an "imprimatur" on some of the worst abuses of the post-conciliar period, including liturgical dance, lay lectors, lay Eucharistic ministers, pop-music at Church functions, slovenly and immodest dress during Mass, pagan rituals surrounding Sunday Mass, and Eucharistic sacrilege. Canada's Vision Television broadcast close-ups of Pope John Paul II continually administering Communion in the hand at his Papal Mass on Sunday.[1]

A Guitarist's Testimony

Before we get to the actual report on World Youth Day, and why it constitutes a revolution against Catholicism, a few comments may be in order.

I wish to state from the beginning that my reports on WYD are not intended to be hard on the youth themselves. It is my belief, based on observation, that a great number of them were never taught basic Catholic modesty, reverence and numerous doctrinal points.

On this point, I speak from experience. I went through twelve years of Catholic school, graduated in 1976, and was taught virtually nothing about Catholicism, especially in high school, when the teachings of the Faith need the most reinforcement. Between first and third grade (1964 to 1966), I received a more traditional formation, but this was eclipsed when the *aggiornamento* of Vatican II steam-rolled through Catholic schools and parishes. In short, when I was in first grade, we were learning the *Kyrie*. By the time I got to fourth grade, we were learning *Kumbaya*.

The "updated" religion classes were often full of discussions such as, "What does love mean to you?" In high school, sin was never mentioned, unless it was to tell us that certain sins were not sins, especially regarding the Sixth and Ninth Commandments.

I learned my Catholic Faith once I got out of Catholic school, and developed a voracious appetite for pre-Vatican II Catholic texts, especially stories of Our Lady, the Infant of Prague, the lives of the saints, traditional apologetics, and pa-

---

[1]For a detailed treatment of this liturgical abuse, see John Vennari, "The Truth About Communion in the Hand," *Catholic Family News,* September 1995, p. 1, and posted at www.cfnews.org/comhand.htm; Michael Davies, *On Communion in the Hand and Similar Frauds,* rev. ed. (St. Paul, MN: Remnant Press, 1998).

pal encyclicals of the nineteenth and early twentieth centuries.[2]

Thus, when it comes to World Youth Day, my primary frustration is not with the youth, many of whom I believe are well-meaning but even more defrauded than was I. My primary frustration is with the adults who promote, organize, take part in, and praise World Youth Day, as though it were a legitimate means to transmit Catholicism.

I also speak from experience on another subject bearing on World Youth Day. I was a full-time guitarist from 1970 to 1980. My father, God rest his gentle soul, was an outstanding jazz guitarist who played in the style of Charlie Christian (the guitarist with Benny Goodman). I grew up in a house where music literally puffed out of the chimney. I too studied jazz guitar, and added classical studies later.

In 1970, about two weeks after starting on guitar, I joined the local Guitar Mass. I could do this as a beginner because in order to play the vapid Guitar Mass songs, one needed no talent, but just the ability to strum a few basic chords. By eighth grade, I had walked away from the Guitar Mass, wearied by the cheap music.[3]

Throughout my teen years, I was instinctively repelled by the oxymoron, "Christian Rock." I preferred my rock 'n' roll to be rock 'n' roll, and my sacred music to be sacred music. "Christian Rock" is an artificial hybrid marketed to teens by adults who believe that today's youngsters are incapable of practising traditional Catholic piety. As a teen, I found this notion to be an insult, and rejected it early on. To me, it is as degrading as an English professor whose "new approach to the youth" is to teach his students Shakespeare through Ebonics. Not only do the youth learn nothing of Shakespeare, but the adult teacher looks like a fool. And if the students can only handle Shakespeare through the me-

---

[2]Thankfully, my parents had mostly pre-Vatican II books around the house. It was these books that kept me on track during my high school years and served as a springboard for further study after I graduated. Time after time, when reading these magnificent pre-Vatican II texts, I remember exclaiming to myself, "Why was I never taught this in Catholic school?"

[3]I played in Guitar Masses at high school only if one of the priests asked me to.

dium of Ebonics, then the deficiency is with the students, not with Shakespeare; and this deficiency should be *remedied* by the teacher, not encouraged.

Nonetheless, from 1970 to 1980, I spent the first five years playing weddings, parties and proms, and the remaining five years playing in night clubs. I worked with bands that played Led Zeppelin, Elton John, Grand Funk Railroad, the J. Giles Band and the Moody Blues. I worked with eight-piece ensembles during the disco era, where we played selections from Harold Melvin and the Bluenotes; the Temptations; Kool and the Gang; James Brown; Earth, Wind and Fire; Average White Band; and other pop artists. I also worked with five-piece club bands that played the Bee Gees (*Saturday Night Fever*), Edgar Winter, Foreigner, The Rolling Stones, Donna Summer, and even the pop-hit of the time, "Boogie-Oogie-Oogie."[4]

I neither play nor listen to this music anymore, but I still know a rock concert when I see one. And World Youth Day was primarily a rock 'n' roll festival, pervaded by the superstition that today's young people are the first generation in Church history that are incapable of knowing and practising the Catholic piety of the centuries. I do not understand why this insult to our young people is broadcast as a "love of the youth."

The New Evangelization

World Youth Day, started in 1985, is a pep-rally version of pop-Catholicism and a sample of what is called the

---

[4] I also co-wrote a "fusion rock" piece that was a winner in a city-wide competition held by WZZD radio in Philadelphia, the "prize" being free studio time for the band to re-record the song, wherein it was cut onto a record album that contained all the winners of the competition. This album was sold in local stores. My purpose in relating this is to let the reader know that I have a background in playing and "creating" pop music. It's not something foreign to me. So in my comments about World Youth Day, I cannot be accused of "not understanding today's generation."

"New Evangelization"[5]: an evangelization that is "new in its ardour, its methods, and its expression."[6] It is also new in its *teaching* and its *orientation*.[7] It seeks to mainstream the most radical elements of Vatican II, especially liturgical innovations, ecumenism, inculturation, and lay involvement in priestly duties.

Various new movements in the Church, such as the Charismatic Movement, rock 'n' roll Eucharistic Congresses (featuring, for example, Bob Dylan singing "Knock, Knock, Knocking on Heaven's Door," and Italian pop stars singing John Lennon's atheistic "Imagine there's no heaven, ... no hell..., and no religion too"[8]), the Neocatechumenal Way with its Protestantized theology,[9] World Youth Day, and other such gimmicks, come under the umbrella of the "New Evangelization." The New Evangelization admits of almost anything that is enthusiastic, energetic, modern, and that inspires excitement (new ardour, new method, new expression). Hence, World Youth Days, with their pep-rally spirit and rock-concert atmosphere in which traditional Catholic reverence is eclipsed, fall precisely into the New Evangelization

---

[5]For a fuller treatment of the New Evangelization, see John Vennari, "Catholicism Dissolved: The 'New Evangelization,'" 4-part series, *Catholic Family News*, October 1998 — January 1999.

[6]Father Avery Dulles, SJ, "John Paul II and the New Evangelization — What Does it Mean?", in *Pope John Paul II and the New Evangelization,* ed. Ralph Martin and Peter Williamson (San Francisco: Ignatius Press, 1994), p. 28.

[7]Regarding the New Evangelization, Pope John Paul II stated in 1985 that the "reference point for all contemporary evangelization must remain the Second Vatican Council." In the 1988 Pontifical Document *Ecclesia Dei*, he openly admits, however, that the teachings of Vatican II, upon which the New Evangelization is based, are *new*: "Indeed, the extent and depth of the teaching of the Second Vatican Council call for a renewed commitment to deeper study in order to reveal clearly the Council's continuity with Tradition, especially in points of doctrine which, *because they are new*, have not been well understood..." (emphasis added). See Vennari, ibid., November 1998, p. 1.

[8]This Bob Dylan rock 'n' roll concert in the presence of Pope John Paul II took place on September 27, 1997, during the 23rd World Eucharistic Congress in Bologna, Italy. The Associated Press reported that a Congress spokesman had called a press conference to "ask 'forgiveness'" for the Church's belated attention to rock 'n' roll," and at the concert the pope would "give his blessing to rock 'n' roll." See ibid.

[9]See Mark Alessio, "The Neo-Catechumenal Way: What do the Founders *Really* Believe?", *Catholic Family News*, March 1996, p. 1.

mould. In fact, Charismatic leader Ralph Martin has mentioned that the rock 'n' roll approach to religion is one of the "new methods" encouraged by John Paul II's New Evangelization.[10] Rock 'n' roll, of course, is a form of inculturation for Western countries — the incorporation of the popular "culture" into Catholicism.

Within this context, World Youth Day is one of the most colourful, expensive, earthy and noisy novelties of the post-conciliar period. It delivers a false rendition of Catholicism that demeans the youth. It is also childish. As I witnessed World Youth Day's *Sesame Street* version of the Faith, I looked around expecting to find a billboard that said, "World Youth Day, brought to you by the letter 'J.'" Throughout World Youth Day's proceedings, a visit from Big Bird would not have been out of place.

Registration

I arrived late Wednesday afternoon, and had the good fortune to stay in Toronto with the family of Cornelia Ferreira. She and I went to the registration area, where I received my World Youth Day back-pack, cross, program, plastic rosary, World Youth Day pin, post cards from Niagara Falls, transit pass and other items. The city of Toronto granted all Youth Day registrants free transportation for the week, provided we showed our pass. (It must be said that Toronto was a good host. No complaints on that score.)

My first surprise came when the volunteer registrar handed over my meal tickets. The registration fee was $240 (Canadian), and $255 for all meals included. When I sent in my registration money four weeks previously, I had signed up for the meals. But when the WYD volunteer handed me the food tickets on the day of my arrival, he said, "The meals are served in groups of six."

"What does that mean?" I asked.

---

[10]Vennari, ibid.

"It means you have to find five other people and get your meals with them."

"I can't take a meal on my own?"

"No," he said. "The meals are only served in groups of six." Sensing my consternation, he encouraged, "It's a great way to meet people!"

I resolved then and there to chalk up the food tickets as fifteen dollars lost, and to buy my vittles from the vendors. I did not relish the thought of bursting into groups of strangers, like Casper the Friendly Ghost, to ask if they would be my friends, at least for the sake of the next meal.

The "Catechesis" Sessions

The next morning, Cornelia Ferreira and I went to some catechesis sessions. These sessions were held in 127 churches throughout Toronto, as well as at Exhibition Place, and were conducted by bishops from various countries. We arrived at one church just in time to hear a French-speaking bishop invite the youth to get acquainted. In the presence of the Blessed Sacrament, those in the crowd turned to each other for a loud, chattering mini-friendship-fest. This died down after a few minutes, and then the bishop resumed his talk.

We left this church, came upon another French-speaking bishop in another parish, and finally found an English-speaking bishop at St. Rose of Lima Church. Bishop Reis, a Caribbean bishop, I think, was better than most.

The theme of the 2002 World Youth Day was "You are the light of the world. You are the salt of the earth." The bishop spoke on the theme of "light," and had some good things to say about purity, chastity and resisting friends who mock religion.

A lot of his talk was on a humanistic level. For example, he told the youth, "If you are chaste before you marry, then after you marry, your spouse will trust you." Not a bad observation. But there was no mention that sins against purity are mortal sins that offend God and send us to hell for eternity, which is a stronger motive to keep oneself pure than all other arguments combined. There was also no mention of the sober words of Bl. Jacinta of Fatima: "More souls go to hell for sins of the flesh than any other reason." [11]

Sadly, using graphic terminology, the bishop also stated that it is the Catholic schools' "duty" to teach the biology of human sexuality to young people, because parents cannot be relied upon to transmit this information to the youth. He seems to have forgotten this so-called "sex education" was condemned by Pope Pius XI in 1929.[12]

Despite these foibles, the bishop's talk was better than I expected. But the good points in his speech were undermined by the surroundings. The young people in the church dressed in a manner that was unfit for the House of God. Their dress ranged from slovenly to immodest. They looked as if they were going to a picnic, to hike through the woods, or to attend a sporting event: shorts, T-shirts, sneakers, many young women in short-shorts, some scanty tops, and lots of matching T-shirts for various youth groups. A young man in the pew in front of me had printed on the back of his shirt the words "Tuned for Trash."

After the bishop's session, the youngsters were told to stand up and stretch before the Mass began. Those in the crowd stood in the church chatting with each other in full voice; some were scratching each other's backs. They milled in and out of pews, and wandered around the church aisles. I did not see one of them genuflect, even though the Sanctuary lamp and tabernacle were clearly in view. One young man stood drumming a rapid funky rhythm with his hands on the side of the pew. Others swigged water from plastic bottles. These poor young people, whom Pope John Paul called "the

---

[11]Cited in Father John de Marchi, IMC, *The Crusade of Fatima* (Fatima: Edições Missões Consolata, 1947), p. 161.

[12]In his Encyclical Letter On the Christian Education of Youth *Divini Illius Magistri*, December 31, 1929. Most of today's prelates, including those in the Vatican, choose to ignore Pope Pius XI's Catholic directive against sex education.

hope of the future," are completely devoid of reverence before the Blessed Sacrament. They don't seem to have a clue. But what can we expect? They are the children of the children of Vatican II.

The young congregation was told to quiet down just before the Mass began. The Mass was full of modern rock 'n' roll, Guitar Mass-styled songs (one could not call them hymns). One modern church-tune was sung during the Offertory by two young men in shorts and sneakers, and a young lady in a scanty outfit — short-shorts, skimpy top — that revealed more flesh than it covered. The three youngsters stood in front of the altar as they performed.

This liturgy did not contain a raucous party atmosphere, as do Charismatic liturgies. It was simply the Novus Ordo, bland and loud. At the Kiss of Peace, there was lots of noise, handshakes and hugs. Young people wandered around the church to hug friends and strangers. We left before the service ended.

Inculturation and Raves

The catechesis session that we attended was tamer than others conducted simultaneously. *The Toronto Star* reported that Our Lady of Lourdes Church held a Mass drenched in Polynesian ceremonies, with the boom-boom of Polynesian drums. This is all part of inculturation, the post-Vatican II novelty that encourages pagan and secular elements to be incorporated into liturgy. The *Star* reported:

> There was the beating of hands on thighs, and — stepping through the small wooden doors and into the yellow brick church — the guttural chanting of men who lined the aisle like sentinels.
> "Who — Who — Ha," they puffed, their yellow and orange shirts glimmering.... With each "Ha," they raised their arms toward the back of the church to where a group of women in the same bright fabric lifted up a silver chalice

and tray....

From the altar, Cardinal Frédéric Etsou-Nzabi-Bamungwabi lifted his head, freshly circled by necklaces of hand-painted seeds and shells. He offered blessings, communion, and then a cultural gift of his own — a hymn in his native language from the Democratic Republic of Congo.

"The Pope says we should celebrate the Eucharist in our own culture," [one observer] whispered....[13]

The *Star* also ran a story called "Youth Rave as Church Service Rocks," a report on a riotous catechesis session and "Mass" held at Santa Cruz Church. "This mass was anything but dead," said the report. This was why:

> The most striking difference was the music. Instead of subdued 200- to 300-year-old hymns, a full band, with bass guitars, keyboard, a drum set, congas and bongos, trumpet and tambourine, filled the sanctuary with the sounds of rock, folk and even, as one woman put it, techno-funk.
>
> Frequently, the church would erupt in song and 400 young people would start to sway or gesticulate to the music. Near the end of the mass, with a chorus that repeated "Yes Lord," they began jumping up and down as if at a rave. Passersby outside cocked their heads in startled curiosity.
>
> They [the youth in the congregation] offered each other peace with high-fives and knuckle jabs. Some danced in the aisles. They even sang the Lord's Prayer with verve.[14]

Likewise, St. Louis' Archbishop Justin Rigali led a catechesis session that closed with two musicians breaking into a rowdy version of the Beatles' "Twist and Shout," wherein "the Catholic pilgrims began to rock."[15]

Thus, when you hear that World Youth Day provided "catechesis sessions," keep in mind that this is the "catechesis" the youth received.

---

[13]Catherine Porter, "Unified in Faith, Rich in Diversity," *The Toronto Star*, July 26, 2002, p. B3.

[14]Andrew Chung, "Youth Rave as Church Service Rocks," ibid.

[15]Maureen Murray, "Fearless in their Belief," ibid. Since this time, Archbishop Rigali has been made a Cardinal and appointed Archbishop of Philadelphia.

Chapter 8
On Reverence

It seems necessary to explain why the WYD "catechesis" sessions, as those here related, constitute an offence against Our Lord in the Blessed Sacrament. Fifty years ago, the reasons would have been self-evident to any Catholic and would have required no explanation. But thanks to the "new springtime of Vatican II," many Catholics today, young and old, have no idea of what constitutes reverence, modest dress or proper behaviour in Church.

In our dealings with God, reverence must come first. All traditional catechisms teach this as a principle that flows from the First and Second Commandments. The homage and adoration we owe to God should be manifest in our reverence towards Him and the things that pertain to Him.

Saint Benedict, the great founder of the Benedictine Order, wrote in his Holy Rule on the necessity of reverence in prayer:

> When we wish to suggest our wants to men of high station, we do not presume to do so except with humility and reverence. How much the more, then, are complete humility and pure devotion necessary in supplication of the Lord who is God of the universe![16]

It follows that when in church, which is the House of God wherein Our Lord resides in the Blessed Sacrament, we must conduct ourselves at all times with humility and reverence. *The Catechism Explained* teaches: "The Church admonishes us to pay homage to the Holy Sacrament of the altar."[17]

---

[16]*St. Benedict's Rule for Monasteries*, trans. Leonard J. Doyle (New York: Benzinger Bros., 1935; reprint ed., Collegeville, MN: The Liturgical Press, 1948), Chap. 20, "On Reverence in Prayer," p. 41.

[17]Father Francis Spirago, *The Catechism Explained* (New York: Benzinger Bros., 1899; reprint ed., Rockford, IL: Tan Books, 1993), p. 593.

This homage also applies to our behaviour at Mass, whether the Mass be held indoors or outdoors.

We pay homage to the Blessed Sacrament by genuflections, absolute silence in church, modest attire, reverential comportment, and also by wearing our "Sunday best" for Sunday Mass, because God deserves the best.[18] This is also why, until the time of Vatican II, only Sacred Music was allowed in church, since it is the only music befitting the reverence we owe to God. This point will be examined more closely in Chapter 15.

The reverence we show to Our Lord is nothing more than what we owe to Him as our Creator and Redeemer. "Since the devil has never ceased to tempt the Christians to irreverence," says the renowned Redemptorist, Father Michael Müller, "and since there are so many in whom the love of the world soon deadens the appreciation of the most holy mysteries of our religion, the Church has always found it necessary to exhort Christians to behave with great reverence in the house of God. 'Reverence My sanctuary: I am the Lord' (Lev. 26:2). 'For My house shall be called the house of prayer' (Matt. 21:13)."[19]

The Question Box explains,

> Genuflection, or bending the knee, is a natural sign of adoration or reverence (Luke 22:41; Acts. 9:40; Phil. 2:10). Catholics genuflect before the tabernacle where the Blessed Sacrament is reserved as a mark of adoration to Jesus Christ, who is really present on the altar.[20]

This duty of reverence before the Blessed Sacrament was reiterated forcefully by Blessed Abbot Marmion, one of

---

[18]For an explanation on how God, in the Old Testament, always commanded His faithful ones to give Him their best, see Gerry Matatics, "How and Why I Returned to the Old Mass," *Catholic Family News,* February 1999, p. 7.

[19]Father Michael Müller, CSSR, *The Holy Sacrifice of the Mass* (New York: Fr. Pustet & Co., 1874; reprint ed., Rockford, IL: Tan Books and Publishers, 1992), pp. 368-69.

[20]Father Bernard Conway, CSP, *The Question Box (*New York: [The Paulist Press], 1929; reprint ed., Stratford, CT: Orthodox Roman Catholic Movement, 1979), p. 238.

the greatest masters of the spiritual life of the twentieth century. "Profound reverence amounting to adoration," said Abbot Marmion, "is the only attitude fitting for man in the presence of the Divine Sacrament. This religious veneration is a condition precedent for the communication to us by God of His graces through the Eucharist." He further warned, "God cannot approve a want of respect towards His Son Who continues in the Eucharist the gift of Himself to men."[21]

Reverence in church thus automatically extends to proper dress and mature comportment. An example of the guidance Catholics used to receive in this area is found in the 1961 book *American Catholic Etiquette*, written by Kay Tone Fenner, with the advice and assistance of the Vice Chancellor of the Diocese of Albany, NY. Herein the author explains:

> Women must *always* dress modestly for any church service. *There is no possible exception to this rule.*

In continuity with the traditional teaching and practice of the Church, she explains that women should always wear their Sunday best, within the proper bounds of modesty and decorum. She also notes, "Regardless of how warm the weather may be, a low-cut dress or one without sleeves should not be worn...." She reaffirms the traditional Church regulations against women wearing slacks or shorts to church. A much-needed reminder for our own day, she speaks specifically against wearing "sports clothes such as a gymnasium suit, tennis dress, bathing suit" to church. She also reaffirms the obligation of women to wear head-

---

[21]Abbot Columba Marmion, OSB, *Christ the Ideal of the Priest* (St. Louis, MO: Herder, 1952), pp. 137, 139. Abbot Marmion further teaches (p. 75) that love and gratitude should also be the motive for our reverence before the Blessed Sacrament. He explains that faith in our Lord's Divinity "commands the most profound respect for Christ. If Jesus hides His splendor, we must adore *all the more* the mysterious reality of His presence in the Blessed Sacrament.... It is out of consideration for us that Christ hides His glory from our eyes, so that in our weakness we may not fear to approach Him. Encouraged by this kindness, our faith should pierce the veil and *prostrate us in adoration* at the feet of the Son of God."

coverings.[22]

Men are bound to dress properly as well. *American Catholic Etiquette* prescribes a suit and tie or at least a sports coat and tie for men, and reminds them, "It is in poor taste to come to Mass in a sports shirt or jersey without a coat, regardless of how warm the weather may be." Likewise, "Men do not wear shorts to Mass."

The same book says,

Children should not come to church dressed sloppily in denims, jerseys, etc.... Children should learn young to bathe and dress carefully for church, and to present as neat and attractive an appearance as possible; this training will then carry over into adult life.[23]

Interestingly, *American Catholic Etiquette*, published in 1961, does not even bother to remind Catholics that it is forbidden to speak in church in the presence of the Blessed Sacrament, much less to hold loud conversations or laugh and socialize as if one were in a sports bar. Absolute silence in church was so much a part of pre-Vatican II parish life that the author presumed it unnecessary to remind Catholics of their duty of silence at all times before the Blessed Sacrament.[24]

The Dominican authors of the college text, *Christ in His Sacraments,* further explain the reason for suitable dress in

---

[22]Kay Tone Fenner, *American Catholic Etiquette* (Westminster, MD: Newman Press, 1961), p. 229 (emphasis in original). The specific recommendations Fenner gives for women's dress may reflect in some details the styles of the early 1960s. Nonetheless, they give today's reader a picture of the beauty and formality of women's dress that was the norm at parish churches for Mass. She says, "The preferred costume is a suit, coat or dress with long sleeves and a modest neckline, hat, gloves, stockings, and street shoes. A head covering, preferably a hat, is obligatory, but a scarf or veil is permissible" (this obligation dates from Apostolic times: see 1 Cor. 11). Papal statements on modesty and proper attire in church are presented in Chapter 13.

[23]Fenner, pp. 229-30.

[24]The reverence we owe God while in church is also based on the Catholic teaching on the Seven Gifts of the Holy Ghost, especially the Gifts of Fear and Piety. See Father Adolphe Tanquerey, *The Spiritual Life* (Tornai, Belgium: Desclee & Co., 1923), pp. 609-37.

church:

> No more than a king's guest would dishonor his host by his disgraceful vesture or physical appearance, should the Christian, by his manner of dress or of bodily cleanliness, evidence irreverence for Christ. Certain garments may not be out of place on the dance floor or the bathing beach, or for hauling rubbish ... [but] are they signs of one's attitude toward the Most Blessed Sacrament? Surely the King deserves above all others the small respect that can be given by men by proper dress and appearance; surely His love merits a little effort on our part....[25]

Sadly, the youth at World Youth Day were not given any reminders of the necessity of reverence and proper dress in church. Practically every one of the immodestly and slovenly dressed youngsters received Communion at the catechesis Mass at St. Rose of Lima. Immodest and slovenly attire was the norm at the Papal Mass on Sunday, and has been so since the first World Youth Day in 1985. Yet no one reminded these young people that they were dressed in a manner unfit for attending church, hearing Mass or receiving Holy Communion.[26]

---

[25]Fathers Thomas C. Donlan, OP, Francis L. B. Cunningham, OP, and Augustine Rock, OP, *Christ in His Sacraments,* unnumbered vol. in the series *College Texts in Theology* (Dubuque, IA: Priory Press, 1958), p. 396.

[26]It should be noted that WYD also had an Adoration Chapel where, I was told, there was Perpetual Adoration of the Blessed Sacrament. I tried unsuccessfully to find this chapel (an aerial map of the Exhibition Centre would have been helpful for those of us who were at WYD alone). There were no signs at Exhibition Place directing the youth to it, nor were there any announcements about it while I was there. I am sure there were devout young people at this chapel, behaving properly. But Catholics must show respect for the Blessed Sacrament at all times, and the catechesis sessions were rife with disrespect for Our Lord in the tabernacle. The fact that the organizers set up an Adoration Chapel does not excuse them from the massive irreverence that went on in front of the tabernacle during other WYD attractions.

Chapter 9
Jacinta: "Our Lady Does Not Want People to Talk in Church"

Thankfully, we live in a time when Heaven gave us clear directions about reverence, probably because Heaven knew that our Church leaders would fail us in this regard. I speak primarily about the apparitions at Fatima, which not only reinforced the Catholic doctrine of the Holy Eucharist, but also reinforced *man's duty of reverence towards the Holy Eucharist* as the Body, Blood, Soul and Divinity of Jesus Christ.[27]

In 1916, a year before Our Lady came to Fatima, Jacinta, Francisco and Lucy were favoured with three separate apparitions of an angel, a precursor to Our Lady's visitations. The third and last of the angelic apparitions occurred in the Autumn of 1916.

Lucy tells us that it was midday, and the children were prostrate, reciting the prayers of reparation taught to them by the "Angel of Peace" that preceding spring. Lucy writes:

> I don't know how many times we had repeated this prayer, when we saw shining above us an unknown light. We sprang up ... and beheld the Angel. He was holding a chalice in his left hand, with the Host suspended above it, from which some drops of blood fell into the chalice. Leaving the chalice and the Host suspended in the air, the Angel knelt down beside us and made us repeat three times:

---

[27]This is of immeasurable importance, since the brilliant Catholic author Romano Amerio, who had been a theological expert at Vatican II, explains that the primary reason for today's irreverence towards the Blessed Sacrament is the New Mass. Thanks to the Protestantized Novus Ordo, Amerio explains, many Catholic churchmen and laity have lost belief in the Real Presence of Our Lord in the Holy Eucharist. See Romano Amerio, *Iota Unum: A Study of Changes in the Catholic Church in the Twentieth Century* (Kansas City, MO: Sarto House, 1995), pp. 590-98.

"Most Holy Trinity, Father, Son and Holy Spirit, I adore You profoundly, and I offer You the most precious Body, Blood, Soul and Divinity of Jesus Christ, present in all the tabernacles of the world, in reparation for the outrages, sacrileges and indifference with which He Himself is offended. And through the infinite merits of His most Sacred Heart, and the Immaculate Heart of Mary, I beg of You the conversion of poor sinners."

Lucy writes that the angel arose, took again into his hands the chalice and the Host, and administered Communion to the three children, placing the Sacred Host on Lucy's tongue. He "shared the Blood from the chalice between Francisco and Jacinta, saying as he did so: 'Take and drink the Body and Blood of Jesus Christ, horribly outraged by ungrateful men! Make reparation for their crimes and console your God.'"

After this, Lucy relates that the angel prostrated himself again on the ground "and repeated with us three times more the same prayer: 'Most Holy Trinity ...,' and then disappeared."[28]

Is it possible for Heaven to send mankind a more forceful instruction on how the Holy Eucharist should be reverenced and venerated? By his actions, the angel not only instructed the three Fatima children, but the entire twentieth century and all nations until the end of time.

Notice how the angel's mannerism towards the Eucharist conformed perfectly to the traditional teaching and practice of the Church, as well as the holy authors we have already quoted:

- The angel was on his knees, prostrate with his face to the ground. By doing so, he was acknowledging the Sovereign Majesty and Divinity of Jesus Christ, truly present in the Eucharist, and reminding us of the great reverence that

---

[28]Sister Lucia's memoirs, *Fatima in Lucia's Own Words*, ed. Father Louis Kondor, SVD, trans. Dominican Nuns of Perpetual Rosary (Fatima: Postulation Centre, 1976), edition without photographs, pp. 60-65, 154-57.

we owe to the Blessed Sacrament.

- The angel recited prayers of reparation for blasphemy and sacrileges against the Blessed Sacrament, as if foretelling the countless outrages that would occur against the Blessed Sacrament, especially after 1960.
- The angel prayed, through the Immaculate Heart of Mary, for the conversion of poor sinners, especially, we may infer from the context, for those who sin against the Holy Eucharist.
- The angel did not give Lucy Communion in the hand.[29]

The three children of Fatima knew that the angel was sent for their instruction, and that his example was to be followed. Lucy writes:

> Impelled by the power of the supernatural that enveloped us, we imitated all that the Angel had done, prostrated ourselves on the ground as he did, and repeating the prayers that he said.... We stayed a long time in this position, repeating the same words over and over again.[30]

Thus, God's angel gave us the example of the profound reverence that we owe to the Blessed Sacrament. And the angel taught this to children aged nine, eight and six. The children were expected, as were all children up until Vatican II, to practise the same Catholic devotion as their parents. There was no "kiddie-version" of worship to make it bouncy and fun. Thus the three children of Fatima, aged nine and under, practiced Catholicism in a manner that was more mature than what I saw practised by 30-year-olds at World Youth Day.

Jacinta learned her lesson well, and received further instruction on the subject by the Mother of God, an instruction that seems to be dead-aimed at the misled youth at WYD, as well as at countless modern Catholics.

---

[29]Clearly, on the impossible chance that the angel had attempted to give Lucia Communion in the hand, Lucia would have been shocked and made note of it, as it was rightly regarded as a sacrilege.

[30]Sister Lucia, pp. 157, 65.

In 1920, during Jacinta's final illness, before going to the hospital, she stayed for a while at an orphanage run by a holy religious named Mother Godinho. Mother Godinho relates that while in the house, Jacinta would go to a room that overlooked a chapel next door to the orphanage. From there she could see the tabernacle, and she would pray with her eyes fixed with love and fervour upon it. From her vantage point, Jacinta could see the activities in the nave of the chapel, and Mother Godinho described her reaction:

> She remarked that several people did not have the necessary attitude of recollection, and she said to me: "Godmother …, these people should not be allowed to behave this way before the Blessed Sacrament. In church, we must be tranquil and not talk…. Our Lady does not want people to talk in church![31]

Our Lady does not want people to talk in church!

What would Jacinta have said about rock 'n' roll music and dancing in front of the Blessed Sacrament at World Youth Day?

No! The atmosphere of reverence, proper attire and holy deportment were not found in WYD catechesis sessions, nor were they present in the Saturday afternoon "Vespers" or at the Papal Mass on Sunday (a WYD volunteer told me he had to stop a soccer game that was going on inside the "congregation" during the Pope's Mass).

Thus, WYD liturgies actually scandalize the youth. World Youth Day transmits a false version of Catholicism that is contrary to the reverence we owe to Our Lord in the Blessed Sacrament, as enunciated by the holiest teachers of the Catholic Church and by the angel and Our Lady of Fatima.

There is no expiration date stamped on the reverence

---

[31] Frère Michel de la Sainte Trinité, *The Whole Truth About Fatima*, 3 vols. (Buffalo, NY: Immaculate Heart Publications, 1988-90), vol. 2: *The Secret and the Church*, trans. John Collorafi (1989), pp. 145-46, 148. Note: "Godmother" is the way Jacinta addressed Mother Godinho.

we owe to God. Thus, those who attended World Youth Day, or watched it on television, came away with the idea that shabby attire, immodest clothes and worldly mannerisms are acceptable for church, for Mass and for reception of the Holy Eucharist. "If there were anything wrong with it," the youth will argue, "the Pope and the bishops would have told us at World Youth Day. But they have not reminded us, not even since the first World Youth Day in 1985, wherefore we've always behaved and dressed as you saw us in 2002!"

(It should be noted that the papal liturgies for Pope John Paul's trips were drawn up at the Vatican by progressivist Abp. Piero Marini, his Master of Ceremonies since 1987.[32] The liturgies were not "sprung" on the Pope unexpectedly when he arrived in a foreign land. In fact, *The National Catholic Reporter*, one of the most leftist Catholic journals on the planet, gave John Paul high marks for his inculturated liturgies during his 2002 trip to Mexico, especially for the pagan Aztec ceremonies that took place in the Basilica of Our Lady of Guadalupe during the canonization of Juan Diego.[33])

I personally believe that most young people would respond positively if the Pope and bishops were to do their duty and insist on proper dress and comportment in Church, at Mass and at other liturgical functions. This is why I say that WYD's encouragement and tolerance of this irreverence is an affront to God and an insult to our youth.[34]

[32]Marini was the protégé and personal secretary of Freemason Abp. Annibale Bugnini, main architect of the Novus Ordo Mass. See Cornelia R. Ferreira, "Mother Teresa 'Beatified' With Idolatrous Rites," *Catholic Family News*, January 2004, p. 13.

[33]John Allen, "Inculturation at Papal Masses," nationalcatholicreporter.org, August 9, 2002.

[34]Is it asking too much to insist upon nothing but the most perfect Catholic example in Papal ceremonies? If Catholics do not receive good example at *Papal ceremonies*, then where will they receive it?

Chapter 10
To Exhibition Place!

After the catechesis sessions, I travelled alone to Exhibition Place, which was World Youth Day Central in Toronto. It is a massive outdoor plaza, with an adjacent indoor arena. I looked for something — anything — that Popes Pius IX, Leo XIII, St. Pius X, Benedict XV, Pius XI or Pius XII would recognize as Catholic. After the close of WYD, I can say that I saw practically nothing they would approve, and plenty they would condemn.

Outside on the main stage, a Catholic rock musician, with his electric guitar strapped on, performed "Catholic pop" music, similar to what I heard when covering Charismatic events.[35] The hokiest performance of his repertoire took place when he sang "I'm a Believer":

> *Then I saw His face*
> *Now I'm a believer.*
> *Not a trace*
> *Of doubt in my mind.*

For those who may not know, "I'm a Believer," by The Monkees, is a pop love song from the 1970s containing the lyrics, "Then I saw her face/Now I'm a believer." The WYD singer changed "her" to "Him," in reference to Our Lord. Deep, man. Deep! Various youngsters in the crowd danced and boogied to the upbeat numbers. As for the crowd, at the time we were told there were 200,000 registrants, which was 150,000 less than what the organizers needed to break even. Now it is known that there were only 187,000 registrants, which left the Catholic Church in Canada with a debt of over 30 million Canadian dollars (that's 19 million

---

[35]See John Vennari, *Close-ups of the Charismatic Movement* (Los Angeles: Tradition in Action, 2002).

dollars in U.S. funds).[36]

Media Image vs. Reality

The press has called World Youth Day a Catholic "Woodstock," and though there is a ring of truth to this description, I don't think it fully communicates what was there. Of course, it is a Woodstock-type of event, because the dominant atmosphere at World Youth Day is not Catholicism. It is the rock 'n' roll culture. There is rock 'n' roll music everywhere. "Catholic Rock" blares relentlessly. Life is a holy "groove" to be enjoyed. The Toronto newspapers continually referred to WYD as a festival. A party atmosphere prevailed.

In fact, the *Globe and Mail*, Canada's national daily, reported two World Youth Day teens stripping down to their bikinis to frolic in a fountain behind the Pope's stage. One young man seized the opportunity, turned on the charm, introduced himself to the scantily clad ladies, and secured their phone numbers, which he immediately penciled into his little black book.

Some of those interviewed for the *Globe and Mail* stated openly (and shamelessly) that their real purpose for coming to World Youth Day was to mingle and carouse with the opposite sex. Some found it especially attractive that they could flirt with those from other countries. The *Globe and Mail* noted correctly that this type of behaviour is bound to take place when tens of thousands of young people are herded together, far away from home, unsupervised. The same newspaper quoted a 19-year-old from Paris, who, speaking in broken English, admitted in somewhat graphic terms his immoral practices. He then said, "The Pope say don't choose that. But we humans are bad, you know...."[37]

Granted, many young people did not attend WYD in

---

[36]Rajiv Sekhri, "Canada's Catholic Youth Fest Ends Up in the Red," *Reuters*, August 9, 2002. Also see Chapter 5 of this book.

[37]Graeme Smith, "Playful Delegates Get Down to Some Fun," *Globe and Mail*, July 25, 2002, p. A8.

order to be naughty. The *Globe and Mail* reported the words of a 17-year-old Philadelphia girl who said, "Those people who are just here for the sex shouldn't be here." The same report quoted a young man who believed he had found the proper "moral" balance. He stated, "There's a time and place for everything. Inside the Mass we're not hitting on girls."[38]

Yet, as mentioned, "Woodstock" does not adequately communicate the spirit of World Youth Day. I would have to call it a Catholic Rock 'n' Roll Olympics, not because there were any competition sports, but because of the way the crowd behaved. There were huge contingents of young people walking together, often wearing matching shirts, carrying the flags from their countries: Italy, Poland, Switzerland, Lebanon. They cheered each other (especially the Americans) when they recognized another party from their country walking by: Yayeee! Wooooooooh! and all the other cheers and jeers one finds at rock concerts and sporting events.

I was inside the huge Exhibition Hall when the Pope arrived. He was scheduled to show up at five o'clock, but he came early, so I missed his grand entrance. The crowd greeted him as if he were a superstar, rock star or pop personality, rather than the visible representative of Christ on earth. There was no reverence. Sure, there were young girls in the crowd crying for John Paul, but in the 1960s, there were even more crowds of young girls crying for John, Paul, George and Ringo.

The newspapers have reported the Pope's words, so I will not recount them here. Rather, I want to describe what it was really like at WYD when John Paul II was on stage greeting the youth, the hope of the future, as he called them.

The Pope addressed the crowd in French, Spanish, Italian and English, so most of the time those in the crowd did not know what he was saying. When he first greeted the crowd in a new tongue, for example, Italian, the Italians would cheer, jump up and down, and wave their flags. It gave the impression that the various nationalities come to

---

[38]Ibid.

World Youth Day primarily to celebrate themselves.

A large crowd in front of the stage listened to and cheered the Pope's words. Much farther back, there was a large screen and speakers in front of which the youth gathered to listen and applaud.

Whenever I saw World Youth Day coverage on television, I was under the impression that the entire crowd was cheering for the Pope. This was not the case. At the same time the Pope was speaking, a massive amount of people, young and old, were "doing their own thing," not paying the slightest attention.

I saw crowds of people milling around, visiting the vendors, while the Pope was speaking. I saw young people sitting on the ground, chatting away, while the Pope was speaking. I saw six long lines of people buying pizza at a pizza truck, while the Pope was speaking. A plump Franciscan slurped an ice cream cone, while the Pope was speaking. And lots of young people were stretched out on the ground for a nap, some young girls using their boyfriends' tummies as pillows, while the Pope was speaking.

After John Paul's greeting, a vague address in which he encouraged the youth to be "Children of the Beatitudes," the crowd dispersed, ate supper, and then spread out to the various attractions scheduled for the evening. I felt sad for these children of the children of Vatican II. This "fusion Catholicism" is practically all the post-conciliar Church offers them.

I wandered in and out of the evening attractions that were composed of rock 'n roll bands, pop dancing and an outdoor rock 'n' roll dance rendition of the Gospel that was simply pathetic. The story of the Gospel was recounted by a narrator, according to a modern version of the Bible. Then a live rock band played a rock-styled song that had something to do with the Gospel reading, I could only guess.

While they played, a group of dancers, young men and women, performed modern, interpretive dance. The young man depicting Our Lord did a dance where he embraced another man with an intensity and duration that gave me the willies, especially in light of recent ecclesiastical scandals. The girls were in tight outfits, dancing away, twirling around the young man who played Our Lord. There was no reverence whatsoever. Though it was not openly lewd, the performance was humid with sensuality.

The dance took place on the main outdoor stage at Exhibition Place, the same stage on which the opening Mass was held, and where the Pope had appeared hours earlier. Loudspeakers blared out the rock music. Huge screens, the same screens that had carried the Pope's image, projected the dancers to the crowd. But the crowd wasn't paying attention. It had dwindled to a small number who wandered around the area in front of the stage. One group of young people kicked a soccer ball back and forth.

It was dusk. I left before the dance-concert ended, and made my way to the train, only to find a group of young American girls, as they descended the steps to the subway, shouting at the top of their lungs Bruce Springsteen's "Born in the USA." I got on the subway and was confronted with another group of WYD Americans dancing a loud version of the hokey-pokey in the centre of the car, with the vehicle in transit.

Granted there are many worse things that young people could do at night than dance the hokey-pokey in a subway car, and I'm not really complaining about it. I'm just giving the reader a feel for the party spirit that grips a city when WYD rolls in. I do not have a problem with young people getting a little rowdy when they get together, provided no one pretends that this youthful enthusiasm, which is solely in the natural order, is some sort of "religious experience" or "encounter with Christ."[39]   Otherwise, we would have to regard the rock group Def Leppard as a "spirit-filled" music ministry.

---

[39]It is common at these pep-rally-type gatherings to falsely interpret the natural, rock 'n' roll enthusiasm of the crowd as a "movement of the Holy Spirit." Charismatics do this all the time. See Vennari, pp. 122-25.

Friday's Punk Rock Concert

At midday on Friday, I returned to Exhibition Place. There were no outside attractions going on. The crowd was small, scattered, milling around. Everything looked promising for me to look forward to a dull afternoon. But it was not to be.

I wandered into the huge "Vocations" room at Exhibition Place, wherein a large number of religious orders had set up booths in the hope of gaining recruits: Jesuits, Franciscans, Carmelites, the charismatic Companions of the Cross, Daughters of St. Paul and many others. As I wandered around, looking at the booths, I heard a hideous, loud noise coming from an adjacent room. I walked in and saw a full-blown rock concert in progress by a freaky punk rock band called dAYZ wAGE.

This performance did not even *feign* a Christian veneer. It was a no-holds-barred rock concert with crashing drums, thumping bass, screeching electric guitar, rap lyrics and a huge crowd of WYD youngsters in front of the stage, going wild.

The band members jumped and leapt and slid all over the stage. The long-haired singer announced the band was about to play a song called "Loud Enough to Rock the Crowd Enough." The crowd went wild in response. The band thundered out heavy-thumping tunes of its own, as well as popular songs from other bands. The youngsters especially went berserk when it launched into an energetic performance of "YMCA," by The Village People, a pop band from the late '70s that was brazenly homosexual.

Those in the crowd were rocking full-tilt, screaming, cheering, throwing water on each other. The hard-driving music had aroused the rock 'n' roll animal that lives inside these children of the children of Vatican II. It was no different — *no different* — from a riotous performance at nightclubs or rock concerts. Some young men ran around without shirts. Young girls danced furiously. The band was sweaty, pounding relentlessly.

Young men and young women were being "body-surfed" over the top of the crowd. I stood and watched bodies bobbing up and down over the heads of the dancers. They were surfed throughout the crowd and lowered down again. There were hands touching up and down the entire bodies of young women as they were body-surfed. They were having the time of their lives. Young men and women would jump up on stage, dance furiously with the band, and then leap back into the rocking crowd, where they would be body-surfed again.

The security guard tried to calm things down. Finally, a Toronto policeman grabbed centre stage and told the crowd, by then in a riotous rave, to settle down or he would close the concert. He laid down the law: no more body-surfing, no more throwing water, no more jumping up on stage.

I filmed a good twenty-five minutes of this pandemonium, which must be seen to be believed.[40] And yes, the dAYZ wAGE concert was a *scheduled World Youth Day event*. Nothing like fighting the culture of death with the culture of death!

WWJD?

World Youth Day is designed for "youth" aged 16-35. This means that Our Lord Himself, Who started His public ministry at age 30, would have qualified for World Youth Day. I cannot imagine Our Lord as one of the defrauded World Youth Day participants, grooving to an aging rocker singing songs by The Monkees that have been awkwardly converted to a "holy" purpose.

---

[40] I have assembled the photographs and video footage I shot while I was at WYD into a "multi-media" lecture. Anyone interested in organizing such a lecture, please contact me through *Catholic Family News* (MPO Box 743, Niagara Falls, NY 14302) or via e-mail at cfnjv@localnet.com. I ask no honorarium or stipend for these presentations. My purpose is to show Catholics what World Youth Day truly is. Parents especially need to know.

I did not see any WWJD (What Would Jesus Do?) T-shirts at Toronto. But I can guess one thing Jesus would *not* do. He would not degrade Himself by participating in the rock 'n' roll antics and pop gimmicks that constitute World Youth Day.

Chapter 11
The Stations of the Cross

Friday evening's "Way of the Cross," despite its many anomalies, was probably the best feature at World Youth Day. I was among the thousands of participants[41] who poured onto University Avenue in downtown Toronto to watch the WYD Stations on July 26th.

The ceremony lasted approximately three hours, and was a fusion of traditional Catholic practice with trendy, World Youth Day gimmicks. The more the gimmicks, the worse the production was. By contrast, the more the traditional aspects of the Stations were emphasized, the more edifying was the event.

Fourteen professional stages were set up on the avenue, one for each stop on the Way of the Cross. A young man and young woman alternately shouted a narration while a group of young amateur actors dramatized each Station. The actors spoke no words, but simply acted out the scene. They dressed in a mixture of period costume and modern clothes. The young actor depicting Our Lord, in my opinion, did a good job. He was solemn and noble from beginning to end. There was nothing clownish or sentimental about his portrayal.

A detailed commentary on these Stations is beyond our present scope. But I will recount some of the anomalies that spoiled what could have been an edifying production.

The two young narrators tended to shout the text of the Stations into the microphone, especially the young lady, who did it with a touch of hambone dramatics. Their constant shouting made me wonder what these narrators thought the purpose of the microphone was. A microphone connected to a state-of-the-art amplification system should

---

[41]Friday's Way of the Cross was free, not restricted just to those who had paid the World Youth Day admittance fee.

preclude the need to "belt it out."

The female narrator was a full-figured young lady in a tight dress. Many people I know were rightly scandalized by her appearance. The young man was casually dressed, with a light goatee and some sort of bun or ponytail. In fact, because I had been watching at a distance (without my glasses) one of the large screens on University Avenue, it wasn't until much later that I learned he was a man. For the better part of the evening, I thought he was a woman with a deep voice. The narrations were not exactly the high point of the ceremony.

The music accompanying the Stations was a mixture of traditional and pop-modern: everything from a beautiful organ rendition of Bach's "O Sacred Head Surrounded," to the "*Dies Irae*" sung to a throbbing rock 'n' roll beat, to hokey modern numbers with crooning singers who sounded as if they came straight from a TV evangelical program.

The Fourth Station

By chance, I ended up in front of the stage on which was depicted the Fourth Station: "Jesus Meets His Sorrowful Mother." The Station contained a flashback to the Annunciation, depicted by two young women in tight, black, pants outfits; then it returned to the Fourth Station, wherein Our Lady was dressed in a handsome period costume. Here the text of the Stations was supremely disappointing, and disturbed me more than anything else I saw that night.

At the flashback to the Annunciation, the narrator recounted the prophecy of the Angel regarding Our Lord: "... and the Lord God will give to Him the throne of His father David, and He will reign over the house of Jacob for ever, and His Kingdom will have no end." The text of the Stations, as narrated, continued as follows:

Mary heard these words. She often returned to them in the secret of her heart. When she met her Son on the Way of the Cross, perhaps these very words came to her mind with particular force. "He will reign, His Kingdom will have no end," the heavenly messenger had said. Now, as she watches her Son condemned to death, carrying the cross on which He must die, she might ask herself all too humanly, "So how can these words be fulfilled? In what way will He reign over the house of David? And how can it be that His Kingdom will have no end?" Humanly speaking, these are all reasonable questions. But Mary remembered that when she first heard the angel's message, she had replied, "Behold, I am the handmaid of the Lord. May it be done to me according to Your Word."

This text gives the false impression that the Passion and Crucifixion of Jesus was something that took Our Blessed Mother by surprise. It was as if, during the Way of the Cross, she was baffled as to how the prediction of "His Kingdom shall have no end" could square with the present reality of her Son on His way to His death, before He had "established" His Kingdom. In one sense, it puts the Queen of Prophets on the same level as the blind Pharisees who had no idea of what Our Lord was talking about when Jesus told them He was establishing His Kingdom, which is the New Covenant of His Holy Catholic Church, purchased by His Precious Blood. The text then merely claims that Mary made an act of faith, "Be it done to me according to Thy will," in order to accept something that she did not understand.

Yet nothing could be further from the truth. This, in fact, is a Protestant reading of the Blessed Mother that emphasizes her "humanity" over the unique exalted supernatural gifts she received as Mother of God. Perhaps the writer of the text did not intend it, but this depiction is actually a denigration of Our Lady, and the first who would say so is St. Alphonsus Liguori.

In *The Glories of Mary*, one of the greatest treatises on Our Blessed Mother, St. Alphonsus explains that Our Lady's understanding of the Old Testament prophecies surpassed even that of the prophets themselves. Citing saints and holy teachers, St. Alphonsus writes that the Blessed Virgin, even before she became Our Lord's Mother, "[knew] how much the Incarnate Word was to suffer for the salvation of men...." He explains that this profound understanding of Our Lord's suffering was one of the great sufferings of her life, for when she gave birth to Our Lord, when she nursed Him and warmed the baby Jesus in her arms, she was aware of the bitter death that awaited Him, and this sword continually pierced her Immaculate Heart. This is why St. Alphonsus teaches that Our Lady was the Queen of Martyrs, for her martyrdom was "longer and greater than that of all the martyrs."[42]

In short, the Passion and Crucifixion of Our Lord *did not* take Our Lady by surprise, as Friday's Way of the Cross text implied, nor was she clueless as to what Our Lord meant when He spoke of establishing His Kingdom.[43]

The Stations improved somewhat towards the end. It is nearly impossible for a Christian soul to witness a dramatization of the Crucifixion, to hear the thud of the hammers driving in the nails, to see Our Lord's body hoisted on the Cross, and His subtle writhing in agony, without being moved to prayer and adoration. At this moment of the production, the WYD organizers finally had the good sense to surround it with nothing but solemn-sounding music, even if this music did contain hymns from the ecumenical Taizé community, as well as the black spiritual, "Were You There When They Crucified My Lord?" (The "*Stabat Mater*," the traditional "At the Cross Her Station Keeping," was not played at all.) Nonetheless, I would have liked to have thought that this face-to-face encounter between 150,000 young people and a dramatized crucifixion and death of Our Lord actually did these youngsters some spiritual good.

---

[42]See St. Alphonsus de Liguori, *The Glories of Mary*, ed. Father Eugene Grimm, CSSR, 4th reprint rev. (Brooklyn, NY: Redemptorist Fathers, 1931; reprint ed., Brookings, SD: O. B. L. Victory Mission, n.d.), pp. 463-67. The 250th Anniversary edition, published in 2000 by Liguori Publications, Liguori, Missouri, has an introduction by Fr. Dennis Billy, CSSR, wherein he apologizes (pp. xviii-xix) for St. Alphonsus Liguori's lack of ecumenical sensitivity.

[43]Sadly, the text of the WYD Way of the Cross was written by Pope John Paul II, and was published in *L'Osservatore Romano* (May 10, 2000, p. 7). Yet it is not surprising that Pope John Paul, who was first and foremost a promoter of Vatican II, would take a post-conciliar ecumenical approach to Our Lady.

But the solemnity would not last long. The next day, it was back to the rock 'n' roll party atmosphere, this time at Downsview Park for the World Youth Day sleepover.

Chapter 12
Not-Very-Solemn Vespers

World Youth Day participants were urged to go to a Saturday night Vespers and "vigil" in an open field, to sleep overnight in the field, and then to attend the Papal Mass there on Sunday morning. This is precisely what I did. I arrived at Downsview Park (a former air base) in mid-afternoon on Saturday, shortly before the Pope's helicopter touched down for Vespers.

Loudspeakers and gigantic screens were placed throughout the huge field to broadcast the vigil to the crowd. The so-called "Vespers" was a far cry from anything that the Catholic Church has ever termed Vespers. It was a tedious three-hour ceremony full of Novus Ordo-styled pop-songs, complete with insipid lyrics and dead melodies. As I said earlier, I felt very sad for the youth at WYD, the children of the children of Vatican II. This "fusion Catholicism" is practically all the Conciliar Church offers them.

At one point in this vigil, the World Youth Day choir sang beautifully the *"Adoremus Te,"* but this was ruined by a jazz saxophone solo that played overtop the choir's voice. The jazz solo wove in and out of the beautiful Latin hymn, so it sounded as if two radios were simultaneously playing two different stations. And this was the *most* traditional part of what was misnamed "Vespers."

There was also an upbeat version of Psalm 149, performed by a smiling baritone, which also featured a troupe of liturgical dancers, young men and women, performing interpretive dance on the massive stage. The whole dance was contrived and pathetic. (Liturgical dancers always bear the most serious expressions on their faces, as if they are actually doing something worthwhile.) Pope John Paul II presided over the entire ceremony, which also included countless cheers from the crowd at various points.

I wandered around the huge field and came upon a patch of land where many makeshift confessionals were set up. I saw practically no one going to confession. I heard that earlier in the week, the "confession garden" at World Youth Day had had many penitents. But on Saturday night, the confessionals were empty.

They were set up with purple partitions and folding chairs. All the confessions were face-to-face. I did not see one person kneeling for the sacrament. All was outdoors, so a good lip-reader could pick up everything that was said. The priests, for the most part, were dressed in some sort of priestly garb. I did not see any priests in shorts hearing confessions, as has happened at previous World Youth Days, particularly in Denver, in 1993.

Time to Boogie!

The Pope was spirited away in his helicopter at about 10:30 p.m., and then the party began.

Acres and acres of young people, girls and boys, sat sprawled on their blankets and sleeping bags, and inside makeshift tents. They were dressed no differently from youngsters on the town during spring break in Daytona Beach: casual slovenliness, shorts, short-shorts, T-shirts and highly immodest tops on the girls. Many of the young ladies were literally "poured into" their tight, scanty outfits in a fashion that resembled Britney Spears and other such pop tarts. Mind you, this is how they would be dressed for the Papal Mass the next morning.

Young people were chatting and laughing with each other, as is to be expected at such a gathering. Here and there, couples were hugging and smooching. Acoustic guitars were being strummed throughout the field. I came upon one group that was standing in a circle around a guitarist. They clapped and danced as they sang over and over "Sweet Home Alabama" by Lynyrd Skynyrd. The party atmosphere prevailed. I saw no one at prayer.

In numerous places, I saw enormous crowds of youngsters doing a line dance to the beat of heavy-jungle rhythms. These line dances went on for hours, literally. And the crowd of dancers seemed to grow continually.

I also came upon a group doing the "front-to-front-to-front" dance. Here's how it works. The crowd forms two circles, one inside the next, and each circle turns in an opposite direction. At one point, a boy and girl stop in front of each other, about 10 inches apart, and shake their front sections at each other while singing, "Front-to-front-to-front, my baby." Then they turn and shake their backsides to one another as they sing, "Back-to-back-to-back, my baby." Then they stand beside each other and sing as they shake, "Side-to-side-to-side, my baby — this is how we do it!"

I meandered away and then passed by this "front-to-front" crowd forty-five minutes later. They were still at it, but the number of dancers had increased. A priest walked by, looked at their dancing, and kept walking. It seems that most of the clergy at this festival left these young people to themselves and their pop culture, and gave the youngsters no firm Catholic direction.

Chapter 13
World Youth Day vs.
Catholic Teaching on Modesty

An example of the guidance that youngsters should have received at World Youth Day from the Pope, bishops and priests can be found in the Catholic teaching on modesty — teaching that has all but disappeared since the "new springtime" of Vatican II.

We recounted earlier the Catholic teaching on proper attire at Mass, which forbids slovenly and immodest dress in church and at religious functions. Here we will discuss the traditional Papal teaching on Catholic modesty itself,[44] which is to be observed not only in church, but also at all times. The teaching is clear: immodesty is a grave matter that offends God. It leads to impure thoughts and actions that send souls to hell.

In his encyclical *Sacra Propediem* (1921), Pope Benedict XV condemns immodesty in strong terms:

> ... one cannot sufficiently deplore the blindness of so many women of every age and condition; made foolish by desire to please, they do not see to what a degree the indecency of their clothing shocks every honest man, and offends God. Most of them would formerly have blushed for those toilettes as for a grave fault against Christian modesty; now it does not suffice for them to exhibit themselves on the pub-

---

[44]Basic Catholic standards for modesty can be found in the following directive issued in 1928 by the Cardinal-Vicar of Pope Pius XI: "... a dress cannot be called decent which is cut deeper than two fingers breadth under the pit of the throat, which does not cover the arms at least to the elbows, and scarcely reaches a bit beyond the knees. Furthermore, dresses of transparent material are improper...." Rufino J. Cardinal Santos, Archbishop of Manila, quotes these standards as "The Church's stand concerning modesty in dress" in his Pastoral Letter of December 6, 1959. Attributing them to Pius XI himself, he says they were issued on September 24, 1928. See "Rome's Decrees on Modesty in Dress ...," national-coalition.org (click on the link to "Modesty").

lic thoroughfares; they do not fear to cross the threshold of the churches, to assist at the Holy Sacrifice of the Mass, and even to bear the seducing food of shameful passions to the Eucharistic Table where one receives the Heavenly Author of purity.[45]

Likewise, on January 12, 1930, Pope Pius XI directed the Sacred Congregation of the Council to issue a strongly-worded "Letter on Christian Modesty" to the whole world. The letter, in part, reads:

... Our Most Holy Father Pope Pius has never ceased to in-culcate, both verbally and by his writings, the words of St. Paul (1 Tim. 9:9-10), namely, *"Women ... adorning them-selves with modesty and sobriety ... and professing godliness with good works."* ... In order to facilitate the desired effect, this Sacred Congregation, by the mandate of the Most Holy Fa-ther, has decreed as follows:
    1. The parish priest, and especially the preacher, when occasion arises, should, according to the words of the Apos-tle Paul (2 Tim. 4:2), insist, argue, exhort and command that feminine garb be based on modesty, and womanly orna-ment be a defense of virtue. Let them likewise admonish parents to cause their daughters to cease wearing indeco-rous dress.
    2. Parents, conscious of their grave obligations toward the education, especially religious and moral, of their off-spring, should see to it that their daughters are solidly in-structed, from earliest childhood, in Christian doctrine; and they themselves should assiduously inculcate in their souls, by word and example, love for the virtues of modesty and chastity; and since their family should follow the example of the Holy Family, they must rule in such a manner that all its members, reared within the walls of the home, should find reason and incentive to love and preserve modesty.[46]

Keep in mind that the type of immodesty that these Popes warned against was relatively tame compared to to-

---

[45]On the Third Order of St. Francis *Sacra Propediem*, January 6, 1921, no. 19.
[46]"Rome's Decrees on Modesty."

day's fashions. Today, being scantily clad is the norm, even in church.

In 1940, Pope Pius XII, addressing a group of Catholic Action girls, stated,

> Many women ... give in to the tyranny of fashion, be it even immodest, in such a way as to appear not even to suspect that it is unbecoming. They have lost the very concept of danger: they have lost the instinct of modesty.[47]

Pope Pius XII, basing himself on St. Thomas Aquinas, reiterated the inescapable duty of being modest in another address:

> ... the good of our soul must take precedence over that of our body, and to the good of our body we must prefer the good of the soul of our neighbour.... [If] a certain form of dress ... becomes a grave and proximate danger for the soul, ... you must reject it.

Pius XII continued,

> O Christian mothers, if you only know what a future of worries and dangers, ... of hardly suppressed shame you lay up for your sons and your daughters by imprudently accustoming them to live barely attired, making them lose the natural sense of modesty, you yourselves would blush, and take fright at the shame you inflict upon yourselves, the harm which you occasion to your children, entrusted to you by heaven to be brought up in a Christian manner.[48]

Yet none of these solid Papal teachings were reiterated at World Youth Day. Tragically still, the immodesty and irreverence of these misguided young people, and the negligence of those in Church authority, who should correct

---

[47] Allocution to the girls of Catholic Action, October 6, 1940. Cited in The Monks of Solesmes, eds., *The Woman in the Modern World* (Boston: St. Paul Editions, 1959), p. 51.

[48] Allocution to the girls of Catholic Action, May 22, 1941: ibid., pp. 59-60.

them,[49] was actually predicted four centuries ago by Our Lady of Good Success in Quito, Ecuador. It is a prediction that also includes a warning of dire punishments for these sins.

In the 1600s, Our Lady of Good Success told Mother Mariana de Jesus that in the twentieth century, "impurity ... will permeate the atmosphere.... Like a filthy ocean it will run through the streets," so that "there would be almost no virgin souls." Also, "Innocence will almost no longer be found in children, *nor modesty in women.* In this supreme moment of need of the Church, *those who should speak will fall silent.*" Further, "The vices of impurity, blasphemy and sacrilege will dominate in this time...." In one of these apparitions, Mother Mariana saw swords above the head of Christ that read, "I shall punish heresy, blasphemy and impurity."[50]

Thus, the sacrilege, immodesty and heresy that are so much a part of the post-Vatican II Church — and of World Youth Day — will, sadly, not invoke God's grace, but incur His wrath. Yet today's Church leaders seem too blind to see it, and continually speak of World Youth Day as a "sign of hope" for the Church of the Third Millennium.

---

[49]Church leaders have a duty to correct all immodesty, not just immodesty in young people. And though the focus is often on women's modesty, men have a duty to be modest as well. Through the Letter of the Sacred Congregation of the Council to the Bishops of the world, August 15, 1954, Pius XII exhorted bishops on their duty to bring about the reform of morals: "'You above all, whom the Holy Spirit hath placed you Bishops, to rule the Church of God' (Acts 20:28), you, Bishops, must give careful consideration to this state of affairs, strive by every attention and take every initiative to protect modesty, and to restore Christian morals.... Hence it is absolutely essential to warn and exhort every class of society and especially youth, to get rid of these great dangers which are indubitably contrary to Christian and civic virtue, and which lay them open to the greatest perils.... The Holy Father is very anxious ... that the Bishops especially leave nothing undone to remedy this evil; that under their ... leadership the rest of the clergy ... labor with energy and constancy to attain success prudently in this matter; that fathers and mothers ..., first by their example and then also by appropriate exhortations, inspired with the austere fortitude of genuine Christians, remove their children from these dangers and be not content until they see in their faces the lustrous charm of purity." Cited in Monks of Solesmes, pp. 231-33, and at olfatima.com/modesty.html.

[50]Marian Therese Horvat, *Our Lady of Good Success: Prophecies for Our Times* (Los Angeles: Tradition in Action, 1999), pp. 52, 43, 45, 25. (Emphases added.)

Chapter 14
The World Youth Day Sleepover

Back at Downsview Park, at the WYD sleepover, the hour was growing late. I trudged along with travel-pack and sleeping bag strapped on my back, and purposely walked myself to exhaustion. I figured it was the only way I would be able to sleep. Finally, at about 12:20 a.m., I found a place to bed down. Huge, bright lights glowed on the massive field. The noise from the partying crowd was incessant. I lay down on my bag at 12:25 a.m., hoping to sleep.

Suddenly, at 12:30 a.m., a screeching, Jimi Hendrix-styled electric guitar blasted from every loudspeaker on the field. It was deafening. The "music" intensified in volume. Synthesizers, electric bass and drums kicked in. Those around me rose from their sleeping bags, blinking in bewilderment. One young girl screamed, "QUIIIIIIEEEET!!!" at the offending loudspeakers. Another yelled in desperation, "SHUT UUUUUUUUP!"

This was followed by wailing vocals from the loud-speakers. Then a young woman's voice over the PA shouted the explanation of what was happening: They were starting a rock concert — at 12:30 a.m.!

The enthusiastic young announcerette exclaimed, as if it should have made us happy, that this was the beginning of a "vocations concert" being broadcast live to millions of young people in Asia. Some people up front applauded, but those who wanted to sleep were furious. A voice from behind me screamed at the announcer, "*You're going to go to hell for this!*"

To my knowledge, this concert was unannounced. It took us by surprise, and lasted over two hours. It started with young people boasting of how they were "salt" and "light," followed by a rock 'n' roll celebration of the vocation of marriage. The violence with which this post-midnight "concert" burst upon us, coupled with the blazing lights on the field, reminded me of stories of prisoners in Communist countries who were forced to work all day, then brutally awakened in the middle of the night by loud noise and bright lights.

I grabbed my camera and made my way down towards the massive stage, which was about a quarter-mile away. I was staggering with disbelief. I chanced upon a priest who stood in a walking path holding his breviary.

"Father," I asked, "do you have any idea why they are holding a rock concert *in the middle of the night?*"

The priest answered, "I haven't got a clue."

I responded, "Father, this is dementia." He nodded and walked away, obviously as baffled as I.

Thousands of youngsters were still in their sleeping bags. Many, to my amazement, continued their sleep. Meanwhile, up on stage, young couples were screaming, "Thank you, Lord, for the Sacrament of Marriage!" This went on for some time, followed by a celebration of the vocation of "Deacon." I think they meant "permanent lay-deacon," but I cannot be certain, because I had bedded down again in a vain attempt to sleep.

Diverse groups made slick "vocation" pitches, such as Madonna House, Focolare, the Franciscan Friars of the Renewal, and various others. This was followed by a "celebration" of religious life. Nuns were brought on stage so that millions of youth in Asia could see the Sisters celebrating life under bright stage lights in the middle of the night. I lay there, reciting my Rosary. Sleep was impossible.

As the night wore on, the music became a bit more subdued, but it still blared from every loudspeaker on the field. Then at 2:30 a.m., the announcer said that it was time to "celebrate" the vocation of the priesthood. Priests were about to come on stage, and they would bring the Blessed Sacrament with them.

After two hours of noisy pop music, those on stage suddenly began to sing traditional Latin hymns. I gather, though I was semi-delirious by now, that they had some form of Benediction of the Blessed Sacrament — at 2:30 a.m.!

Finally, at 10 minutes to 3 a.m., the announcer said, "Good night!" and the loudspeakers fell silent.

But sleep was still impossible. Every nerve in my body was rattled and enraged. Lying on the ground, with an umbrella pitched next to me to block the blaring lights, I finally fell asleep at a quarter to 4 a.m.

TWO HOURS LATER, we were awakened again by voices over the loudspeaker. This time, a woman's voice gave instructions on how to work the breakfast meal tickets. I looked at my watch. I had had only two hours' sleep. Five minutes later came a cloudburst of sudden, drenching rain. I quickly sat up under my umbrella in an unsuccessful attempt to shield myself from the storm.

By 6:00 a.m., I was soaked, shivering and in a foul temper. I walked about a mile to get coffee, and then left the field for over ninety minutes.[51] When I returned to the field around 8:30, another cloudburst hit, a veritable deluge. Those in the crowd huddled under umbrellas. Many abandoned their makeshift tents because the field now streamed with mud.

Crossing the Threshold of Heathenism

The Papal Mass was free of charge, so thousands more who had not participated in World Youth Day poured onto the field. I stood in front of a large screen that beamed a close-up of the Pope's helicopter gliding in. The choir sang

---

[51]Being a son of Adam, I had to tend to the "necessities of nature" as St. Benedict put it. I refused to use the reeking battery of port-a-potties in the field that had been cooking in the sun all day previously. In fact, as I walked by this standing army of stalls on Sunday morning, a teenaged girl came racing full-speed out of one of them, screaming to her friend, "Oohh, it's soooooo disgustinnnnnnnng!" I walked almost a mile to the subway restroom only to find a line of men *and* a line of women going into the men's room. I left, hopped on the subway and finally found a doughnut shop a couple of stops down. The whole adventure took more than ninety minutes. These are some of the "joys" of World Youth Day.

some good pieces, including Handel's "Hallelujah Chorus," as the Pope's chopper touched down. The rain intensified.

I stood there deciding whether to stay or leave. I knew we were in for "creative liturgy," but did not know what form it would take. Further, I had had barely two hours' sleep. My resistance was down. I had no idea if or when the rain would stop. And even if it stopped, the ground was soaked. I would have had to stand for another three hours, rain or shine.

My mind went back to a story told to me by *Catholic Family News* writer Ed Faust. When Pope John Paul II visited Newark, New Jersey, some years ago, a parish priest from South Jersey went to the sports arena to attend the Pope's outdoor Mass. He considered it the greatest event of his life. Everyone coming to the stadium had their umbrellas confiscated upon entering the arena, for security purposes. It rained all through the Mass, but the priest stood in the downpour anyway, so happy to be there. The same priest died two months later from pneumonia contracted from standing in the storm at the stadium.[52]

"This sure isn't worth dying for," I thought to myself.

Suddenly I heard loud, ungodly screams and shrieks coming from the loudspeakers, accompanied by native drumming. Immediately after the Pope's arrival-music (the "Hallelujah Chorus") had finished, Native American Indians were given the platform to do a no-holds-barred native ceremony. It had the most ungodly shrieks I had ever heard. Dancing, drumming, wailing and full-tilt pagan superstition captured the stage.

---

[52]According to medical staff at Downsview, "thousands" of pilgrims suffered dehydration due to Saturday's heat. Furthermore, "As the rain beat down during the papal mass ..., patients wrapped in thermal blankets [because now they suffered from hypothermia due to the rain and a cold night] and barely able to stand filed into WYD field hospitals. By 8 a.m., just 24 hours into the Catholic celebration, 2,500 people had been treated. Forty-five people were taken to hospital." One doctor said staff "saw twice as many people as we had anticipated.... We knew there would be a big influx of people before the mass. Everyone was wet and exhausted." See Chris Doucette, "Too Pooped to Pray," *The Toronto Sun*, July 29, 2002, p. 4; Prithi Yelaja, "Nasty Weather Keeps Medics Hopping," *Toronto Star*, July 29, 2002, p. B4.

At this point, something inside me snapped. I turned and headed for the exit. This pagan ceremony was the final straw. In short, I walked out on the Papal Mass.

As I trudged the mile or so to the exit, I watched the confusion and consternation on people's faces as they viewed the heathen ritual. Predictably, some young people danced around in joyful mockery of an Indian dance. How xenophobic! One older woman caught my eye as I was leaving. I said to her, "I bet you thought you were attending something Catholic." She rolled her eyes and shrugged.

The downpour continued. There was a stream of people walking out of the field. The native ceremony was still screeching and drumming and wailing behind me. Two young girls asked a bunch of us, "Why are you leaving?" Most responded by pointing up to the cloudburst, but I said to them, "Because this is not Catholic." The two girls looked at me with shocked eyes, spun around, and quick-stepped towards the stage. Obviously, I was an extremist to be avoided at all cost.

Our Lady of Fatima Not Invited

But if Native Indians with their superstitious dance were invited to World Youth Day, there was one person who was barely invited, and that was the Blessed Mother. Her image was nowhere to be found at any of the functions over which the Pope presided. He mentioned her briefly in his Sunday homily, but did not exhort the youth to pray to her, did not exhort them to consecrate their lives and their chastity to her. And in the fight to preserve purity and modesty, who needs Our Blessed Mother more than the world's youth? We all need her.

There was also no mention of Our Lady of Fatima, who told us, "God wants to establish in the world devotion to my Immaculate Heart."[53] At Toronto, John Paul II did not

---

[53] After the three children of Fatima were shown a terrifying vision of hell and

remind the world's youth of what God wants in this regard. There was no public recitation of the Rosary when the massive crowds were together. This was a missed opportunity on a grand scale, as it would have been easy for the Pope, or someone delegated by him, to lead the Rosary through the state-of-the-art PA system set up for World Youth Day events. Individual groups, here and there, recited the Rosary on their own. I did not see recitation of the Rosary listed on any of the lists of scheduled WYD activities.

Sadly, Pope John Paul II, at World Youth Day in Toronto, did nothing to lead young people to the Holy Rosary, which Our Lady of Fatima asked us to recite every day. And even though the Pope's next stop was the canonization of Juan Diego in Mexico, there was no mention of Our Lady of Guadalupe, who came to free Native Americans from their paganism.[54]

No, Our Lady was barely invited to World Youth Day. For the most part, she was replaced by the Youth of the World boasting that *they* are the light of the world, and *they* are the salt of the earth. These "youth" at World Youth Day, were often treated as if they had already successfully achieved this commission to be salt and light, even though they had not been asked to give up their rock 'n' roll culture, their immodesty or their adolescent mannerisms. Pumped up with unmerited self-esteem, the "youth" left World Youth

the tortured souls of human beings in the conflagration, Our Lady told them, "You have seen hell where the souls of poor sinners go. To save them, God wishes to establish in the world devotion to my Immaculate Heart. If what I say to you is done, many souls will be saved...." See Sister Lucia, p. 167.

[54]The Catholic website, Seattlecatholic.com, posted some of my WYD reports in late July 2002. After they were posted, a learned Franciscan wrote me the following regarding John Paul II's inculturation ceremonies: "It seems the Pope is intentionally making it a point of order that in every trip he includes some sort of native pagan ritual.... I have a B.A. in Anthropology from the University of Florida, Gainesville, USA, and made a particular study of meso-American and south-American Indian history and culture, which is entirely demonic and satanic in every aspect of its organized religious practices. I do not believe anyone not ignorant of indigenous American culture could conclude otherwise, certainly not someone who is supposed to be well informed, as the Pope. For the Vicar of Christ to act thus so publicly will have the invariable consequence of raising an entire generation of Catholic youth who will mix all kinds of false worship together with Catholic worship, while believing they are doing nothing evil."

Day believing that *they* are now "going to make a difference." In this respect, World Youth Day was no different from Woodstock.

Remember Fatima

I would never allow my own children to attend World Youth Day. It does not transmit the Catholic Faith, but delivers a counterfeit, emotional religion. It is permeated by the rock 'n' roll culture. It corrupts the youth.

I will close this chapter by calling to mind two warnings from Fatima.

Before her death in 1920, Bl. Jacinta warned:

> Certain fashions are going to be introduced which will offend Our Lord very much. The Church has no fashions. Our Lord is always the same.[55]

These "certain fashions" that "offend Our Lord very much" were in full romp at World Youth Day. I wonder what Jacinta would have had to say about all these scantily clad ladies boasting that *they* are the light of the world. And what would she have said of our high-level churchmen who do nothing — *nothing* — to correct the WYD immodesty?

The Fatima Message also admonished us, "Pray a great deal for the Holy Father!"[56] Let us do so with zeal.

---

[55]Father de Marchi, ibid.
[56]Jesus Himself said this to Sr. Lucy in 1936 (Frère Michel de la Sainte Trinité, p. 158), reinforcing the message given to the three children in Fatima. Cf. Sister Lucia, pp. 112-13.

Chapter 15
World Youth Day:
Showcase of Liturgical Abuse

Father Joseph de Sainte-Marie, OCD, was an outstanding theologian who taught in Rome in the 1970s and '80s. He was an expert on Fatima and a loyal son of Pope John Paul II. He worked closely with John Paul, and is said to have helped compose the formula that the Pope used for the Consecration of the World to the Immaculate Heart of Mary in 1982.[57]

Yet even Fr. Joseph de Sainte-Marie uttered, in 1977, the following warning about those who now occupy the highest levels of the Church:

> In our day, and it is one of the most obvious signs of the extraordinarily abnormal character of the current state of the Church, it is very often the case that acts of the Holy See demand of us prudence and discernment.[58]

Father Joseph de Sainte-Marie thus tells us, in a respectful, gentlemanly manner, that our Holy Church is now passing through an extraordinary period in history. He uses the word "abnormal."

Yet in the face of the "extraordinarily abnormal character of the current state of the Church," he does not advise us, "Well, if the Pope changes the traditional teachings or practices of the Church, then you just bow down your head and follow blindly." No. Aligning himself with the traditional teaching of the popes and saints (for example, that of

---

[57]For an example of Father Joseph de Sainte-Marie's work on Fatima, see his article, "The Church's Duty in the Face of the Fatima Message," *Catholic Family News*, July 2000, p. 13.

[58]Cited in A. S. Fraser, "The New Catechism," *Apropos* (Portree, Isle of Skye, Scotland), no. 16 (1994), p. 5.

Pope Innocent III and St. Robert Bellarmine), Fr. Joseph de Sainte-Marie tells us that we have to be careful these days; we have to exercise "prudence and discernment" when it comes to the actions of the Holy See itself — that is, even when it comes to papal actions. Notice too, he tells us it is "*very often the case*" that we have to exercise this caution.

There is no doubt that the rock 'n' roll riot known as World Youth Day is one of the "actions of the Holy See" concerning which we should exercise "prudence and discernment." It is demonstrable that World Youth Day is a revolution against the papal teachings of the centuries, especially regarding liturgy, reverence, modesty, sacred music and many other fundamental Catholic principles.

As mentioned in the previous chapter, I walked out on the Sunday Mass during the opening pagan ceremony of screaming Native American Indians. The Third Commandment obliges us, "Remember thou keep holy the Lord's Day," but there is nothing holy about opening a Sunday Mass with a no-holds-barred pagan ritual. Neither can the presence of the satanic here be ruled out. The early Catholic missionaries, especially the Jesuits, consistently identified these Native religious ceremonies with superstition and sorcery.[59]

This pagan rite fused to the Papal Mass is an example of the post-conciliar novelty called "inculturation." We will now focus on the details of the Sunday Papal Mass that immediately followed the opening "inculturated" ceremony.

Liturgical Abuses at Papal Mass

In a way, I was sorry to leave the Sunday Mass, as I

---

[59]See *The Jesuit Relations and Allied Documents*, posted at puffin.creighton.edu/jesuit/relations/. Sister Eva Solomon, a post-conciliar "Native American Catholic" who promotes inculturation, denounces the early Catholic missionaries as well as traditional, pre-Vatican II teaching. "Before Vatican II," says. Solomon, "our traditions were denounced as pagan. In order to be Christians, we had to set aside all our traditions, all the teachings of our elders". See Paula Elizabeth Holmes, "We are Native Catholics," *Studies in Religion* (Waterloo, ON) 28, no. 2 (1999): 153.

had wanted to see first-hand what goes on in the crowd. (I have already mentioned that a World Youth Day volunteer later told me he had to stop a soccer game that was going on in the middle of the Pope's three-hour Sunday Mass. Also, a young woman subsequently told me of her girlfriend who went to WYD and who, during the Pope's Sunday Mass, fell asleep in the arms of a boy she had just met.)

I had also wanted to see if conditions had improved since the 1993 World Youth Day in Denver, especially in regard to Communion time. Gerry Matatics, the Catholic apologist and convert from Protestantism, attended the 1993 WYD, and was eyewitness to the Eucharistic sacrileges in full romp at the Papal Mass. Mr. Matatics explains:

> We had camped out the night before on the ground to be sure that we would have a place for the papal Mass. We all had grimy faces and 'sleeping-bag' hair. The assisting priests who were to distribute Holy Communion, implementing inculturation, accommodated themselves to the heat and humidity by wearing t-shirts, shorts, flip-flops and baseball caps along with their stoles. Priests similarly attired were listening to confessions beforehand.
>
> The crowd had been roped off into quadrants, about a hundred of us in each one. When the time came for reception of Holy Communion I knelt at the front of my little quadrant in an attempt to receive the Sacred Host on my knees. Hosts were being distributed from big, shallow bowls that could have been used for punch or potato chips. People were reaching over each other's shoulders to grab the consecrated Hosts from the priests. I saw Hosts falling into the mud, where they were being trampled on. I reached down and rescued as many as I could and consumed them.
>
> I had been going to the Tridentine Mass since the fall of 1992 and [to] the Novus Ordo on weekdays. At that moment I realized that if this kind of sacrilege could occur at a *papal Mass* because of the Novus Ordo rubrics, I could no longer be a party to the new liturgy. It was the last Novus

Ordo Mass I ever attended.[60]

Likewise, a friend wrote to me after I returned from Toronto's World Youth Day, saying, "... an elderly friend who once attended one of these events said that after the thing was over, she walked the grounds picking up hosts that people had discarded."

I was not present to observe whether these sacrileges occurred at the 2002 World Youth Day, but later viewed a video of the Pope's Sunday Mass from a broadcast of Canada's Vision Television.

Tragically, the Papal Sunday Mass at World Youth Day implicitly placed an "imprimatur" on some of the worst abuses of the post-conciliar period, including liturgical dance, lay lectors, lay Eucharistic ministers, pop music at Church functions, slovenly and immodest dress during Mass, pagan rituals attached to the Mass, and Eucharistic sacrileges. Vision Television broadcast close-ups of Pope John Paul II continually administering Communion in the hand at his Mass.

The following was showcased at the Sunday Papal Mass at World Youth Day 2002:

- The Mass opened with a pagan Native American ritual, already discussed.
- A rock 'n' roll band on the "altar" with the Pope, including electric guitars and full drum set. This did not produce a reverential Catholic atmosphere, but rather, advanced that false notion that Mass should be a jolly, fun time. The WYD choir and participants added to the worldly atmosphere by singing, smiling and cutesy raised-arm swaying to upbeat rock 'n' pop "hymns."
- When the Pope opened the Mass with the words, "In the name of the Father, and of the Son, ...," the crowd responded "YAAAHY!" as they do at rock concerts when the band starts one of their favourite tunes, thus trampling

---

[60]Christopher Ferrara and Tom Woods, *The Great Façade* (Wyoming: Remnant Press, 2002), pp. 388-89.

on the notion of reverence that should surround the Holy
Sacrifice of the Mass.

- The *Gloria* was put to an insipid melody accompanied by
  tinkling electric piano.
- Men in albs incensed the stage while pop music played.
- Altar girls.
- An all-girl liturgical dance ceremony after the First Reading. (Liturgical dance was also performed at the Pope's
  Saturday evening "Vespers" service.)
- Before and after the Gospel, the band broke into an upbeat, handclapping, footstompin' "Alle-Alle-Luia" song
  sung by two young girls and a young man with an ear-
  ring.
- The Pope's homily during Mass, as with all his speeches,
  was constantly interrupted by applause. This created the
  atmosphere of a political rally rather than a holy sermon.
- Throughout the homily and even during Mass, the youngsters would chant his name over and over, especially to
  the pep-rally beat, "John Paul II, we love you." The Pope
  did nothing to stop the constant cheering and celebration
  of his name.[61]
- After the homily, the Pope led the young people in a Renewal of the Baptismal Promises. He led the prayer while
  a tinkling piano played lounge-style "mood music" in the
  background. The youngsters responded with an upbeat,
  pop music-styled "*Credo, credo*. Amen. Alleluia." This
  constant infusion of hokey gimmicks robbed the ceremony
  of all sense of the sacred. Further, the renewal of the baptismal vows was according to a new formula that contained no mention of renouncing the devil and his works.
- The "Prayers of the Faithful" seemed to go on endlessly.
  Six sets of young people from six different countries,
  speaking six different languages, led the "Let us pray to

---

[61]Contrast this with Pope St. Pius X, the greatest Pope of the twentieth century, who forbade crowds to applaud him. "It is not fitting," also said the humble Pius X, "that the servant should be applauded in His Master's house." See
F. A. Forbes, *Pope St. Pius X* (n.p.: 1918; reprint ed., Rockford, IL: Tan Books,
1987), p. 69.

the Lord" prayers.

- During the Offertory, twelve young people presented the gifts. Everything about this liturgy gave the impression that all was done in order to make the ceremony as drawn-out as possible.

- The Our Father was sung in the traditional Gregorian manner. Many of the bishops on stage with the Pope, however, chanted this prayer with arms raised in Charismatic fashion.

- There was, once again, lounge-style "mood music" of a tinkling piano providing background music for the "Kiss of Peace."

- As mentioned, the youngsters who had spent the night in the field were dressed in a manner that ranged from slovenly to immodest. Yet this is how they attended the Papal Mass and how they received Communion.

- There were innumerable lay Eucharistic ministers in slovenly dress administering Hosts to the youngsters. Countless people received Communion in the hand.

- Vision Television broadcast a total of thirty-five people receiving Communion from the Pope; twenty-five of these communicants received Communion in the hand.

- A nun in a gray habit, plucking an acoustic guitar, sang a folk-styled "Communion song," after which there was audience applause.

A word must be said about the approximately four hundred bishops who were on stage with the Pope for the Sunday Mass. The bishops sat together in one clump, all dressed in custom-made "World Youth Day" vestments. These vestments looked as if they were designed by an individual who hated the Catholic Church and was determined to make the bishops look as ridiculous as possible. They were white and streaked with World Youth Day colours — red, yellow and blue — in broad strokes. They looked as if they were the end-result of a pre-school finger-painting class. Making matters worse, some of the bishops, with arms uplifted, sheepishly swayed along with the youth during the upbeat songs at the Papal Mass.

A Scandal to the Youth

I would never allow my children to attend World Youth Day. Why would a Catholic parent want his son or daughter to attend an event that makes the Barque of Peter look like a Civilization-of-Love Boat? Nor would I allow my children to attend the World Youth Day Papal Mass. It is a source of scandal because of what young people are implicitly taught at this Papal Mass.

They are taught that during Mass, there is nothing wrong with the novelty of liturgical dancing.

They are taught that there is no problem with lay lectors, despite the fact that lay lectors are an import from Protestantism.

They are taught that there is nothing wrong with worldly pop and rock 'n' roll music at Mass, despite the fact that all pre-Vatican II popes taught that no profane music is allowed in church or during sacred liturgy. Pope St. Pius X said in his 1903 *Motu Proprio* on Sacred Music:

> ... *the more closely a composition for church approaches in its movement, inspiration, and savour the Gregorian form, the more sacred and liturgical it becomes; and the more out of harmony it is with that supreme model, the less worthy it is of the temple....*
>
> ... since modern music has risen mainly to serve profane uses, ... the musical compositions of modern style which are admitted in the Church may contain nothing profane ... and be not fashioned even in their external forms after the manner of profane pieces.[62]

Furthermore, as Cardinal Sarto, Pope St. Pius had banned string orchestras, drums, trumpets, tambourines and

---

[62]Pope St. Pius X, *Motu Proprio* on Sacred Music *Inter Sollicitudines*, November 22, 1903, nos. 3, 5. Of course, in a blending of the "old and the new," there were also some traditional hymns at the WYD Sunday Mass.

whistles. Only the organ could be used in church; and "[t]he words of the Mass were to be sung to the Gregorian chant with solemnity and dignity, and by men and boys alone."[63]

These teachings on sacred music, which reflect the consistent teachings of the popes, were trampled underfoot at World Youth Day's Sunday Mass.

The young people are taught at World Youth Day that there is nothing wrong with immodest dress, or slovenly and immodest dress during Mass — again, in defiance of traditional papal teaching on the subject.

They are taught that there is nothing wrong with pagan and superstitious religious ritual surrounding Mass.

They are taught that there is nothing wrong with lay Eucharistic ministers. And even in the case of the huge crowd at World Youth Day, there is *still* no reason for lay ministers of the Eucharist. Most of the youth groups that comprised WYD attendees came with their own chaplain, so the needs of the laity could have been taken care of without lay "ministers." Further, there were about four hundred bishops on stage with the Pope — but they did not even attempt to administer Holy Communion to the laity. And as for any concern that the Sunday liturgy would have been "unduly prolonged," many of the time-consuming, hokey gimmicks that were part of the Sunday Mass, such as the all-girl liturgical-dance routine, could have been cut to allow for the extra time needed to administer Communion in a reverent manner to the massive crowd.

Lastly, at World Youth Day, our children and our young people are taught that there is nothing wrong with the sacrilege of Communion in the hand.[64]

Thus, World Youth Day delivers a counterfeit, emotional, pep-rally religion. Its ceremonies contain countless novelties, practices and sacrileges that have been condemned

---

[63]Forbes, p. 44.

[64]St. Thomas Aquinas wrote that only the consecrated hands of the priest should touch the consecrated Sacred Host. See Vennari, "The Truth About Communion in the Hand." Also see Francis Alban, *Fatima Priest* (Pound Ridge, NY: Good Counsel Publications, 1997), app. V.

by the constant teaching and practice of the popes throughout the centuries. WYD is a scandal to our young people. It *corrupts* the youth.

Which John Paul II Do You Follow?

There are those who claim that we should have followed whatever Pope John Paul II said and did. Even if this were true, the question must be asked: Which John Paul should one have followed? This is a valid question especially in regard to Communion in the hand and lay Eucharistic ministers. For it is here that the later John Paul II contradicted the earlier John Paul II.

In 1980, Pope John Paul II spoke against Communion in the hand and Eucharistic ministers. He said, "[T]o touch the sacred species and to administer them with their own hands is the privilege of the ordained."[65]

This was a good statement, and it conformed to the traditional papal teaching of the centuries. In one sentence, Pope John Paul II spoke clearly against both Communion in the hand and Eucharistic ministers. To say, "to touch the sacred species is a privilege of the ordained," is to speak against Communion in the hand. To say, "to administer (the sacred species) with their own hands is a privilege of the ordained," is to speak against lay Eucharistic ministers.[66]

Yet twenty-two years later, at the 2002 World Youth Day, Pope John Paul II — in practice —went against his own former teaching. He allowed lay Eucharistic ministers at his Mass, and he freely gave Communion in the hand.

So, how does a Catholic know which John Paul II was right? A Catholic knows which John Paul II was right when his words and actions *conformed to the traditional Catholic teach-*

---

[65]Apostolic Letter *Dominicae Cenae*, February 24, 1980, no. 11.

[66]I use the term "speak against" since *Dominicae Cenae* was actually a contradictory document. The Pope spoke against these abuses, but the document left existing concessions for Communion in the hand and lay Eucharistic ministers on the books.

ing and practice of the centuries. This is the criteria that Catholics must employ at a time when progressivist novelties emanate from the Papal Office, whether it be that of Pope Paul VI, Pope John Paul II or his successor.

As Catholics, we are obliged to be faithful to Peter. But at the same time, *Peter is obliged to be faithful to Peter.* And if today's Peter, by his words and actions, contradicts the consistent teaching and practice of Peter throughout the centuries, then we resist the novelties of today's Peter, and cling to the traditional papal teaching and practice of all times. This is why Fr. Joseph de Sainte-Marie, quoted earlier, warned, "In our day, and it is one of the most obvious signs of the extraordinarily abnormal character of the current state of the Church, *it is very often the case that acts of the Holy See demand of us prudence and discernment.*" Later, we will see that this is the same counsel given by the popes, saints and Doctors of the Church.

Chapter 16
Abuses "Imprimatured"

Here is another problem that World Youth Day presents to us.

As I said earlier, the Sunday Papal Mass at World Youth Day placed an "imprimatur" on many of the liturgical abuses that concerned Catholics have been fighting for the past thirty-five years. But now, thanks to WYD liturgies, Catholics who continue to fight these abuses will find their efforts undermined by the fact that Pope John Paul II's liturgies contained the very abuses they rightly deplore.

Thus, if you complain that your local parish church has lay Eucharistic ministers and Communion in the hand, your pastor will respond, "Well, Pope John Paul II did it at his Mass!"

If your pastor allows pagan, Native American ritual, or even Aztec ritual, to take place in your parish church, and if you complain about it, he will say, "What's your beef? Pope John Paul II had Native American ritual at his Masses."

If you try to stop the rock 'n' pop music at your local Sunday Mass, the priest will say, "Hey, Pope John Paul II had rock music at his Sunday liturgies."

If you protest against liturgical dancing at your Sunday Mass, your pastor and your bishop will respond, "John Paul II had liturgical dancing at his Sunday Mass. What's your problem?"

And we shall mention here just one *concrete example* of Pope John Paul II's actions undermining those Catholics who still try to fight certain liturgical abuses.[67] On Monday, July 29th, the day after World Youth Day, Francis Cardinal George of Chicago took part in a Native American sweet-grass cere-

---

[67]Another example is mentioned in Chapter 3 of this book. A pastor who had always forbidden rock 'n' roll Masses in his parish now allows them because of Pope John Paul II's rock 'n' roll Masses at World Youth Day.

mony in Canada. This is a ritual wherein sweet-grass is burned as some sort of "purification." Again, this is nothing but heathen superstition, since burning sweet-grass does nothing to "purify" one's soul. The pagan ceremony was incorporated into Cardinal George's Mass.

The Wanderer then blasted Cardinal George in a front-page story. The article called the Cardinal's ceremony a mockery. It rightly accused him of scandal for taking part in a heathen ritual. However, immediately after this, the newspaper for the Archdiocese of Chicago, *The Catholic New World,* defended Cardinal George, saying he should not have been criticized because he was only imitating John Paul II. The rebuttal read as follows:

> Cardinal George was the target of an outrageous and ill-conceived attack in a recent issue of a purportedly Catholic newspaper. He was criticized for participating in a ceremony at a Catholic Church in Toronto during World Youth Day in which Native American symbolism was incorporated into a liturgy....
>
> Using words like "mockery" and "pagan," the front-page piece sputtered that acknowledging Native American symbolism in a Catholic ritual was an "affront" because of the martyrdom of Jesuits and other missionaries in the New World.
>
> Nonsense.
>
> During the canonization ceremony of Juan Diego last month in Mexico City, Pope John Paul II did much the same thing, celebrating with incense presented by an indigenous woman.... Native Americans in traditional costumes danced, as they did a few years ago when bare-chested Polynesian men danced at the Vatican during the Synod for Oceania.[68]

This is what I mean when I speak of the scandal that was perpetrated at World Youth Day. The result is clear to see. If you try to oppose blatant liturgical abuses, such as pagan ceremonies incorporated into Catholic liturgies, many

---

[68]Tom Sheridan, "Spread the Word," *Catholic New World,* August 18, 2002.

Catholics will dismiss you out of hand.   They will only respond, "Well, Pope John Paul II did it!"[69]

---

[69]One of the main themes of Ferrara and Woods in *The Great Façade* is that
"neo-Catholic" news media will oppose an abuse until the Pope "approves" it.
Then they will defend the very same abuse they formerly opposed. Worse, they
will then attack traditional Catholics who continue to oppose the abuse. Ferrara
summed up this typically schizophrenic position: "So the neo-Catholic establishment condemns Cardinal George for doing what the Pope does, and praises
John Paul for doing what Cardinal George does" (Christopher Ferrara, "Propping
Up the Great Façade," *The Remnant,* August 31, 2002).

Chapter 17
Papal Office:
Custodian of Tradition or
Change Agent?

This brings us then to the next question: Is it possible that Pope John Paul II — even if he had been well-meaning — was mistaken in encouraging (or permitting) these novel practices that have always been condemned by the Church? I propose this question because many Catholics erroneously believe that it is impossible for a Pope to make mistakes on this scale.[70]

The answer is found in the Papal Coronation Oath. The full text of the Oath reads:

> *I vow* to change nothing of the received Tradition, and nothing thereof I have found before guarded by my God-pleasing predecessors, to encroach, to alter, or to permit any innovation therein.
>
> *To the contrary*: with glowing affection as her truly faithful steward and successor, [I vow] to reverently safeguard the passed-on good, with my whole strength and utmost effort.
>
> *To cleanse* all that is in contradiction to the canonical order, should such appear; to guard the holy canons and decrees of our Popes as if they were the Divine ordinances of Heaven, because I am conscious of Thee, Whose place I

---

[70]It should be noted here that the radical *aggiornamento* of Vatican II has taken place with the full-throttle encouragement of the post-conciliar Popes, who even before their elevation to the Papacy, were kin to the progressivist brotherhood. Before he became Pope Paul VI, Cardinal Montini was one of a clique of progressivist cardinals in Europe. He was a close friend and collaborator of Cardinal Suenens, probably the most progressivist Cardinal at Vatican II (see Vennari, "The Charismatic Cardinal Suenens," in *Charismatic Movement*, part III). Likewise, Fr. Ludvik Nemec, a "conservative" Catholic, writes in praise of John Paul II that "Bishop Wojtyla took a progressive stand" at Vatican II, and that he "interacted with progressive theologians" at the Council. See Father Ludvik Nemec, *Pope John Paul II: A Festive Profile* (New York: Catholic Book Publishing, 1979), p. 98.

take through the grace of God, Whose Vicarship I possess with Thy support, being subject to severest accounting before Thy Divine Tribunal over all that I shall confess....

If I should undertake to act in anything of contrary sense, or should permit that it will be executed, Thou willst not be merciful to me on the dreadful day of Divine Justice.

Accordingly, without exclusion, we subject to severest excommunication anyone — be it Ourselves or be it another — who would dare to undertake anything new in contradiction to this constituted evangelic Tradition and the purity of the orthodox Faith and the Christian Religion, or [who] would seek to change anything by his opposing efforts, or [who] would concur with those who undertake such a blasphemous venture.[71]

Thus the Pope here says in so many words: "If I deviate from the traditional teaching and practice of the Church, may God not have mercy on me." This Papal Oath is part of our Catholic heritage. It began around the sixth or seventh century. And even though it has not been said for a number of centuries, it is, if you will, the Church's "Job Description" of the Papacy.

This Papal Coronation Oath is a wealth of instruction for us:

1) It demonstrates that *even the Pope* is forbidden to deviate from Tradition.

2) The fact that a Pope takes this Oath shows that it is *possible* for a Pope to deviate; otherwise, there would be no need to take such a solemn, terrifying oath.[72]

In fact, there are examples in history of Popes who deviated, such as Honorius I, John XXII and Nicholas I.[73]

---

[71]*Liber Diurnus Romanorum Pontificum*, P. L105, S. 54.

[72]When Pope St. Pius X condemned Modernism in *Pascendi*, he opened that encyclical stating that if he took no action against Modernism, he would have failed in his primary duty. This shows that *it is possible* for a Pope to fail. See The False Doctrines of the Modernists *Pascendi Dominici Gregis*, September 8, 1907, no. 1.

[73]*Pope Nicholas I*, whose declaration on the validity of the minister of Baptism (whether it could be a Jew or a pagan) noted in passing (according to Bellarmine) that "Baptism was valid, whether administered in the name of the Three Persons or in the name of Christ only." In this Pope Nicholas was mistaken. Baptism in

Archbishop M. Sheehan in his magnificent *Apologetics and Christian Doctrine*, points out that far from undermining the Papal Office, the occasional weaknesses and mistakes of the Popes serve as proof of the Papacy's Divine institution. "We may, indeed, make no difficulty," says Bishop Sheehan, "admitting that in the long history of the Papacy, there have been errors of policy. It seems as though God wished to make the occasional weakness of the Papacy a motive of credibility, a proof that the Church is Divinely supported."[74]

It is necessary to understand this in order to counteract the false notion of Papal Infallibility held by many Catholics who claim that the Pope can pretty much do or say any-

---

the name of Christ only is not valid. See John Henry Newman, *Certain Difficulties* (1876), cited in Michael Davies, *Lead Kindly Light: The Life of John Henry Newman* (Long Prairie, MN: Neumann Press, 2001), pp. 181-82.

Likewise, "*Honorius* is, among all the Popes in any way guilty of heresy, both the best known and the most culpable — even though this concerned only a single episode in an otherwise great Pontificate. The phrase he used when justifying his compromise with the heretics has a surprisingly up-to-date ring about it, for all that it was spoken in 634: 'We must be careful not to rekindle ancient quarrels.' On the strength of this argument, he allowed error to spread freely, with the result that truth and orthodoxy were effectively banished. St. Sophronius of Jerusalem was almost alone in standing up to Honorius and accusing him of heresy. Eventually the Pope came to his senses, but he died without having repaired the immense damage caused to the Church by his lack of decision. For this reason the Sixth Council of Constantinople cast its anathema upon him, and this was confirmed by Pope Leo II. All the great Ecumenical Councils since then have endorsed this verdict; even while proclaiming the dogma of Papal Infallibility, the Church of Rome upheld the anathema cast many centuries ago upon one of her Pontiffs on account of heresy. *John XXII* said at Avignon, on the Feast of All Saints, 1331, that the soul does not enter the Beatific Vision until the resurrection of the body, at the last day. Protests followed, and a rebuke from the University of Paris, whose theologians were consulted. John XXII died in 1334, admitting and recanting his error.... The Testament of *Gregory XI*, dated 1374, is both moving and instructive. For in it he recognizes in effect that he [Gregory] may have committed 'errors against the Catholic Faith or adopted opinions at variance with the Catholic Faith' in his teaching given 'in public or in private'; and he now abjures and detests any such thing of which he may have been guilty. John XXII, upon his deathbed, solemnly recanted every opinion, every teaching, contrary to the Catholic Faith, alluding to his heretical sermon given on the Feast of All Saints in 1331, 'submitting all that he may have said or written on the subject to the judgment of the Church and of his successors: *determinationi Ecclesiae ac successorum nostrorum.*'" See Abbé Georges de Nantes, ed., "The Question of Papal Heresy, Schism or Scandal," *The Catholic Counter-Reformation in the XXth Century*, June 1973.

[74]Archbishop M. Sheehan, *Apologetics and Christian Doctrine* (Dublin: M. H. Gill and Son, 1951), pp. 16-17.

thing he wants simply because he is Pope. This is not what the Church teaches.

In a sermon on the subject, the eminent nineteenth-century Cardinal, John Henry Newman, quoted a Pastoral Letter from the Bishops of Switzerland that had received the approval of Blessed Pope Pius IX. The letter was on the subject of Papal Infallibility, and what a Pope may or may not teach. The Swiss bishops clearly stated:

> It in no way depends upon the caprice of the Pope, or upon his good pleasure, to make such and such a doctrine the object of a dogmatic definition. He is tied up and limited to the divine revelation and to the truths which that revelation contains. He is tied up and limited by the creeds, already in existence, and by the preceding definitions of the Church. He is tied up and limited by the divine law, and by the constitution of the Church....[75]

The Pope himself, then, is bound to teach what has always been taught by the uninterrupted teaching of his predecessors throughout the centuries.

What Do We Do?

Throughout the ages, the popes, saints and holy Doctors have taught that the first duty of all Catholics, including the hierarchy, is to maintain Tradition, that is, to maintain the purity of the Faith in doctrine and practice. We are also commanded to abhor novelty. Pope St. Pius X wrote in his Encyclical against Modernism:

> But for Catholics nothing will remove the authority of the second Council of Nicea, where it condemns those "who dare, after the impious fashion of heretics, to deride the *ecclesiastical traditions*, to invent novelties of some kind ... or endeavor by malice or craft to overthrow *any one of the legitimate*

---

[75]Cited in Davies, p. 184.

traditions of the Catholic Church".... Wherefore the Roman Pontiffs, Pius IV and Pius IX, ordered the insertion in the profession of faith of the following declaration: "I most firmly admit and embrace the apostolic *and ecclesiastical* traditions and *other observances* and constitutions of the Church."[76]

And the Second Council of Nicea (787) teaches infallibly: "If anyone rejects all ecclesiastical tradition either written or not written ... let him be anathema."[77] Yet the discarding of tradition and the introduction of novelties has been the *defining element* of the post-conciliar Church.

On the subject of maintaining tradition, St. Peter Canisius, Doctor of the Church, wrote in his *Summa Doctrinae Christianae,* "It behooves us unanimously to observe the ecclesiastical traditions, whether defined or simply retained by customary practice of the Church." St. Peter Damian, another Doctor of the Church, teaches, "It is unlawful to alter the established customs of the Church.... Remove not the ancient landmarks which the fathers have set." Likewise, in the early twentieth century, Pope Benedict XV repeated almost verbatim the words of Pope St. Stephen I, when he declared, "Do not innovate anything. Rest content with tradition."[78]

Then what if a pope *does* deviate from tradition and inaugurates novelties such as ecumenism and pop-music liturgies and the other liturgical aberrations from World Youth Day? Are we bound to follow him in these novelties? Are we bound to defend these innovations? According to the teaching of Pope Innocent III, and according to the great theologian Juan de Torquemada and other saints and Doctors of the Church, the answer is No! We are not bound to follow. We are encouraged to resist all novelties.

---

[76]Pius X, no. 42. (Emphases added.)

[77]Henry Denzinger, *The Sources of Catholic Dogma*, 30th ed., trans. Roy J. Deferrari (St. Louis, MO: B. Herder Book Co., 1957; reprint ed., Powers Lake, ND: Marian House, n.d.), no. 308.

[78]Pope St. Stephen (254-57) said, "Let them innovate in nothing, but keep the traditions." All quotes cited in Father Paul Kramer, *A Theological Vindication of Roman Catholic Traditionalism*, 2d ed. (Nazareth, Kerala, India: Apostle Publications, n.d. [ca. 1996]), p. 28.

Juan Cardinal de Torquemada (1388-1468) was a revered medieval theologian responsible for the formulation of the doctrines that were defined at the Council of Florence. Cardinal Torquemada teaches:

> Were the Pope to command anything against Holy Scriptures, or the articles of faith, or the truth of the sacraments, or the commands of the natural or divine law, he ought not to be obeyed, but in such commands he is to be disregarded.[79]

Citing the doctrine of Pope Innocent III, Cardinal Torquemada further teaches:

> Thus it is that Pope Innocent III states *(De Consuetudine)* that it is necessary to obey the Pope in all things as long as he, himself, does not go against the universal customs of the Church, but should he go against the universal customs of the Church, "he need not be followed...."[80]

If a father tells his son not to go to Mass on Sunday and instead to help Dad clean the garage, the son would not

[79]*Summa de ecclesia* (Venice: M. Tranmezium, 1561), Lib. II, c. 49, p. 163B. This English translation of the statement by Juan de Torquemada is found in Patrick Granfield, *The Papacy in Transition* (New York: Doubleday, 1980), p. 171. This book received high praise from Father (now Cardinal) Avery Dulles, SJ.

[80]Cited in Father Kramer, p. 29. The full quotation from Cardinal Torquemada reads: "By disobedience, the Pope can separate himself from Christ despite the fact that he is head of the Church, for above all, the unity of the Church is dependent on its relationship with Christ. The Pope can separate himself from Christ either by disobeying the law of Christ, or by commanding something that is against the divine or natural law." It follows, then, that if it is possible for a Pope to *command* something against divine law, then it is likewise possible for a Pope to *permit* something that is against divine or natural law, or to go against the traditional teaching of the Church. Cardinal Torquemada continues: "By doing so, the Pope separates himself from the body of the Church because the body is itself linked to Christ by obedience. In this way the Pope could, without doubt, fall into schism.... Especially is this true with regard to the divine liturgy as, for example, if he did not wish personally to follow the universal customs and rites of the Church.... Thus it is that Pope Innocent III states (*De Consuetudine*) that it is necessary to obey the Pope in all things as long as he himself does not go against the universal customs of the Church, but should he go against the universal customs of the Church, 'he need not be followed....'" It must be stressed that I am not suggesting that Pope John Paul formally "separated himself from Christ." I am only demonstrating that the popes and saints of the past have explained that if the Pope deviates, then the duty of the Catholic is to resist.

follow his father, but would respond, "You are my father, and I obey you in all things. But because you command something against the law of God, I will resist this order." Similarly, if and when a pope deviates from tradition and introduces novelties that are contrary to the perennial teaching and practice of the Church, we do not claim he is not the Pope, that he is not our father; nor do we withdraw all obedience from him. But we could not follow him on these points; rather, we would have to resist him. Our first allegiance must be — as the Church teaches — to the perennial faith of the Catholic Church, and not to a pope's personal innovations.

Saint Robert Bellarmine, the great champion of the Counter-Reformation, taught the following regarding lawful Catholic resistance:

> Just as it is licit to resist the Pontiff that aggresses the body, it is also licit to resist the one who aggresses the soul or who disturbs civil order, or, above all, who attempts to destroy the Church. I say that it is licit to resist him by not doing what he orders and preventing his will from being executed; it is not licit, however, to judge, punish or depose him, since these are acts proper to a superior.[81]

Thus we can make no moral judgement on anyone's soul, especially that of the Pope of the Catholic Church. But we *do* have the duty to maintain the traditional doctrine and devotions of the Catholic Church, and to resist novelty, even if it comes from the Church's highest places.[82] We must be firm in our resistance for the sake of our children as well.

---

[81] *De Romano Pontifice,* Lib. II, c. 29, in *Opera omnia* (Neapoli/Panormi/Paris: Pedone Lauriel, 1871), vol. I, p. 418.

[82] Resisting unorthodox novelties goes even further. St. Thomas Aquinas, in many passages of his works, upholds the principle that the faithful can question and admonish prelates. For example: "There being an imminent danger for the Faith, prelates must be questioned, even publicly, by their subjects. Thus, Saint Paul, who was a subject of Saint Peter, questioned him publicly on account of an imminent danger of scandal in a matter of Faith. And, as the *Glosa* of Saint Augustine puts it [on Gal. 2:14], 'Saint Peter himself gave the example to those who govern so that if sometime they stray from the right way, they will not reject a correction as unworthy even if it comes from their subjects'" (*Summa Theologica* [Taurini/Romae: Marietti, 1948], II.II, q.33, a.4).

The Fathers of the Church have given us the same firm guidance as to what a Catholic must do during a time of ecclesiastical crisis. St. Vincent of Lerins (ca. A.D. 445) teaches:

> What shall a Catholic do if some portion of the Church detaches itself from communion of the universal Faith? What other choice can he make if some new contagion attempts to poison, no longer a small part of the Church, but the whole Church at once, *then his great concern will be to attach himself to antiquity [tradition] which can no longer be led astray by any lying novelty.*[83]

We attach ourselves to Tradition by:

- Resistance to the post-conciliar revolutionary novelties, such as Communion in the hand, pan-religious ecumenism, inculturation, pop-music at Church functions, and World Youth Day itself;
- Uncompromising fidelity to the unchangeable, perennial Magisterium, and fidelity to the traditional practices of Catholic piety;
- Firm commitment to Our Lady's requests at Fatima, and to the message to "pray a great deal for the Holy Father," as noted earlier;
- Fierce attachment to the Latin Tridentine Mass and all the traditional sacramental formulae, in which the liturgical aberrations can find no home.

Finally, we must draw courage from the words of St. Athanasius, who teaches, "Even if Catholics faithful to Tradition are reduced to a handful, they are the ones who are the true Church of Jesus Christ."[84]

We must also draw strength from Pope St. Pius X, who assures us, "Indeed, the true friends of the people are neither revolutionaries nor innovators, they are *traditionalists*."[85]

---

[83]Cited in Father Kramer, p. 94. (Emphasis added.)

[84]*Coll. Selecta SS. Eccl. Patrum* (Caillau and Guillou), vol. 32, pp. 411-412.

[85]Pius X, Encyclical *Our Apostolic Mandate*, August 25, 1910, trans. and commentary by Yves Dupont (Kansas City, MO: Angelus Press, 1998), no. 44. (Emphasis added.)

PRAYER TO ST. MICHAEL THE ARCHANGEL
Composed by Pope Leo XIII

MOST GLORIOUS prince of the heavenly hosts, Archangel St. Michael, defend us in the battle and in the tremendous struggle we carry on against the Principalities and Powers, against the rulers of the world of darkness and all evil spirits. Come to the help of man, whom God created immortal, fashioned to His own image and likeness, and rescued at a great price from the tyranny of the devil. With the great army of the holy angels, fight today the battle of the Lord as thou didst of old fight against Lucifer, the leader of the proud, and his apostate angels, who were powerless against thee, and they had no longer a place in Heaven; and that monster, the old serpent who is called the devil and Satan, that seduces the whole world, was cast into hell with his angels.

But now that first enemy and homicide has regained his insolent boldness. Taking on the appearance of an angel of light, he has invaded the earth, and with his whole train of evil spirits he is prowling about among men, striving to blot out the name of God and of His Christ, to capture, to destroy, to drag to eternal perdition the souls destined to the crown of eternal glory. That malignant dragon is pouring abroad, like a foul stream, into the souls of men of ruined intellect and corrupt heart the poison of his wickedness, the spirit of lying, of impiety and blasphemy, the pestilent breath of impurity and of all vice and iniquity. Most cunning enemies have filled with bitterness and drenched with gall the Church, the Spouse of the Lamb without spot, and have lifted impious hands against all that is most sacred in it. Even in the holy place where the See of Blessed Peter and the chair of truth was set up to enlighten the world, they have raised the abominable throne of their impiety with the iniquitous hope that the Shepherd may be stricken and the flock scattered abroad.

Arise, then, unconquerable Prince, defend the people of God against the assaults of the reprobate spirits, and give them the victory. Holy Church reveres thee as its guardian and patron; it glories in thee as its defender against the malignant powers of hell; to thee God has committed the souls that are to be conveyed to the seats of the Blessed in eternal happiness. Pray, then, to the God of peace, that He may put Satan under our feet, so completely vanquished that he may no longer be able to hold men in bondage and work harm to the Church. Offer up our prayers before the Most High, so that the mercies of the Lord may prevent us, and lay hold of the dragon, the old serpent, who is the devil and Satan, and hurl him bound in chains into the abyss where he may no longer seduce the souls of men. Amen.

V. Behold the Cross of the Lord, fly ye hostile ranks.
R. *The Lion of the tribe of Juda, the Root of David, has conquered.*

V. May Thy mercies, O Lord, be fulfilled in us.
R. *As we have hoped in Thee.*

V. Lord, hear my prayer.
R. *And let my cry come unto Thee.*

Let us pray.

O God, and the Father of Our Lord Jesus Christ, we call upon Thy holy name and humbly beseech Thy clemency, that through the intercession of the ever-immaculate Virgin and our Mother Mary, and of the glorious Archangel St. Michael, Thou wouldst vouchsafe to help us against Satan and all the other unclean spirits that are prowling about the world to the great peril of the human race and the loss of souls. Amen.

His Holiness, Leo XIII, *Motu Proprio*, September 25, 1888, granted to the faithful who recite the above prayer **an indulgence of three hundred days, once a day.**

(Reprinted from *The New Raccolta or Collection of Prayers and Good Works to which the Sovereign Pontiffs have Attached Holy Indulgences*, which was published in 1898 by order of His Holiness, Pope Leo XIII.)

Index